About the editors

Isabelle Guérin is a socioeconomist and senior research fellow at the Institute of Research for Development/Centre d'études en sciences sociales sur les mondes américains africains et asiatiques (Cessma), and an associate researcher at both the French Institute of Pondicherry (India) and the Centre for European Research in Microfinance (CERMi, Belgium). She specializes in the political and moral economics of money, debt and finance. Her current work focuses on the financialization of domestic economies, looking at how financialization produces both new forms of inequalities and domination, but also alternative and solidarity-based initiatives.

Marc Labie is full professor at the Warocqué School of Business and Economics of the University of Mons (UMONS), where he teaches management and organization studies. He is also a co-founder and co-director of the Centre for European Research in Microfinance (CERMi), an excellence centre based in Mons and Brussels, Belgium. In 2011, he co-edited *The Handbook of Microfinance* with Professor Beatriz Armendariz.

Jean-Michel Servet is professor emeritus at Lyon University, and currently professor in development studies at the Graduate Institute of International and Development Studies in Geneva. His research deals with social finance, local exchange trading systems, financial globalization, the history of economic thought, and interdisciplinary methods. He has carried out field research on financial inclusion in western and northern Africa, southern India, Latin America and western Europe.

THE CRISES OF MICROCREDIT

edited by Isabelle Guérin, Marc Labie and
Jean-Michel Servet

Zed Books
London

The Crises of Microcredit was first published in 2015 by Zed Books Ltd,
The Foundry, 17 Oval Way, London SE11 5RR, UK

www.zedbooks.co.uk

Editorial copyright © Isabelle Guérin, Marc Labie and Jean-Michel Servet 2015
Copyright in this collection © Zed Books 2015

The rights of Isabelle Guérin, Marc Labie and Jean-Michel Servet to be identified as
the editors of this work have been asserted by them in accordance with the Copyright,
Designs and Patents Act, 1988

Typeset in Plantin and Kievit by Swales & Willis Ltd, Exeter, Devon
Index: ed.emery@thefreeuniversity.net
Cover designed by www.roguefour.co.uk

A catalogue record for this book is available from the British Library.

ISBN 978-1-78360-375-6 hb
ISBN 978-1-78360-374-9 pb
ISBN 978-1-78360-376-3 pdf
ISBN 978-1-78360-377-0 epub
ISBN 978-1-78360-378-7 mobi

CONTENTS

FIGURES, TABLES AND BOXES

Figures

Tables

Boxes

ACKNOWLEDGEMENTS

This edited volume is the outcome of the research project 'Microfinance in Crisis' (www.microfinance-in-crisis.org) supported by the European Investment Bank (EIB), through its EIB University Research Sponsorship Programme. The research project was led by the research unit 'Development and Societies' (Paris I Sorbonne University/Institute of Research of Development), in partnership with the Centre for European Research in Microfinance (CERMi, Belgium), the Department of Political Economy of Fribourg University and the Laboratoire de Statistique Appliquée à l'Analyse et la Recherche en Economie (Lasaare, Casablanca). Except for Chapter 2, which draws on a report done for Planet Rating, and Chapter 8, all chapters come from this research project.

We are very grateful to the many practitioners in the field in the various countries on which this research is based, for their open-mindedness and their capacity to engage with us in critical discussions about microcredit, microfinance and financial inclusion policies. By suggesting fresh ways of analysing finance for the low-income sectors of the world's population, we hope that this volume will be of use to them and to all those who consider themselves as politically engaged scholars and practitioners concerned with financial inclusion policies and with development and social change in general.

ACRONYMS AND ABBREVIATIONS

ACEP	Alliance de Crédit et d'Epargne pour la Production (Sénégal)
ADA	Appui au Développement Autonome (Luxembourg)
AP	Andhra Pradesh
AP-SFD	Association professionnelle des systèmes financiers décentralisés (Sénégal)
ASOMIF	Asociación Nicaragüense de Instituciones de Microfinanzas (Nicaragua)
ASPIRE	Asociación para Inversión y Empleo (Dominican Republic)
BANADES	Banco Nacional de Desarrollo (Nicaragua)
BCEAO	Banque Centrale des Etats de l'Afrique de l'Ouest
BIMAO	Banque des institutions mutualistes d'Afrique de l'Ouest
BIO	Belgian Investment Company for Developing Countries
CMS	Crédit mutuel du Sénégal
CGAP	Consultative Group to Assist the Poor
Cordaid	Catholic Organization for Relief and Development Aid (Netherlands)
DOP	Dominican pesos
DRS-SFD	Direction de la Réglementation et de la Surveillance des Systèmes Financiers Décentralisés (Sénégal)
DWCRA	Development of Women and Children in Rural Areas (India)
ENABAS	Empresa Nicaragüense de Alimentos Básicos (Nicaragua)
EWI	Early-Warning Index
FAMA	Fundación para el Apoyo a la Microempresa/Financiera Fama (Nicaragua)
FDL	Fondo de Desarrollo Local (Nicaragua)
FENACREP	Fédération Nationale des Caisses Rurales d'Epargne et de Prêt
FINDESA	Financiera Nicaragüense de Desarrollo (Nicaragua)
FONDESA	Fondo para el Desarrollo, Inc. (Dominican Republic)
FSS	Financial Services Society (Andhra Pradesh)
FUNDENUSE	Fundación para el Desarrollo de Nueva Segovia (Nicaragua)

FUNDESER	Fundación para el Desarrollo Socioeconómico Rural (Nicaragua)
GDP	gross domestic product
GEC	*groupement d'épargne et de crédit*
GNI	gross national income
HDI	Human Development Index
ICICI	Industrial Credit and Investment Corporation of India
IFC	International Finance Corporation
ILO	International Labour Organization
INR	Indian rupee
IRAM	Institut de Recherches et d'Applications des Méthodes de développement (France)
LMDF	Luxembourg Microfinance and Development Fund
MCA	microcredit association
MFI	microfinance institution
MIMOSA	Microfinance Index of Market Outreach and Saturation
MIV	microfinance investment vehicle
Mix	Microfinance Information Exchange
MPCMAN	El Movimiento de Productores, Comerciantes, Microempresarios y Asalariados del Norte (Nicaragua)
NBFIs	non-banking financial institutions
NGO	non-governmental organization
PADME	Association pour la Promotion et l'Appui au Développement des Micro-Entreprises
PAMECAS	Partenariat pour la Mobilisation de l'Epargne et le Crédit
PAPME	Agence pour la Promotion et l'Appui des Petites et Moyennes Entreprises
PAR	portfolio at risk
PARMEC	Programme d'Appui à la Réforme des Mutuelles d'Epargne et de Crédit (Sénégal)
PRESTANIC	Fondo Nicaragüense para el Desarrollo Comunitario (Nicaragua)
RBI	Reserve Bank of India
REDCAMIF	Red de Microfinanzas en Centroamérica y del Caribe (Dominican Republic)
ROSCA	rotating savings and credit association
RUME	rural microfinance and employment
SGBS	Société générale de banques au Sénégal
SHG	self-help group
SIBOIF	Superintendente de Bancos y otras Instituciones Financieras (Nicaragua)
SKS	Swayam Krishi Sangam (India)

TAPIR	Tácticas y Armas Policiales de Intervención y Rescate (Nicaragua)
TDP	Telugu Desam Party (Andhra Pradesh)
UBA	United Bank for Africa
USAID	United States Agency for International Development
WAEMU	West African Economic and Monetary Union
XOF	West African CFA franc

INTRODUCTION

Microcredit[1] programmes have long been acclaimed as efficient development tools, but have been facing unprecedented crises over the past few years. While the relative success of these programmes was largely attributable to high repayment rates, these rates have now fallen sharply in various regions of the world. In contrast to the apparently unlimited growth prospects of the past, the number of poor clients is now on the decline. Data from the Microcredit Summit Campaign has shown that after a temporary slowdown in 2011 owing to crisis in India, the microcredit industry started growing again. But the poor are increasingly less targeted than before. The number of poor clients peaked at 138 million in 2010, which went down to 125 million in 2011 and 116 in 2012 (Reed 2014). Is this the end of microcredit, or just a critical phase in its development? Are these crises due to mission drift, or should microcredit per se be considered a dead end? Should we put a stop to microcredit, or rethink how it is implemented?

This edited volume draws on case studies from various parts of the world to offer a number of answers to these questions, combining various angles of analysis to the microcredit chain as a whole, from investors and donors to clients. It highlights how diverse these crises have been, both in terms of their severity and their specific features. Some of the crises have been systemic, others crises of maturity, or latent crises. Some have been a sign of a governance deficit and non-adherence to ground rules, others of over-indebtedness among clients who took out credit. But they can also result from strategies of resistance and struggle from above and below. This volume also highlights the diversity of the roles of actors in this field. We will encounter microcredit organizations that were unprepared for massive growth, along with donors who had been urged to spend money, greedy investors and shareholders attracted by profit, opportunistic local leaders using microcredit to strengthen their patronage networks, and regulators and policy-makers who fail to implement proper regulatory measures, or who instrumentalize microcredit for electoral purposes.

But these weaknesses should not bring us to condemn microcredit out of hand: the poor and unbanked do need financial services, provided that they are understood for what they are – financial tools – and not a magic bullet. Moreover they must be considered as commons, and not as a private and lucrative tool.

Microcredit crises

The first crises broke out in Bolivia in the late 1990s, in Bangladesh in 1999 (Rhyne 2001), Kenya in 2003 (Johnson et al. 2003) and Zambia in 2006 and 2007 (Siwale and Ritchie 2013). They were limited in scope and duration. Nicaragua, Bosnia Herzegovina, northern Pakistan and Morocco experienced major crisis from 2007. Default rates were above the 10 per cent threshold the microcredit industry deems an indicator of crisis[2] (Chen et al. 2010). By early 2013, after several years of chronic difficulties, the portfolio at risk had gone back down in Bosnia, but at the cost of a massive debt cancellation policy. In Morocco in 2008, one of the biggest microcredit providers, Zakoura, had to write off almost 50 per cent of its portfolio – and was then taken over by one of its competitors (Attawfiq[3]). The sector lost a third of its clients over five years (2007–12). In Nicaragua, the default rate grew considerably in 2010 (by over 14 per cent across the whole sector, but with considerable disparities between regions) and the industry went into a dramatic slump. Over three years (2008–11), client numbers fell by 30 per cent, outstanding volumes fell by 34 per cent, and the overall portfolio shrank by 53 per cent (Servet 2013).

The Andhra Pradesh crisis has undoubtedly been on a great and tragic scale. As early as 2006, some clients were recorded as having committed suicide after experiencing a poor return on production, and over-indebtedness, but this first crisis was temporarily resolved. Since October 2010, however, the Andhra Pradesh state has failed to emerge from a deep crisis characterized by contagion and systemic risk. In September 2011 repayment rates fell to 10 per cent. By May 2013, micro-lending activities had almost come to a halt. David Picherit discusses the 'end' of microcredit in some areas of Andhra Pradesh (see Picherit in this volume), when many microfinance institutions (MFIs) ceased operations. Others are still operational but have diverted most of their activities to other Indian states. Basix, a very high-profile Indian MFI, had to make 9,000 people redundant, which amounted to 90 per cent of its staff. The collapse of the microcredit industry in Andhra Pradesh, a state which had been at the forefront of microcredit in India, also accounts for the global slowdown of 2011 (Reed 2013).

At the time of writing (March 2015), other than in Andhra Pradesh, the sector seems to have reconsolidated. Many practitioners, observers and researchers believe that the crises are behind us. We believe that there are still grounds for concern, however, and that lessons have still not been learnt.

Microcredit growth is currently at its highest in Africa, but here too, and far beyond Morocco, there are ongoing problems. In Benin in the 2000s, the four largest microfinance institutions[4] saw a steady decline in portfolio quality while cooperative-based MFIs – whose role is central in the microfinance landscape in Benin – struggled to collect savings (see the case of FECECAM Bénin) (Acclassato and Goudjo 2012). In Cameroon and Niger, several MFIs were placed under state supervision. In Senegal, various small organizations, some of which had been in operation for a long time, closed down or are on the verge of doing so because of massive defaults. Out of the country's three largest institutions which dominate most of the market, two no longer publish their default rates, while the third has a portfolio at risk of almost 10 per cent (see Baumann et al. this volume).

These crises are all the more worrying considering that some of the countries in difficulty have been taken as 'role models' for their regions, including Benin for West Africa, Morocco for the Arab world, and Andhra Pradesh for India. The crises have varied in scope, development and origin. Some have involved a sub-region (Andhra Pradesh in India), or specific pockets (four towns in Karnataka) or, in some cases, a whole country (Morocco). Sometimes only urban (Bolivia) or rural areas (Nicaragua, Andhra Pradesh) have been affected, sometimes both (Morocco). Certain crises are systemic, as with Andhra Pradesh (southern India), where most microcredit organizations have entirely stopped their activities and where, more fundamentally, the local state has now stepped in to manage all development activity (see Picherit this volume). Other crises can be considered 'maturity' crises, in the sense of being the transient signs of temporary growth-related difficulties. This is the case, for instance, in Morocco, where regulatory measures have been implemented, both by the public authorities and microcredit organizations and donors (Mourji 2014; Rozas et al. 2014). This does not mean, however, that all the problems have been solved, as Morvant-Roux and Roesch argue in this volume. Some crises have almost broken out but preventive measures have avoided the worst, as in Bangladesh in 2008 (Chen and Rutherford 2013). Last but not least, there are 'latent crises': good repayment rates are maintained but combine with a number of worrying indicators, whether in terms of repayment, client over-indebtedness, excessive concentration in specific locations or sectors and market saturation, malpractices within microcredit organizations, etc. This is, for instance, the case of Senegal, where there has been an obvious 'malaise' in the microfinance landscape (Baumann et al. this volume). According to various estimates, a number of countries are close to saturation. These include Laos, Cambodia, Bangladesh, Mexico, Mongolia, Kyrgyzstan and Bolivia (see Javoy and Rozas this volume). The situation is particularly troubling in Mexico, where more than half the loans are held by clients with four or more microcredits. This means that the sector's exposure to multiple borrowers is very high (Rozas 2014).

In some places, debt rescheduling practices can hide major repayment difficulties. Refinancing vulnerable clients, either as an official policy, as with the Grameen Bank, or as an informal field practice, hides the true quality of microcredit portfolios (Roodman 2012). The same goes for continued loan portfolio growth, since fresh loans can dilute and thus lower the proportion of arrears.

A multifaceted analysis

This volume combines case studies from the Dominican Republic, southern India (Andhra Pradesh and Tamil Nadu), Morocco, Senegal and Nicaragua, with transversal chapters addressing aspects such as unsustainable growth and market saturation. Andhra Pradesh, Morocco and Nicaragua have been among the worst-hit countries and subject to the highest level of media attention, which is why they have been chosen. We are convinced that the 'malaise' runs deeper than the usual indicators used to define crisis (rising repayment defaults and falling loan disbursements). We have decided to widen our analysis to three other cases. Two of them are not openly in crisis (the 'latent' crises mentioned above), but close to it for various reasons (Senegal and Tamil Nadu). For the third case, all the indicators are green, yet clients are suffering (the Dominican Republic). We take a diversity of locations and 'models' (NGOs and associations in Morocco and Tamil Nadu, cooperatives in Senegal, combination or for-profit and not-for-profit organizations in Andhra Pradesh, Nicaragua and the Dominican Republic). This allows for a certain representativeness although we do not claim to be exhaustive. Our aim is not to provide a systematic analysis of all microcredit crises, but to address several of their facets that have not been discussed to date. Far beyond the specific cases presented here, which cannot bring out the full diversity and complexity of the phenomenon, our ultimate goal is to take these crises as an opportunity to analyse the transformation and limitations of the microcredit industry and to critically reflect on its future. This is what the global framework for analysis presented in this introduction looks to support.

According to their objectives and academic backgrounds, researchers have taken different approaches to analyse microcredit crises. Though most such studies acknowledge the complexity of the phenomenon and the fact that there are multiple interactions between various factors, most focus on one particular factor. Some look in depth at the microcredit industry, focusing on governance and regulation issues and pointing out supply-related factors (see, for instance, Chen et al. 2010). Others, taking political-economic and economic-anthropological approaches, situate microcredit crises within a broader context while focusing on demand- and environment-related factors (see, for instance, Taylor 2011). We believe that a true understanding of the processes underlying microcredit crises calls for contextualized analysis. Financial services of all kinds take place in contexts and environments that have their own specificities, their own history and their own trajectory. We need to look at both sides of the coin – supply and demand. This is how the present volume is organized, with three parts (supply, demand, environment), combining various angles of analysis and methods. The authors approach microcredit as a multifaceted phenomenon, engaging in a dialogue between various disciplines and approaches – from political economics and anthropology to management – approaching them as complementary rather than contradictory, even if, on some issues, consensus cannot be reached. Various levels of analysis are equally articulated, by looking at both the lived experience of microcredit and its structural effects. Putting the various cases, studies and levels of analysis together, we can argue that microcredit crises stem from four factors:

- Governance-related factors and mission drift: these include excessive competition, inadequate enforcement mechanisms, delivering credit without any analysis of customer creditworthiness or potential for success in the activity to be financed, focusing on the highest-risk financial products, and mismanagement.
- Regulation-related factors: these include inadequate regulation, political interference, and distortion due to government programmes.
- Saturation effects, and the inability of local economies to absorb external liquidities beyond a certain threshold, or to support the creation of new income-generating activities, with the crises symptomatic of broader economic crisis.
- Collective resistance practices that can be interpreted as political messages to MFIs, the microcredit industry, or more generally to 'authority'.

These various factors are strongly interrelated and mutually reinforcing. Most, if not necessarily all, delinquency crises stem from a combination of these factors. Beyond these direct causes, whether crises break out – or not – depends on how the different parties concerned interact with one another, and whether they overreact or minimize the scale of the problem.

Mission drifts

Concern about mission drift in the microcredit industry is nothing new. A number of scholars have looked at it, most often equating microcredit's social mission with poverty eradication. The proportion of women, rural or poor clients (the latter are measured indirectly through loan amounts) an MFI has has been thought to represent the extent of its concern for social welfare. Most studies have found there to be a trade-off between financial and social performances (Hudon and Sandberg 2013: 577). These types of indicators, as useful as they may be, are problematic. As Armendáriz and Szafarz (2011) have argued, they can be misleading by ignoring the specificity of local contexts. They may also overshadow deliberate strategies of cross-subsidization: benefits made up of loans to richer and more profitable clients can be used to target poorer clients. These indicators give microcredit objectives (such as poverty eradication or women's 'empowerment') far more credit than they deserve. Last but not least, they neglect the issue of the client's well-being.

This is of course difficult to gauge and, furthermore, measure, but cannot be ignored. Here, mission drift refers to constraints that are imposed in favour of profitability and that serve to detract from the objectives of social welfare and high-quality services. By high-quality services, we mean services tailored to the diversity of financial needs and at affordable costs. A CGAP[5] study has argued that 'uncontrolled' growth was the main explanatory factor for the crises in Nicaragua, Bosnia Herzegovina, Pakistan and Morocco (Chen et al. 2010). From 2004 to 2008, annual outstanding loans grew by 67 per cent in Pakistan, 59 per cent in Morocco, 43 per cent in Bosnia Herzegovina, and 33 per cent in Nicaragua. Beyond growth – which is not necessarily higher than the 43 per cent average recorded by the Mix Market[6] – it is the pattern of growth that is highlighted: excessive competition focused on specific areas, increasing amounts lent to former clients, multiple borrowing from various MFIs, a loosening of control and governance regulation, and the erosion of 'disciplinary' measures. The CGAP study also highlights the fragility of growth driven by credit supply: in the four countries, saving represents less than 10 per cent of the amount borrowed (as opposed to 46 per cent on average for MFIs reporting to the Mix Market).

A key question, however, is the sustainability of growth, which D'Espallier et al. directly address in this volume, considering whether growth can ever be deemed 'too strong'. There is, of course, no single authoritative answer to this question. D'Espallier et al. instead propose a list of indicators, from the supply side, that should be kept in mind to ensure that microcredit providers don't lose sight of their original objectives. Most of the other chapters also indirectly tackle the issue of sustainability, to which we shall return later.

Governance factors also include mismanagement and corruption. If they persist and become public knowledge, they can weaken the entire sector. Although such factors have often been seen as unique to state-sponsored credit programmes, the evidence shows that private MFIs are also widely affected. In Benin, the problems the microcredit industry has seen in recent years are partly due to widespread corrupt practices, whether in private institutions (e.g. PADME) or public programmes (Acclassato and Goudjo 2012). In Cameroon, a large proportion of funds have been concentrated on a minority of clients, including MFI leaders, which looks to be a common practice. Morocco, which was long seen as a model of transparency and good governance, has also had many internal management problems (Mourji 2014). In Niger, a number of MFIs accused of fraud have been placed under strict controls. Two of Senegal's three largest MFIs, Crédit Mutuel du Sénégal and PAMECAS, have had substantial amounts of funds misused by management.

The concept of mission drift is not limited to excessive and uncontrolled growth or the targeting of better-off clients: another dimension is the intensive use of local patronage networks to recruit clients and win their loyalty. In southern India, for instance, political and patronage networks have fuelled the sector's dramatic growth. MFI managers, facing growing pressure to get new clients and issue new loans, have often relied on local male or female 'leaders' to select new clients and enforce repayments. This in no way involved looking for potential entrepreneurs or creditworthy clients, but rather for guaranteed loyalty (Guérin and Kumar 2007; see also Guérin et al. this volume). Ramesh Arunachalam, who has been an Indian microcredit specialist for over two decades, has described the emergence of this brokering function as the 'Frankenstein' of microcredit (Arunachalam 2011). Reliance on such key individuals to manage microcredit risk has proved a very effective model for rapid growth, but has also turned out to be extremely fragile (not to mention troubling for serving to reinforce inequalities). We have seen that when a leader declares that clients are not obliged to repay, or when he or she loses credibility, it is possible for a whole system to collapse. It is commonplace in Tamil Nadu and Andhra Pradesh, although probably not universal, for local leaders to have a lynchpin role (Arunachalam 2011). It has also been observed in other contexts such as Bangladesh (Karim 2011), Pakistan (Burki 2009), Egypt (Elyachar 2006) and Senegal (Guérin 2003; Sall 2012).

These governance factors can lead to both customer relations and market concentration deteriorating. They can be the outcome of internal policies, market-based funding and excessive pressures from donors. We also believe that these governance factors illustrate the rising hegemony of a commercial and profit-oriented approach which has turned the initial priorities of microcredit on their head: we have shifted from a social-welfare-oriented project mobilizing financial instruments to the emergence of financial institutions with (or, in some cases, claiming to have) a social-welfare-oriented mission. Not all institutions share this vision (Bédécarrats and Lapenu 2013), but commercial microcredit institutions have the most customers and handle the largest volumes. As various case studies in this volume illustrate, this profit-oriented approach has led to a frantic search for clients, the concentration of funds into small areas to minimize costs, and considerable pressure on loan officers who have profitability targets foisted on them, which in turn affects customers. This profit-driven approach is also apparent in the intense competition between microcredit institutions (see D'Espallier et al. this volume). Rather than sharing markets and spaces and looking for unoccupied segments, they tend to target and accumulate in places that are already taken. They benefit from the learning effects of their predecessors, always with a view to lowering costs (Servet 2015).

The loss of ethical and moral values is, however, a complex reality (Hudon and Sandberg 2013), which goes far beyond a Manichaean opposition between 'social-welfare-oriented' and 'commercial' approaches. Non-profit statuses in no way prevent massive private investments or bankruptcy.

So-called 'social-welfare-oriented' microcredit initiatives, whether under the banner of 'NGOs' or 'cooperatives', are unlikely to succeed in their mission when they are promoted or supported by populist and clientelist public policies, or by local groups and individuals seizing on microcredit to further expand their power (see Baumann et al. this volume). The evidence suggests that it is a constant challenge to find middle ground between social welfare objectives and sustainability. But clearly, for-profit investment in MFIs often constrains them to position themselves in the most profitable segments of the market in order to secure substantial profits. Strong pressure is then put on loan officers, to the detriment of a realistic analysis of client creditworthiness. It follows that there should be critical analysis of the role of the logic of the 'market' in over-indebtedness, and ultimately in repayment defaults.

MFIs are not solely responsible for mission drift: the role of investors and donors should also be pinpointed. Both public and private donors and investors tend to focus their investments on those regions and MFIs that can best publicize the positive impact they make (Servet 2012; Sinclair 2012). A study by MicroRate, one of the microcredit industry's leading rating agencies, has found a correlation between default payments and the number of lenders per MFI, thus highlighting the perverse effects of excessive funding (MicroRate 2013). Several explanations can be given for this. Microcredit supply is sometimes growing more slowly than investment funds are (ADA 2010). At the same time, funders' credit standards often restrict the number of MFIs that they consider to be qualified as borrowers. They rarely have time to carry out audits themselves, so they mostly rely on ratings, and they all consult the same ones. Investments made by others also serve as green lights. Some investors don't even look at ratings, which may be negative and serve as a warning, but simply copy their competitors (Sinclair 2012). All this leads to the concentration of large volumes of funding on a small number of leading MFIs in a particular location. When microcredit grows quickly in a particular area, it may be difficult for the less dynamic (or more cautious) MFIs to find lenders or investors, and some are then tempted – or forced – to grow as quickly as their competitors in order to survive. MFIs in India and Nicaragua, before reaching their peak, engaged in a veritable tug-of-war over increased growth, with attracting donors and investors as their priority. This not only led to a boom, but also a situation in which all stakeholders, starting with investors, lost touch with reality (Servet 2012; Sinclair 2012). Measurement tools of market saturation such as the Microfinance Index of Market Outreach and Saturation (MIMOSA) index (Javoy and Rozas this volume) are supposed to allow investors to avoid excessive concentration of their portfolios. But it is hard to say how willing or able investors are to cooperate over sharing the market.

Microcredit's shift towards the market should be put in its broader context: growing confusion between the 'market' and 'development', with the emergence of pro-poor markets as a concept, and the idea that poverty can reflect the poor's lack of access to markets (Bateman 2010), the financialization of development (Augsburg and Fouillet 2010; Guérin 2015; Young 2010) and poverty (Mader 2015), or even the transformation of poverty into capital (Roy 2010). Though the prevalence of neoliberal ideologies can certainly explain the market turn of the microcredit industry, we would argue that microcredit is not a monolithic project. Its initiatives are contextually specific, complex processes. Our work suggests that microcredit crises should also be analysed in the light of national histories and policies, which all have their own particular features. Microcredit is a global tool in the sense that its terms are shaped by uniform standards set by a very small number of organizations, foundations and lobbies, most of which are very close to multinational and bilateral aid agencies. But a wide range of actors all along the chain, from investors and donors to clients, play a central role in microcredit's interpretation, appropriation and implementation. The role of the state, in particular, cannot be ignored, which is our second key point.

Regulation and public policies

Regulation and public policies are a second important factor. The public authorities of some countries have been making genuine efforts to support MFIs with adequate back-up and monitoring, and have savers' and borrowers' best interests at heart, but state regulation in other countries can be absent, inadequate or unenforced. This can include weak oversight bodies and legislation that promotes only for-profit institutions, undermining other models, or imposing self-sufficiency over the very short term (Bédécarrats et al. 2012). Moreover, existing regulation may go unenforced, owing simply to a lack of human and financial resources. Beyond regulation, states may interfere through their own policies. While the days of public credit programmes were said to be over, this was never the case in some countries, and in some places this type of programme has been springing back up. To name just a few, this is clearly the case in southern India (see Guérin et al. and Picherit this volume), West Africa (see Baumann et al. this volume with regard to Senegal), and in several Latin American countries with the coming of left-wing governments to power (Bédécarrats et al. 2012).

The role of public authorities in microcredit crises should be situated within the context of the long history of credit and employment policies. It can take many shapes: fostering local cultures of 'non-payment', 'unfair' competition due to very cheap rates, pressurizing microfinance organizations to accept certain funds that follow clientelistic criteria (such as in Senegal), or even measures to control the entire sector (as with Andhra Pradesh). For public authorities, microcredit is at the crossroads of several agendas. It can be used to promote employment, poverty eradication, women's empowerment and rural development, but also to capture private capital, to win voters or at least to keep the social peace. The outcome is a wide range of measures that can be multiple and contradictory. In Andhra Pradesh, the collapse of microcredit organizations over a few months and the central role played by the local state in this collapse reflect structural changes in public and political approaches to development issues. As Picherit argues, the microcredit crisis reflects the failure of a development model which has relied on self-help interventions; but it is also part of a broader movement to control the activities of private development organizations as a whole, and to constrain their spheres of intervention to the implementation of state programmes. The various case studies in this volume shed light on the key ways that states directly or indirectly affect how microcredit emerges, develops and at times collapses.

The saturation of local economies

Saturated local economies unable to absorb further liquidity past a certain threshold are a third important factor. The absorption capacity of local economies is affected by the extent to which emerging markets are present, which in turn affects the potential to create or develop entrepreneurial activities and the added value they create. There is now a broad consensus that a large share of microcredits – often more than 50 per cent – is used on consumption rather than income-generative activities (Morduch 2013). Demand for 'productive' microcredit, while varying regionally, has been much lower than microcredit advocates had expected. Market saturation can be measured on national levels, as the MIMOSA index indicates (Javoy and Rozas this volume), showing that a large number of markets are already saturated and the risk of crisis is not over. National markets, however, give an incomplete picture. Given the wide disparity of local economies and the strong concentration of microcredit supply, market saturation should also be investigated on local levels (Guérin and Servet this volume).

Various factors explain why demand is often lower than expected: a lack of opportunities for entrepreneurs (Bateman 2010, 2013), products failing to address the complexity and diversity of demand (Armendáriz and Labie 2011), or micro-entrepreneurs already having access to financing facilities (Collins et al. 2009; Guérin et al. 2011). These facilities are mostly informal, but all things being equal, they can often be much more attractive than microcredit, contrary to popular belief. Microcredit is thus mostly, albeit with regional variation, used for non-income-generative purposes and is sustainable only up to a certain limit. It is more commonplace for microcredit to be used to boost existing businesses, provided that there is local demand and that access to credit is needed. Here too it is essential to look at pre-existing financial or emerging practices, as argued in the three chapters in this volume that focus on the question of demand. Pre-existing practices include consumption credit, which is booming in various parts of the world and is increasingly in competition with microcredit (see the chapters on the Dominican Republic and India). They also include informal credit and saving practices, which can vary in form and degree, but are found everywhere. Our evidence here suggests that these practices can shed new light on microcredit failure. Where a target population is already highly indebted (as, for instance, in many parts of southern India), is microcredit part of the problem or part of the solution (see Guérin et al. this volume)? Where a target population has a preference for saving, as in rural Morocco, not only is the demand for microcredit limited, but clients may also use microcredit sporadically and have little incentive to make repayments (see Morvant-Roux et al. this volume). At the same time, other segments of the market (for instance, medium-sized and large entrepreneurs) are often underserved.

Microcredit delinquency crises should be understood within a broader context and addressed in the light of macroeconomic trends in the regions in question. For Andhra Pradesh, Taylor (2011) and Servet (2011) argue that excessive, uncontrolled growth in the microcredit industry has certainly been a trigger factor. But the two authors argue that the sector's uneven growth (which has shown that there is a strong demand for microcredit) and defaults are first and foremost indicative of the severe agrarian crisis that Andhra Pradesh has been facing for more than two decades. In a context of drought cycles, the massive influx of microfinance met with an eager clientele looking to make ends meet, bolster consumption and roll over informal debt.

For Punjab in Pakistan, Burki (2009) argues that the microcredit crisis resulted from the uncontrolled growth of the industry, excessive concentration in certain locations, and the deterioration of macroeconomic variables (rampant inflation and a fall in real incomes). In Nicaragua, the collapse of the livestock sector, which is the pillar of the economy of the north of the country, and soaring corn prices from rising demand for biofuels, occurred after the microcredit crisis, but worsened it (see Servet this volume). In Mexico, pockets of default payments have in part stemmed from a significant drop in remittances from the USA since the global crisis (Angulo 2013; Hummel 2013). It should also be pointed out that household over-indebtedness pre-dates microcredit, and can occur where there is no microcredit, as has been observed in rural southern India (see Guérin et al. this volume) and in various parts of the world (Guérin et al. 2013).

In other words, household over-indebtedness stems not only from aggressive microcredit policies, but also from the broader context of the evolution of modern societies and economies. Where debt starts to substitute for income, as often seems to be the case and as this volume's case studies illustrate, a massive injection of liquidity obviously creates troublesome issues (Servet and Saiag 2013). The examples given above show how crucial it is to assess the absorptive capacity of local economies: how much external cashflow can a local economy take? This goes beyond the debate over 'productive' (income-generating) versus 'unproductive' uses (consumption). It relates to the nature of local markets: do we have emerging or saturated markets? Can we observe spillover effects (the activities created by microcredit leading to new ones and boosting local economies through trickle-down effects) or do we instead find saturation effects (new businesses saturating local markets and therefore bringing down the profitability of existing businesses) or displacement effects (one business is created but a nearby one closes)? If consumption financed by microcredit concerns goods that are produced locally with potential trickle-down and spillover effects (construction is a typical example), then 'consumption', through rebound effects, may boost local economies and enrich local communities. This leads us to consider the sustainability of growth rates from a different angle: the question should be posed on the supply side, as mentioned above (levels of growth should be compatible with adequate governance, control procedures, proximity, etc.; see D'Espallier et al. this volume), and simultaneously on the demand side: how much debt can people and local economies absorb? A careful, case-specific balance should be sought between economic and debt growth rates.

As the Dominican Republic's case makes clear, in order to achieve financial sustainability, remain competitive and attract funders, MFIs have pre-defined objectives as regards both volume portfolios and repayment performance. While these targets are not necessarily high by global standards, they can push MFIs to concentrate on a specific segment – less risky clients – who are then overwhelmed by credit offers. Pursuing growth becomes a strain – where demand does not exist it must be created. The cases of Tamil Nadu and Morocco are rather similar in this respect: with the delinquency crisis fresh in loan officers' minds, they have targeted an increasingly narrow segment: not necessarily where demand is greatest, but where there is the most security. In Senegal, where some signs of crisis have emerged, targeting wage earners has successfully given security to microcredit providers, but has raised questions as to the nature of their objectives. Across the board, the security of the providers seems to have come at the expense of borrowers, who either have plentiful choices and are therefore exposed to the dangers of over-indebtedness, or are excluded.

The issue of the absorption capacity of local economies is all the more critical given that timely repayment is not a fully reliable indicator of repayment capacity. Various studies point out that some mechanisms simply postpone crises: these include informal finance juggling practices (see Guérin et al. on Tamil Nadu and Morvant-Roux et al. on the Dominican Republic this volume), migration (Bylander 2014; Morvant-Roux 2013) or selling assets (Bateman 2010; Joseph 2013). As for MFIs, rescheduling practices – disbursing a new loan to a defaulting client – are common in places such as India (see Guérin et al. this volume), Pakistan (Burki 2009), Bangladesh (Karim 2011), and quite probably elsewhere.

Good repayment rates cannot rule out client over-indebtedness (and vice versa, as we shall see below). In Ghana, excellent repayment rates were found to run alongside a high share (around one-third) of customer over-indebtedness (Schicks 2013). Since the pioneering study of Rahman (1999), several studies in Bangladesh have pointed out clients' over-indebtedness. But repayment rates are still excellent, owing to what Lamia Karim (2011) calls an 'economy of shame'. This works through public denunciations that mostly target women as the guardians of family honour in the local social culture. In Bolivia, though the crisis officially ended in the early 2000s, various studies have found that clients' financial fragility has been ongoing (Brett 2006; Gonzales 2008). This is also clear from the Dominican Republic case presented here (Morvant et al.): despite good performance indicators, a large number of clients are struggling to repay their loans, including some whom the MFIs would view as 'good clients'.

Struggle and resistance

Microcredit crises can also reflect resistance practices whereby borrowers are able, but unwilling, to repay. Repayment defaults can be interpreted as political messages to microcredit organizations, the microcredit industry or more globally towards 'authority'. These practices may be the result of inadequate financial services, a sense of injustice following aggressive marketing and strong-arm enforcement mechanisms, a lack of integration and legitimacy within local contexts, or conflicts of interest. They can happen spontaneously, or be encouraged by the perceived or publicly proven corrupt practices of some leaders. They can be individual or collective, initiated by a clientele as a whole, or only a particular interest group. These resistance practices can also arise from a climate of distrust stemming from a specific political situation. They occur more readily when borrowers can access alternatives such as consumer credit or informal finance.

Borrowers' failure to repay doesn't imply a lack of ethical standards, but rather that borrowers are using their own specific criteria. Economic anthropology has shown that debt is considered not only a financial transaction but a social tie. Diversity in debts reflects, updates, reproduces or challenges diversity in individual and collective social identities. Individuals often accumulate debt and credit and repay loans on the basis of their own informal hierarchies and frameworks of calculation (Shipton 2010). This transcends material or self-centred motivation to reflect issues of status, honour, power and individual as well as group identity. It also reflects the trust – or lack thereof – between microcredit providers and their clients.

Various reports on the microcredit crises have highlighted the role of political or religious pressure groups in microcredit's loss of legitimacy. There is no doubt as to the opportunism of some of these groups, and it is clear that public calls for non-payment have dramatically accelerated waves of defaults. But in-depth field observation makes clear that some of the revolts started at a grassroots level, and were spontaneous.

The clients themselves first began the non-payment movement in Punjab (Pakistan). They then turned to a politician for back-up (Burki 2009). Clients disclosed the highly unethical practices of MFIs, which included making heavy use of local leaders and gangs to screen and monitor clients, stealing borrowing groups from other MFIs by bribing group leaders, and extorting clients. In Karnataka, where defaulting clients are often portrayed as having been manipulated by a Muslim organization (Anjuman Committee), closer analysis shows that the borrowers themselves, some of whom were over-indebted, decided to defy the rules of MFIs. Others were simply worn out by unethical practices, and they then asked local leaders and local authorities for their support (Joseph 2013).

In Nicaragua, it was President Ortega who was suspected to have played a major role in the *No Pago* movement. Here too, Servet's chapter shows that the mass default movement was a grassroots initiative by property owners against the imprisonment of defaulters and in the defence of property rights: it is a social movement, and not at all a direct political intervention from above. In Senegal, the climate of impunity that has prevailed under the Wade regime and repeated corruption scandals in the microcredit industry have clearly contributed to an atmosphere of defiance and distrust (Baumann et al. this volume).

In Morocco, repayment defaults largely reflect microcredit's lack of legitimacy (Morvant-Roux et al. 2014), owing to aversion to debt for religious and cultural reasons. In some regions, it also stems from confusions between microcredit and the *Maghzen* (central authority, king). Precisely because microcredit is perceived as coming from the state, it is considered a non-repayable debt. On top of this come incentives for non-payment from local leaders, be these clan leaders or politicians using microcredit and promises of debt cancellation as an opportunity to win votes (Morvant-Roux et al. 2014). The Arab Spring probably played a role in the continuation of the crisis in Morocco. In 2011 a revolt took place in Ouarzazat, under the name of the 'victims of microcredit' (Mourji 2014). They publicly accused microcredit providers of exploiting women while citing opaque credit agreements, exorbitant prices, the seizure of material goods in the event of default, the impoverishment of families and the tragedies some had experienced. In the meantime they enjoyed multiple benefits (tax exemptions, preferential rates from banks, multiple grants from foreign donors, and high profits). The case was sent to court and had still not been settled in late 2014.

Should we abandon or rethink microcredit?

Crises vary and so do their consequences. These can include increasing professionalization (which may not mean the same thing to everyone), increased concentration (there is no definitive answer to whether this is good or bad: it depends on the particular context and location), the diversification of products, improved transparency, improved articulation between portfolio growth and quality, and the logics of cross-subsidiarization. Crises can also bring about a loss of trust that might be difficult to rebuild, at least in the short term. They can also strengthen the highly questionable practices of microcredit organizations whose survival is at stake, kill off small organizations that had been offering innovative services, and lead to the abandonment of rural areas and the poorest segments of clientele.

Microcredit crises reveal that clients are facing over-indebtedness and/or that there is a loss of legitimacy and trust in microcredit institutions. Providers have meanwhile been unable to respect the fundamental principles of what microcredit should be. These crises widely confirm that mission drift has indeed taken place in different parts of the world, as has been denounced for several years now, but ignored by many practitioners and policy-makers, and has often been reframed into a dominant single view. The four factors behind the crises – mission drift, regulation and public policies, the saturation of local economies, and struggle and resistance – are strongly interrelated. The way in which they relate to one another varies across countries and sub-regions. They also articulate with social and cultural factors. The inability of microcredit services to fit with local perceptions, be it in terms of their financial needs, aspirations or attitudes towards money, debt and saving, helps to explain the poor social credibility of microcredit in some contexts.

Microcredit crises should also be situated in a broader context of the role of various stakeholders in the regulation of the microcredit industry. Of course, innovative and sophisticated tools of control and good governance can and need to be developed. But the ideology underlying the crises should also be critically addressed. To do so reveals the growing importance of for-profit motivations and the frenetic explosion of the market. At the same time, the ideology of the market has gone hand in hand with the return of populist public credit policies. Will these crises be seized as an opportunity to create compromises that go beyond the pursuit of profit for some, and electoral agendas for others? That is our hope.

Should we conclude that microcredit does more harm than good and that it should be abandoned? Some scholars are extremely critical of microcredit, considering it first and foremost as a new niche for capitalism and a vehicle for neoliberalism that destroys local economies (Bateman 2010) or acts as a new form of power and control over the poor (Fernando 2006; Roy 2010). Microcredit has been deconstructed as shaped by and constitutive of hegemonic discourses and policies that are highly neoliberal (Bateman 2010; Mader 2015), neocolonial (Roy 2010) and patriarchal (Karim 2011). In its most common form, microcredit is more likely to discipline than empower the poor. It directly or indirectly imposes specific behavioural norms, or exploits them, with a large proportion of the poor's income being taken up by debt repayment (Guérin 2015).

It is extremely useful and necessary to critically unpack development discourses and to situate micro-initiatives within a broader framework. There is no doubt that the original alternative, reformist movement has gradually transformed into a standardized, highly commercial platform. It is very clear that the microcredit industry has been built on unrealistic expectations and impossible promises. On its own, microcredit is in no position to eradicate poverty, create jobs or empower women. Furthermore, encouraging people to get into debt without protecting them is risky (Guérin 2015). There is no doubt that the demand for microcredit has been greatly overestimated. The size of the potential market has more to do with fantasy than reality. In many cases it is a dream fuelled by the search for financial sustainability or profitability.

All of these wayward tendencies need to be highlighted and condemned. This is one of the purposes of this book, but it does not mean stopping thinking about what fair and affordable financial services should look like. This is our editorial position, although some of our authors' chapters may disagree.

Whether we like it or not, most of today's societies are, to various degrees, financialized. Nowadays, the poor and those excluded from formal banking need financial services, be this to protect themselves from the risks of everyday life, or to make investments and take advantage of economic opportunities, or to plan for the future. Marginalized local economies also need financial services to support their development. Local populations have not been waiting for microfinance providers to come along in order to borrow, save and self-insure. As various chapters in this volume show, there exists a wide range of sophisticated, often informal financial services to respond to various needs, sometimes more efficiently than microcredit. All too often, microcredit providers ignore pre-existing financial arrangements or misunderstand their meaning and significance. Credit providers are very often perceived as greedy and exploitative moneylenders, which is often wrong. Too often, the multiple roles of pre-existing financial providers are ignored. This includes their protective function (which might be exploitative, but is also key when social protection is lacking), their facilitation of access to markets (which is crucial for small entrepreneurs), and their social and cultural meanings.

This said, pre-existing financial services still struggle to meet all the financial needs of given populations, especially as regards investment credit, saving, insurance, payments and transfers. Even in very remote places, except maybe for few isolated tribes, populations are connected to the global world and aspire to be connected. To give them the opportunity to send and receive money is a way to be connected. In a growing number of countries, social benefits now transit through bank accounts. As such, holding a bank account contributes to citizenship.

This does not mean that we should fatalistically accept today's banking and financialization conditions as unavoidable processes. Since the 1980s, the growing neoliberal mutation of the interdependencies between human activities, happening globally and locally, has resulted in a strong dependence on the financial sector. Under various forms, the multiple mechanisms of the financial sector have consciously increased their draining of productive activities and households, through consumer credits, for example. These accumulated financial volumes are now so significant that they feed on themselves and increase in relative weight. This also explains the widening of the inequality gap, as analysed by Thomas Piketty. However, it has now become impossible to break out of this system – for example, by rejecting financial institutions – because this would mean breaking the links that are essential to the continuation of human societies and communities. Many of the links between and within territories require those financial interdependencies. The links between productive units appear in financial contexts. Yet we shall not conclude that the supply of financial services should be reduced. If we dared to compare the supply of financial services to water supply, it's not because water supply was privatized and generates significant profits that a reduction in water consumption should in any way be advocated. Similarly, the domination of neoliberal finance (of which microcredit has in many cases become one of the mechanisms, and increasingly so at the base of the pyramid) should indeed be reduced, all the while diversifying the offer of financial services. Poor people need, like everyone else, to have access to sound, safe, respectful and reliable systems in order to fulfil their financial needs and all around the world there are people and organizations that are trying to contribute to this desirable objective.

However, the main challenge is to identify the conditions that can allow financial services to benefit poor and local economies, and not just financial providers and their allies. This edited volume calls in its conclusion for a vision of finance and money as 'commons', as a pathway out of the limitations of the current microcredit industry, which are likely to generate repeated crises – be it through saturation effects or over-indebtedness, and so on – and thus to harm or even kill off the credibility of the entire sector.

Notes

1 Microcredit is defined here as the provision of credit services to the unbanked. It is often confused with microfinance, which includes *all sorts* of financial services for the unbanked (microcredit but also savings, insurance, bank accounts, transfers, payments, etc.). Unless otherwise specified, these are the definitions used throughout the book. The present crises, which are the focus of this book, relate to microcredit and repayment defaults. However, when we refer to organizations, since many of them provide services other than microcredit, we often use the term 'microfinance institutions' or its acronym (MFI). For countries where most microcredit providers also provide other services (such as Senegal), we also use the term microfinance.

2 This refers to loan portfolios overdue by more than thirty days.

3 Attawfiq is the new name of the Fondation Banque Populaire pour le Microcrédit.

4 At that time, they were FECECAM, PADME, PAPME and FENACREP (Acclassato and Goudjo 2012).

5 Consultative Group to Assist the Poor (CGAP). The CGAP is an informal network bringing together prominent microcredit

providers and donors, which has played a key role in areas including the professionalization of the industry, the elaboration of 'best practices' and the common rules of management and evaluation.

6 The Mix Market validates and then centralizes on an internet platform a number of indicators (mostly financial, but some social) from MFIs which are willing to divulge their activities.

References

Acclassato, D. and G. Goudjo (2012) 'Pratiques de gouvernance et crise des institutions de microfinance au Bénin', *Techniques Financières et Développement*, 106: 79–97.

ADA (2010) 'La trop forte concentration des investissements étrangers dans un nombre restreint d'institutions de microfinance engendre-t-elle des "mauvaises" pratiques pour le secteur?', *Support de discussion ADA*, 2, Luxembourg: ADA.

Angulo, L. (2013) 'The social costs of microfinance and over-indebtedness for women', in I. Guérin, S. Morvant-Roux and M. Villarreal (eds), *Microfinance, Debt and Over-indebtedness: Juggling with Money*, London: Routledge, pp. 232–52.

Armendáriz, B. and M. Labie (eds) (2011) *Handbook of Microfinance*, Washington, DC: World Scientific Publishing.

Armendáriz, B. and A. Szafarz (2011) 'On mission drift in microfinance institutions', in *Handbook of Microfinance*, Washington, DC: World Scientific Publishing, pp. 341–67.

Arunachalam, R. (2011) *The Journey of Indian Micro-Finance: Lessons for the Future*, Chennai: Aapti Publications.

Augsburg, B. and C. Fouillet (2010) 'Profit empowerment: the microfinance institution's mission drift', *Perspectives on Global Development and Technology*, IX(3/4): 327–55.

Bateman, M. (2010) *Why Doesn't Microfinance Work? The Destructive Rise of Local Neoliberalism*, London: Zed Books.

— (2013) 'The age of microfinance: destroying Latin American economies from the bottom up', ÖFSE Working Paper 39, Vienna: Österreichische Forschungsstiftung für Internationale Entwicklung – ÖFSE.

Bédécarrats, F. and C. Lapenu (2013) 'Assessing microfinance: striking a balance between social utility and financial performance', in J.-P. Gueyie, R. Manos and J. Yaron (eds), *Microfinance in Developing and Developed Countries: Issues, Policies and Performance*

Evaluation, New York: Palgrave Macmillan, pp. 62–82.

Bédécarrats, F., J. Bastiaensen and F. Doligez (2012) 'Co-optation, cooperation or competition? Microfinance and the new left in Bolivia, Ecuador and Nicaragua', *Third World Quarterly*, 33(1): 143–60.

Brett, J. A. (2006) '"We sacrifice and eat less": the structural complexities of microfinance participation', *Human Organization*, 65(1): 8–19.

Burki, H.-B. (2009) 'Unraveling the delinquency problem (2008–2009) in Punjab-Pakistan', *Micronote*, 10, Microfinance Pakistan Network.

Bylander, M. (2014) 'Borrowing across borders: migration and microcredit in rural Cambodia', *Development and Change*, XLV(2): 284–307.

Chen, G. and S. Rutherford (2013) 'A microcredit crisis averted: the case of Bangladesh', *Focus Note* no. 87, Washington, DC: CGAP.

Chen, G., S. Rasmussen and X. Reille (2010) 'Growth and vulnerabilities in microfinance', *Focus Note* no. 61, Washington, DC: CGAP.

Collins, D., J. Morduch, S. Rutherford and O. Ruthven (2009) *Portfolios of the Poor: How the World's Poor Live on $2 a Day*, Princeton, NJ: Princeton University Press.

Dichter, T. and M. Harper (2007) *What's Wrong with Microfinance?*, London: Practical Action.

Dixon, R., J. Ritchie and J. Siwale (2007) 'Loan officers and loan "delinquency" in microfinance: a Zambian case', *Accounting Forum*, 31(1): 47–71.

Elyachar, J. (2006) *Markets of Dispossession: NGOs, Economic Development and the State in Cairo*, Durham, NC: Duke University Press.

Fernando, J. (2006) *Microfinance: Perils and Prospects*, London: Routledge.

Gonzales, A. (2008) 'Microfinance, incentives to repay, and overindebtedness: evidence from a household survey in Bolivia',

Doctoral thesis, Ohio State University, Ohio.

Guérin, I. (2003) *Femmes et économie solidaire*, Paris: La Découverte.

— (2015) *La microfinance et ses dérives: émanciper, exploiter ou discipliner?*, Paris: Demopolis/IRD.

Guérin, I. and S. Kumar (2007) 'Clientélisme, courtage et gestion des risques en microfinance. Etude de cas en Inde du Sud', *Revue Autrepart*, 44: 13–26.

Guérin, I., S. Morvant-Roux and J.-M. Servet (2011) 'Understanding the diversity and complexity of demand for microfinance services: lessons from informal finance', in B. Armendáriz and M. Labie (eds), *Handbook of Microfinance*, Washington, DC: World Scientific Publishing, pp. 101–22.

Guérin, I., S. Morvant-Roux and M. Villarreal (eds) (2013) *Microfinance, Debt and Over-indebtedness: Juggling with Money*, London: Routledge.

Hudon, M. and J. Sandberg (2013) 'The ethical crisis in microfinance: issues, findings, and implications', *Business Ethics Quarterly*, XXIII(4): 561–89.

Hummel, A. (2013) 'The commercialization of microcredits and local consumerism: examples of over-indebtedness from indigenous Mexico', in I. Guérin, S. Morvant-Roux and M. Villarreal (eds), *Microfinance, Debt and Over-indebtedness: Juggling with Money*, London: Routledge, pp. 253–71.

Johnson, S., N. Mule, P. Hickson and W. Mwangi (2003) 'The managed ASCA model innovation in Kenya's microfinance industry', in M. Harper (ed.), *Microfinance: Evolution, Achievements and Challenges*, London: ITDG Publishing, pp. 159–71.

Joseph, N. (2013) 'Mortgaging used saree-skirts, spear-heading resistance: narratives from the microfinance repayment standoff in Ramanagaram, India, 2008–2010', in I. Guérin, S. Morvant-Roux and M. Villarreal (eds), *Microfinance, Debt and Over-indebtedness: Juggling with Money*, London: Routledge, pp. 272–94.

Karim, L. (2011) *Microfinance and Its Discontents: Women Debt in Bangladesh*, Minneapolis and London: University of Minnesota Press.

Mader, P. (2015) *The Political Economy of Microfinance: Financialising Poverty*, London: Palgrave.

Microbanking Bulletin (2012) 'The tipping point: over-indebtedness and investment in microfinance', Mix/MicroRate, microrate.com/wp-content/uploads/downloads/2012/03/MBB-The-Tipping-Point-over-indebtedness-and-investment-in-microfinance_2.pdf, accessed 24 May 2013.

MicroRate (2013) 'The state of microfinance investment 2013 – survey and analysis of MIVs – 8th edition'.

Morduch, J. (1999) 'The microfinance promise', *Journal of Economic Literature*, XXXVII(4): 1569–614.

— (2013) 'How microfinance really works? (What new research tells us about)', CERMi's 5th birthday celebration, Brussels, 18 March.

Morvant-Roux, S. (2013) 'International migration and over-indebtedness in rural Mexico', in I. Guérin, S. Morvant-Roux and M. Villarreal (eds), *Microfinance, Debt and Over-indebtedness: Juggling with Money*, London: Routledge, pp. 171–86.

Morvant-Roux, S. and M. Roesch (2013) 'Analysis of strategic defaults in the Moroccan microfinance sector', *Policy and Research Brief*, 1, Microfinance in Crisis Research Project.

Morvant-Roux, S., I. Guérin, M. Roesch and J.-Y. Moisseron (2014) 'Adding value to randomization with qualitative analysis: the case of microcredit in rural Morocco', *World Development*, LVI: 302–12.

Mourji, F. (2014) 'An overview of microcredit activities in Morocco: from boom to bust and new horizons', Unpublished document, Microfinance in Crisis Research Project.

Planetrating (2013) *Mimosa. Microfinance Index of Market Outreach and Saturation. Part 1 – Total Credit Market Capacity, March 2013*, Paris: Planetrating, www.planetrating.com/userfiles/file/MIMOSA%201_0_final%20110313.pdf, accessed 2 June 2013.

Rahman, A. (1999) *Women and Microcredit in Rural Bangladesh: An Anthropological Study of Grameen Bank Lending*, Boulder, CO: Westview Press.

Reed, L. R. (2013) *Vulnerability: The State of the Microcredit Summit Campaign Report, 2013*, Washington, DC: Microcredit Summit Campaign.

— (2014) *Resilience: The State of the Microcredit Summit Campaign Report, 2014*, Washington, DC: Microcredit Summit Campaign.

Rhyne, E. (2001) *Mainstreaming Microfinance: How Lending to the Poor Began, Grew and Came of Age in Bolivia?*, West Hartford, CT: Kumarian Press.

Roodman, D. (2012) 'Grameen Bank portfolio continues deteriorating', Blog, international.cgdev.org/blog/grameen-bank-portfolio-continues-deteriorating, accessed 20 October 2014.

Roy, A. (2010) *Poverty Capital: Microfinance and the Making of Development*, New York: Routledge.

Rozas, D. (2009) 'Is there a microfinance bubble in south-India?', *Microfinance Focus*, 17, www.danielrozas.com/2009/11/17/is-there-a-microfinance-bubble-in-south-india/, accessed 22 March 2013.

— (2014) 'Microfinance in Mexico: beyond the brink', EMP blog, www.e-mfp.eu/blog/microfinance-mexico-beyond-brink, accessed 20 October 2014.

Rozas, D., K. Pinget, M. Khaled and S. El Yaalaoui (2014) *Ending the Microfinance Crisis in Morocco: Acting Early, Acting Right*, Washington, DC: International Finance Corporation (World Bank group).

Sall, A. (2012) 'Les stratégies et initiatives des femmes dans le secteur de la microfinance. Le cas du Sénégal', Doctoral thesis in sociology, Université Paris Descartes.

Schicks, J. (2013) 'The sacrifices of micro-borrowers in Ghana – a customer protection perspective on measuring over-indebtedness', *Journal of Development Studies*, 49(9): 1238–55.

Servet, J.-M. (2011) 'La crise du microcrédit en Andhra Pradesh (Inde)', *Revue Tiers Monde*, 207(3): 43–59.

— (2012) 'Un facteur externe de crise de microcrédit: la concentration des investissements étrangers dans un nombre restreint d'institutions de microfinance', *Techniques Financières et Développement*, 106: 23–34.

— (2013) 'Origines et impact du mouvement No Pago dans le Nord Ouest du Nicaragua', *Policy and Research Brief*, 2, Microfinance in Crisis Research Project, www.microfinance-in-crisis.org.

— (2015) *La vraie révolution du microcrédit*, Paris: Odile Jacob.

Servet, J.-M. and H. Saiag (2013) 'Household over-indebtedness in northern and southern countries: a macro-perspective', in I. Guérin, S. Morvant-Roux and M. Villarreal (eds), *Microfinance, Debt and Over-indebtedness: Juggling with Money*, London: Routledge, pp. 24–45.

Shipton, P. (2010) *Credit between Cultures: Farmers, Financiers and Misunderstandings in Africa*, New Haven, CT, and London: Yale University Press.

Sinclair, H. (2012) *Confessions of a Microfinance Heretic: How Microlending Lost Its Way and Betrayed the Poor*, San Francisco, CA: Berrett-Kohler Publishers.

Siwale, J. and J. Ritchie (2013) 'Accounting for microfinance failure: insights from Zambia', *International Journal of Critical Accounting*, 5(6): 641–62.

Taylor, M. (2011) 'Freedom from poverty is not for "free": rural development and the microfinance crisis in Andhra Pradesh, India', *Journal of Agrarian Change*, 11(4): 484–504.

Young, S. (2010) 'Gender, mobility and the financialisation of development', *Geopolitics*, 15(3): 606–27.

Part I
SUPPLY

1 | MICROCREDIT CRISES AND UNSUSTAINABLE GROWTH: A MANAGEMENT PERSPECTIVE

Bert D'Espallier, Marc Labie and Philippe Louis

Introduction

Over the last few years, several major crises have drawn the attention of the international community to the limits of microcredit and the risks the industry must be able to face. Of course, different factors play a critical part in these crises, and we need to analyse them from different perspectives, taking demand, supply and environment into account, among other things. The goal of this chapter is to improve understanding of the potential mechanisms that may contribute to the origin of supply crises. The chapter is based on a bottom-up approach. A better understanding of these sources and their consequences will be beneficial for a wide range of stakeholders such as regulators, donors and, evidently, the management of microcredit institutions (MFIs).

We define a supply-side microcredit crisis as a situation in which the industry is disrupted since some MFIs are no longer able to operate properly because the MFIs themselves are having difficulties, often of a financial or operational nature. This covers supply-related problems that should be understood as the MFIs becoming unable to appropriately deliver the microcredit products and services. More specifically, we try to give an overview of the dynamic that may generate crises, focusing particularly on the issue of 'sustainable growth'. Indeed, in many of the crises observed on the ground, it appears quite clear that once the crisis is there, many people consider that it is somehow linked with the way the MFI(s) has developed and more specifically with the way it has grown. So we will try to present here a framework of analysis to discuss this issue. The remainder of this chapter is made up of six sections. The first will discuss the fundamentals of microcredit. The second will review the challenges generated by high growth and how it can represent a danger for the fundamentals presented in the previous section. The third will then discuss to what extent it is possible to identify what is 'too strong a growth'. The fourth will suggest how such excessive growth can affect MFIs. The fifth will suggest a 'preventive check list' resulting from the previous discussions and the last one will provide preliminary conclusions.

Fundamentals of microcredit

In order to be able to discuss how microcredit can get into crisis dynamics, it is important to describe what the fundamental characteristics of successful microcredit institutions are, because when a crisis occurs it is reasonable to assume these fundamentals characteristics will be endangered. Of course, not all cases will be similar and there is plenty of space to discuss to what extent those changes are part of the causes or the consequences of the crisis.

Present-day microcredit is composed of a great variety of actors and practices that aim to offer financial services to people who have no access to the traditional banking sector (Armendáriz and Morduch 2010). Owing to this heterogeneity, it is not straightforward to easily summarize common characteristics. However, generally speaking, successful microcredit institutions operate in a decentralized fashion and offer simple, rather standardized products to well-screened clients who are under enough peer pressure to guarantee their repayments. In a nutshell, there are four key common characteristics of successful MFIs: decentralization, proximity, simple (and usually standardized) products, and growth strategies that allow for a true development of the portfolios while keeping their quality under control.

Decentralization and hence high proximity between clients and institutions is vital for several reasons. First, it offers an in-depth knowledge of the local context in which the clients will undertake their activities and projects. As such, the credit officer has a very good grasp of the economic, social and cultural reality. Besides, knowing this reality will also give some credibility to the credit officer. Second, assessing the clients is essential. Most clients cannot provide documents or definite proof of their reliability. As a consequence, credit officers will be in a better position to assess a client's 'a priori' reliability if they 'belong' to a community. Third, since follow-up is necessary, high proximity allows the credit officer to get in touch with clients if problems should arise. In sum, it is clear that MFIs need to give priority to the proximity with their clients.

Local microcredit branches generally have real decision-making capacity and autonomy. Credit officers are responsible for their clients and have to manage their portfolio in the best possible way. Incentive schemes encourage them to pursue portfolio growth and maintain an appropriate portfolio quality. Yet microcredit institutions limit the size of their branches to prevent bureaucracy, which could dissuade clients.

Credit is often limited – at least officially – to the financing of working capital and to relatively short-term investments. Usually, credits are standardized in order to facilitate the clients' understanding and the MFIs' everyday management of their portfolios. When savings services are provided, they are very often relatively simple and allow clients to save according to their capabilities. They also allow clients to have easy access to their savings when needed. Of course, the various programmes differ, but generally savings programmes that have been successful aim to provide a simple, safe and available product to their clients. Returns on savings are clearly a concern of less importance in those programmes (Rutherford and Arora 2009).

In terms of the institution's growth strategy, several approaches are possible. First, a horizontal growth strategy which intends to increase the number of branches without changing the products offered within each branch. This growth tactic is appropriate when the organization is of the impression that various geographic regions are not properly served. A second possible strategy is to offer new products to existing clients in the current branches. The third possible approach is to diversify the clients, which generally implies targeting less underprivileged clients. Although these different strategies typically stem from internal growth, external development, for instance through joint ventures or mergers, is also possible.

High growth challenges

During the last decade, microfinance experienced unprecedented growth, often with double-digit annual growth rates in terms of both asset volume and number of borrowers. We believe that this tremendous growth is a direct result of governance evolution. The gradual shift from subsidized programmes towards more sustainable microfinance, where the unmet demand would be supplied by financially efficient institutions, has markedly changed the way microfinance is delivered to its audience.

Originally, from the early 1950s to the 1980s, subsidized credit was the cornerstone of many poverty reduction schemes. However, as Robinson (2001) points out, these programmes were not successful, either from a social impact point of view, or from a good corporate governance perspective, since (1) subsidized interest rates combined with a relatively high cost of making small loans ensured that loans were channelled to larger borrowers and not to poorer households; (2) funding was provided by donors, making many subsidized credit programmes susceptible to a high degree of moral hazard, resulting in widespread corruption and high default rates; and (3) the programmes were unable to satisfy the demand for microfinance, resulting in significant unmet demand. As such, in the 1980s, these credit programmes came under increased attack as evidence of poor results mounted (Adams et al. 1984; Robinson 2001). The idea behind commercial microfinance is straightforward: by making MFIs less dependent on donations and steering them towards more self-sufficiency, the aforementioned problems could be resolved (Woller et al. 1999; Morduch 2000). The ideological goal was growing the industry in order to serve the unmet demand in microfinance. Eventually, this should result in the largest possible availability of microcredit at the lowest possible cost to donors and governments (Bateman 2010). The inevitable transitional process is described at length in Ledgerwood and White (2006).

As such, this evolution has brought various challenges into the microcredit sector. The first, financial stress, is mainly due to the change from donor funding to more expensive commercial loans and deposits, which increased the average cost of funds, particularly for institutions facing a high need for additional liquidities in order to match the growth of their credit portfolio. The second challenge, adapting the institution to a novel operational management structure, is not straightforward and is more difficult to quantify, but it is clear that, for many institutions, adapting new management information systems, having to report to bank supervisory bodies (for those institutions which transformed into regulated entities) and matching expectations from new share- and stakeholders represents quite a challenge. A good example of this evolution is the way the industry has been confronted with a rising number of microfinance investment vehicles (MIVs). These profit-seeking investors, including investment banks and private equity funds, channelled capital into microcredit operations, aiming to combine two types of logic: a banking logic and a development logic (Battilana and Dorado 2010; Urgeghe 2013). While the number of MIVs and the amount under their management totalled forty-three and US$1 billion respectively in 2004, these numbers rose to ninety-five and US$8 billion by 2011, representing 61 per cent of the total foreign investment in microfinance (Reille et al. 2010; MicroRate 2013). According to Reille et al. (2010), MIVs' funding comprises 42 per cent institutional investors, 34 per cent individuals, 21 per cent development finance institutions (DFIs) and 3 per cent other sources. While institutional investors value both financial and social impact and returns, DFIs focus primarily on financial performance. Consequently, they steer their investments towards large, profitable MFIs. Given this investment rationale and the fact that they represent a large proportion of the funding in microfinance, their impact and importance cannot be underestimated. Furthermore, MIVs prefer to invest by means of debt (82 per cent), with just 18 per cent equity participation (MicroRate 2013). The high proportion of debt investments is a good example of a proverbial double-edged sword. If more can be earned on the microcredit operations than the institution pays in interest expenses and fees on the debt, the institution is able to pursue strong expansion at a relatively low cost, as debt is normally less expensive than equity. However, debt requires that institutions strictly comply with their repayment commitments, as failure to make these payments can lead to default or loss of control of the institution. In case of an adverse economic situation, equity will act as a financial cushion whereas debt repayments still need to be serviced. Moreover, a higher proportion of debt funding relative to equity results in a higher leverage of the institution, which will magnify losses when the institution runs into problems.

In many contexts, MFIs have gone through a 'professionalization process', becoming closer to 'mainstream financial institutions' and facing the same dilemmas between cost, outreach and sustainability, notably in order to balance their double core objectives of being 'financial self-sufficient' and at the same time 'socially oriented'. This has resulted in debates on what the true priorities of MFIs are and what their impact is. In many markets, a lot has been achieved in terms of development of the sector, even though the true social impact might be much more limited than what has been hoped for originally. In other markets, development has sometimes gone 'wild', and crises have appeared. We believe there exists a potential causative relationship between unhealthy growth (i.e. growth that is too strong) and crises. However, before we elaborate this hypothesis, we will first define the term 'microcredit crisis'. When someone uses this term, it is not always immediately clear to what kind of crisis the person is referring, for the very reason that multiple situations are considered a crisis. From a conceptual point of view, we could broadly distinguish between a demand- and a supply-side crisis. A demand-side crisis arises when many borrowers run into problems, while the MFIs are still able to properly function financially and operationally.

A supply-side crisis occurs when MFIs run into such trouble that they are no longer able to operate properly. Several conditions should be fulfilled in order to designate a problem situation as an industry-wide microcredit supply crisis. First, MFIs must become unable to appropriately deliver their products and services. As such, an obvious, sharp disruption is necessary. Second, MFIs themselves must run into financial woes. Third, the affected MFIs should be located in a clear geographical area. Fourth, this crisis situation should last for a certain period, e.g. several years. Finally, the crisis should profoundly change the way MFIs do business.

But of course, in real life, supply and demand microcredit crises are not mutually exclusive. Indeed, not only can they happen at the same moment but they are quite often highly correlated to each other. Indeed, in many of the famous cases experienced by the industry so far, it is either because MFIs were not operating properly that their clients got into trouble (for example, MFIs generating over-indebtedness or being unable to guarantee sufficient liquidity to provide credits on time or good access to savings) or because clients were being affected by systemic problems (for example, political crisis or weather issues for agricultural schemes). Chapters on Nicaragua (Servet) and Andhra Pradesh (Picherit) presented in this volume are illustrative of this link.

While we accept that borrowers may also experience problems even when crises are not under way (as shown in this book in the case of some clients of Dominican Republic MFIs), in this chapter we will solely focus on supply-related issues and consequences. From 2007 onwards, microcredit started to experience serious problems in some geographic areas. When considering major supply crises in microcredit that hit a geographical area, it is often not surprising to see that these crises developed after a period of unrestrained growth. The crises that hit Bolivia several years ago and, more recently, those that struck Andhra Pradesh, Morocco, Nicaragua and Bosnia and Herzegovina all have different characteristics, but all have in common strong growth prior to the start of the crisis (Gonzalez-Vega and Villafani-Ibarnegaray 2011; Servet 2012; Morvant-Roux et al. 2012; Guérin and Roesch 2012).

The hypothesis we wish to put forward is that when too strong a growth is taking place, institutions lose the grasp they have on their processes and strategies and therefore take initiatives that ultimately may result in a crisis either at the level of the institution (if the problem is limited to a single institution) or at a broader level (if the same trend is experienced by various institutions simultaneously). Based on observation of various crises, the common dynamic seems to be the following. For whatever reason (excess of funds accessible, political pressure, huge 'perceived' potential growth, hubris, etc.) MFIs decide to develop fast (and furiously). They hire quite a lot of people, open new branches, and launch new (sometimes insufficiently tested) products. By doing so, they put a lot of pressure on their financial and operational skills, which they then have a hard time 'upgrading' at the same speed as the growth they are pursuing for their portfolio. The growth of the organization becomes the main objective and 'original' human resource management and corporate culture (and notably the initial 'double bottom line' elements it often includes) are progressively eroded. Then the key elements we mention in the second section of this chapter start to be affected. Decisions (including growth objectives) becomes less decentralized, proximity between operational staff and clients is lost (because growth generates the arrival of many newcomers and the creation of branches that do not have the time to build the type of relationship required in traditionally successful microcredit), portfolio growth is accorded a higher priority than portfolio quality (and to a certain extent the delay between the moment new credits are attributed and the time it takes for them to prove delinquent can be [technically] hidden for a certain period provided that growth is strong enough), and sometimes too many credits (or credits that are too large) are provided to previously sound clients who then turn 'bad' owing to this 'overflow of funding', as experienced to a certain extent in the Andhra Pradesh and Moroccan cases (see later chapters in this book). At this stage, MFIs usually try to react but they are already facing a crisis and the cost of salvation – when possible – is usually substantial. To a certain extent, a parallel can be made with the wild developments experienced by the world banking industry since the beginning of the 1980s. Indeed, the search for tremendous growth (and in this case for the highest possible short-term profits) led very 'old-fashioned' traditional banks to move away from their prudent and well-tested practices to much riskier ones, with the illusion that growth would be unlimited. In the end, it resulted in a huge crisis that swept away some institutions that everyone thought to be extremely sound and strong. In both cases (microcredit and the banking industry), the same strategy gives the same result: aiming for growth that is too strong and too fast leads organizations into trouble. So the key questions should be: 'what is a sustainable level of growth' and when can we say that growth is 'too strong'?

How much growth is too much?

Even if there are exceptions, 'growth' is usually an objective of most companies, irrespective of the industry in which they are operating. In microfinance, it is usually justified through two arguments: first, people need financial services and there are still excluded beneficiaries (even if, as shown by some recent research, the importance of this unmet market may be smaller than many thought – at least if we consider existing products, services and methodologies); second, growth is the best way to benefit from economies of scale and economies of scope as they are believed to be the most obvious ways to reduce the cost of providing services, hopefully (but not always) allowing for cheaper services to customers. In an economic context, growth is defined as 'an increase in the value of goods or services produced and sold by a business' (Longman 2003). With regard to the microcredit industry, growth is often measured as the increase in the number of borrowers or the number of loans, or the evolution of the gross loan portfolio. The Mix Market database reports that the total size of the gross loan portfolio and the total number of borrowers (of the MFIs that report to it) increased from just US$8.37 billion and 10.76 million respectively at the end of 2003 to US$98.36 billion and 77.30 million by the end of 2012 (Mix Market 2014). In Figure 1.1, the growth in the gross

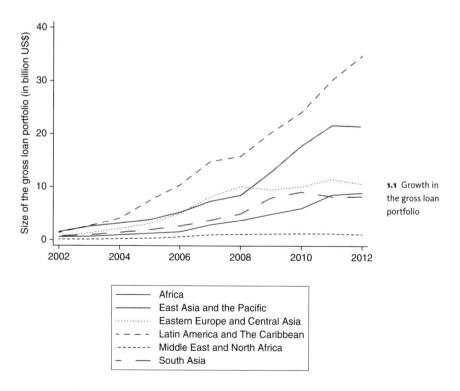

1.1 Growth in the gross loan portfolio

Africa
East Asia and the Pacific
Eastern Europe and Central Asia
Latin America and The Caribbean
Middle East and North Africa
South Asia

Source: Mix Market database and authors' calculation

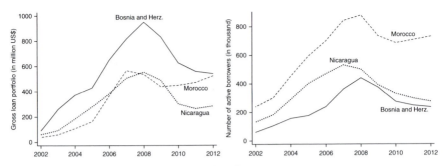

1.2 Aggregate gross loan portfolio and aggregate number of borrowers
Source: Mix Market variables winsorized at 95% percentile and authors' calculation

loan portfolio is further divided by region. As depicted, most regions, except the Middle East and North Africa, experienced strong growth.

In Figure 1.2 (left) plots the size of the aggregate gross loan portfolio of three countries that were recently confronted with a crisis: Bosnia and Herzegovina, Morocco and Nicaragua. Between 2004 and 2007/08, the industry expanded at an unprecedented annual growth rate, with expansion being fuelled by 'a combination of the addition of branches in new markets and growth in existing markets through larger loans and new products'. The total number of borrowers in Figure 1.2 (right) shows a similar growth pattern between 2004 and 2007/08. However, from 2007/08 onwards, the growth tanked and the microcredit industry found itself in a serious crisis.

The stories behind those curves are not identical, but still, it is quite interesting to note that in the three cases there was a sharp increase in the growth rate (either in the portfolio or the number of active borrowers) before the sharp decline identified as 'the crisis'.

A striking example is Morocco. In 2007, the microcredit industry was hit by a major crisis. From 2003 to 2007, Moroccan MFIs experienced very strong growth and their portfolio increased tenfold with 1.35 million loans outstanding by December 2007 (Chehade and Nègre 2013). The industry appeared to be in healthy shape and the major MFIs performed well with respect to profitability and asset quality. However, when the credit risks to which the MFIs were exposed started to increase, MFIs became more wary about rolling over existing loans and reduced new credit, resulting in liquidity problems for some clients. Repayment problems soon spread across the entire microcredit sector, and by the end of 2009 the overall default rate was almost 14 per cent.

In the years leading to the crisis, the growth rate of the Moroccan economy was somewhat on a par with those of its regional peers, which can be seen in Table 1.1.

Given the slightly stronger expansion of the Moroccan economy compared to those of its regional peers, we would equally assume a more pronounced growth of the Moroccan microcredit industry. However, if the latter growth

TABLE 1.1 Economic growth figures in Morocco versus regional peers

		Morocco	Regional peers
GDP annual % growth	average pre-crisis 2002–07	4.65%	4.67%
	average post-crisis 2008–12	4.79%	3.35%
GDP per capita annual % growth	average pre-crisis 2002–07	3.62%	2.15%
	average post-crisis 2008–12	3.08%	1.95%

Source: World Bank World Development Indicators; authors' calculations

is much higher, this could possibly point towards an unsustainable growth pattern in the microcredit industry, which could be a major cause of the crisis. While the annual growth rate of GDP per capita in Morocco was around 68 per cent higher compared with the peer group, we find that the average annual growth rate of the gross loan portfolio during this period was around 81 per cent. This discrepancy argues in favour of a potential overheating of the industry. As such, examination of the average growth rate of the gross loan portfolio and the growth rate of the active borrowers supports the hypothesis that the expansion was out of line with that of its regional peers. Prior to the onset of the crisis, the average Moroccan paces of growth were consistently higher. However, when the difficulties started, this rate plummeted and remained below that of the regional peers.

By themselves, of course, those considerations do not allow us to say that when 'growth' reaches a certain level 'x', it could be considered a reason to be concerned. However, it sustains the intuition that when a crisis happens, it somehow follows a period of 'faster growth than usual'. It is therefore interesting to question how 'fast growth' could translate into 'higher risk' for MFIs.

The paths from growth to risks

In this section, we provide the reader with an analysis of how very strong growth within the microcredit industry might cause a range of unwanted effects. It is apparent that MFIs are, in certain situations, not able to deal with the consequences of the aforementioned unconstrained growth and that this growth influences the internal processes of an MFI in such a way that normal

TABLE 1.2 Growth of the Moroccan microcredit industry versus its peers

		Morocco	Regional peers
Gross loan portfolio annual % growth	average pre-crisis 2002–07	77.43%	42.80%
	average post-crisis 2008–12	–2.10%	30.66%
Active borrowers annual % growth	average pre-crisis 2002–07	49.08%	38.35%
	average post-crisis 2008–12	–3.03%	24.73%

Source: Mix Market variables winsorized at 95% percentile; authors' calculations

day-to-day activities could become impossible. Figure 1.3 provides the reader with a graphical overview of how strong growth could trigger a microcredit crisis through two different channels. These channels will be discussed in the next subsections.

Financial effects While in some crisis situations only a small number of institutions are affected, other cases disturb the entire microcredit market in a certain geographic area. These systemic crises affect all organizations, even those that tried to keep up with 'good practices'. An example is Basix, which was strongly affected by the deterioration of microcredit – as a field – in Andhra Pradesh. As such, institutions that are better managed may get into trouble because the economic environment in which they are operating is evolving, making life particularly hard for them. To some extent, this is the case for some institutions in Nicaragua (and in Morocco). Their business model made sense and they were reasonably well managed, but the crisis that appeared was a combination of a variety of political and social interferences that make their life difficult.

The management of the various assets and liabilities on the MFI's balance sheet is often demanding owing to the nature of the activities. In terms of assets, many short-term credits are granted within portfolios that are characterized by substantial risks, such as credit and concentration risks. Frequently, the clients are relatively concentrated either in a geographical area or in a business sector. As a result, when the risk profile of the portfolio changes, the consequences can become serious very quickly, even if the portfolio was well engineered and diversified at the beginning. In terms of liability management, the situation is also fairly complicated. First, capitalization can be a problem, even if an institution was properly capitalized previously, because it is often not feasible to maintain a constant level of capitalization when fast growth is experienced. Some organizations even become relatively less capitalized when the balance sheet grows as a result of larger portfolios. This is a potentially dangerous situation because capital acts as a buffer against unforeseen difficulties and hence growth warrants a sufficient capital buffer.

Substantial risks in terms of donors' funds also exist depending on the markets. This is due to the fact that the rates (and the speed) of refinancing are, by definition, beyond the MFIs' control. The MFI can somewhat mitigate this risk by adopting savings mobilization strategies but, notwithstanding that

1.3 Schematic overview of causative effects

this choice could be perfectly rational in the long term, savings mobilization strategies still entail a risk for the institutions as they imply important changes in terms of status, procedures, cost ratios, etc. As an alternative, some MFIs finance themselves abroad and resort to the various MIVs that have appeared over recent years. Even if this kind of financing is really interesting in terms of rapidity and reliability, it sometimes entails foreign exchange risks (which are often underestimated by the MFIs) and it can put MFIs under pressure that they sometimes did not anticipate.

Last but not least, high growth may lead to increased competition. Aggressive competition and lending concentration resulted in many clients borrowing from more than one MFI. Chen et al. (2010) estimate that around 40 per cent of active borrowers have multiple loans at different MFIs. In some cases, this results in massive 'merry-go-round lending', whereby clients take credit in an institution to reimburse another and so on. Of course, the situation can be even worse when informal financial sources are added to the scheme, as observed with some customers in the Dominican Republic (see Morvant-Roux et al. on the Dominican Republic in this volume), with formal and informal pressures reinforcing each other. Another way to calculate the amount of competition within an industry is the Herfindahl–Hirschman index (HHI). It is computed by squaring the market share of each microcredit institution competing in a regional market, and then summing the resulting numbers. Consequently, it ranges from >0 to 1, where a number close to zero indicates near-perfect competition and a number close to one indicates a near-monopoly. When one applies this method to the countries we have referred to in this chapter (Morocco, Bosnia, Nicaragua), we observe that in all these countries competition was much harsher than that experienced by the other countries of their peer groups before their own crises.

Operational management effects The control of an organization can be particularly problematic in times of high growth. Several fundamental characteristics of microcredit institutions management allow us to understand why.

The first is the decentralized operational approach that was discussed in the previous section. While this strategy offers various advantages such as close proximity to clients and easier follow-up, an adequate overview of the branches from the institutions' headquarters can be challenging because microcredit institutions very often adopt a somewhat fuzzy structure in which governance is above all based on social control and trust. A good example are the large cooperative networks in West Africa (Ouedraogo and Gentil 2008; Doligez et al. 2012). At a small scale, it may work fine, but when growth appears, the structures become more elaborate and the increased distance between 'the head' and 'the base' of the organization reduces the efficiency of the control mechanisms that were at the core of the original successful operational management of the MFI.

Second, when the institutions grow, with respect to both complexity and scale, to some degree informal control mechanisms are not efficient any more and new, explicit procedures must be adopted in terms of internal oversight, regulation and supervision. The formalization and systemization of procedures through more elaborate management systems is seldom a straightforward task and they thus pose a risk to the survival of MFIs if they fail. However, as multiple studies show, it is no easy task to identify the key elements necessary for reliable governance, as there are many different situations. Considering that governance results from the overall set of mechanisms used in an institution to make sure that it sticks to its mission, we can assume that the existence of a large number of control mechanisms is – a priori – a rather positive element when the institution is experiencing strong growth. Indeed, some studies have shown that efficient governance mechanisms in small organizations can become less efficient in bigger institutions (Périlleux 2011).

Third, many institutions start as tiny organizations that are developed by a small group of motivated people who share a common understanding about the project. When an institution expands, the situation inevitably changes: existing members sometimes leave and new members are hired. Recruiting the right person for the job, and providing valuable human resources training, is often challenging. In particular, when the MFIs expand, many new employees are hired and consequently the relative proportion of experienced staff diminishes, representing sometimes a stiff challenge in terms of maintaining the corporate culture that was often a key element of the original success.

Besides, management practices can evolve. Quite often growth-oriented organizations implement incentive schemes in order to boost their growth but do not pay enough attention to the elements that originally were the main drivers of their success. A thorough analysis of incentive schemes intended for credit officers and all employees is thus justified.

So, by way of a conclusion to this section, we can say that some microcredit crises happen because MFIs experience changes that are too radical in their financial and operational profiles and therefore, in order to prevent crisis, it would be useful to clearly identify the items that need to be followed up. The next section tries to contribute to this goal.

Towards a 'preventive checklist'

Considering all the elements mentioned in the previous sections, it is clear that there are many ways in which excessive growth can damage microcredit institutions. Consequently, there are many aspects that should be scrutinized in order for someone to be able to whistle-blow before things reach a critical point.

Table 1.3 proposes a first approach to these aspects by providing a 'preventive checklist' to be kept in mind. It first focuses on the scale and

TABLE 1.3 Preventive checklist

Nature of growth		Preoccupying (Y/N?)
Balance sheet total growth		Y/N
Loan portfolio total growth (and % of balance sheet total)		Y/N
Evolution of the structure (number of branches, number of intermediary levels, etc.)		Y/N
Evolution of human resources (number of employees, number of credit officers)		Y/N
Levels of control		
of the mission	Clear definition and correct match with the organization's corporate culture	Y/N
	Stakeholders' 'sense of ownership'	
	○ employees (and/or members)	Y/N
	○ (operational) directors	Y/N
	○ members of specific governance structures (board of directors, General Assembly, internal audit, etc.)	Y/N
of the decentralization	Growth in the number of branches (number, size, etc.)	Y/N
	Number of new credit officers	Y/N
	Design of the incentive schemes for credit officers	Y/N
	Turnover of staff	Y/N
of operational strategies	Number and nature of new products	Y/N
	Number and nature of new guarantees or collaterals	Y/N
	Number and nature of new procedures	Y/N
of the portfolio	Increase in PAR 30 and PAR 90	Y/N
	Increase in portfolio loss	Y/N
	Increase in write-offs	Y/N
of the cost structure	Financing costs (short- and medium-term)	Y/N
	Operational costs (short- and medium-term)	Y/N
	Loan-loss provisioning costs (short- and medium-term)	Y/N
of the strategy	Medium- and long-term goals	Y/N
of the governance	Inadequate or non-existent internal audit and control mechanisms	Y/N
	Inadequate or non-existent integration in an appropriate regulation and supervision framework	Y/N

Source: Table elaborated by the authors

the nature of the growth and then goes through different fields that could be affected by this growth.

The ideal solution for an institution would be to move from such a 'generic list' to a more specific one (adapted to the characteristics of the institution and to the market in which it operates), hopefully resulting at the end in the establishment of a real 'balanced scorecard' (Labie 2005).

For each level of control, the idea should be to establish margins that the MFI considers acceptable based on its experience and on benchmarks that should be chosen among peer groups. The review would thus involve considering all the topics and deciding whether any have reached a level where they should be considered 'worrying' (yes or no). Based on the 'red flags' appearing, one could thus have a first warning before a crisis actually develops.

Concluding remarks

In a sector such as microcredit, an organization that is successful will be quickly confronted by strong growth possibilities. In absolute terms, there is no reason to be worried by this growth given that many people still do not have access to microfinance services and many authors believe that better financial inclusion should be promoted, which is a much broader debate than that characterizing the origin of the industry (Robinson 2009). However, as already mentioned, with existing products, services and methodologies, the potential market may often be much more limited than MFIs (and industry stakeholders) have in mind, as will be shown in the various chapters of this book focusing on understanding true demand. Besides, as we have attempted to demonstrate in this chapter, while the reasons that explain the success of microcredit are today relatively well identified, there are also many risks. We thus need to be careful, and MFIs that are achieving strong growth should consider it a reward for the effort invested, but also as an important challenge for their future.

References

Adams, D. W., D. H. Graham and J. D. von Pischke (1984) *Undermining Rural Development with Cheap Credit*, Boulder, CO: Westview Press.

Armendáriz, B. and M. Labie (2011) *The Handbook of Microfinance*, London/ Singapore: World Scientific Publishing/ Imperial College Press.

Armendáriz, B. and J. Morduch (2010) *The Economics of Microfinance*, Cambridge, MA, and London: MIT Press.

Armendáriz, B. and A. Szafarz (2011) 'On mission drift in microfinance institutions', in B. Armendáriz and M. Labie (eds), *The Handbook of Microfinance*, London/ Singapore: World Scientific Publishing/ Imperial College Press.

Austin, J., R. Gutierrez, M. Labie and E. Ogliastri (1998) 'Finansol: Financiera para Microempresas' (in Spanish); 'Finansol', Harvard Business School Case, Harvard University (in English), February.

Bastiaensen, J., P. Marchetti, R. Mendoza and F. Pérez (2013) 'After the Nicaraguan non-payment crisis: alternatives to microfinance narcissism', *Development and Change*, 44(4): 861–85.

Bateman, M. (2010) *Why Doesn't Microfinance Work? The Destructive Rise of Local Neoliberalism*, London: Zed Books.

Battilana, J. and S. Dorado (2010) 'Building sustainable hybrid organizations: the case of commercial microfinance organizations', *Academy of Management Journal*, 53(6): 1419–40.

Chehade, N. and A. Nègre (2013) 'Lessons learned from the Moroccan crisis', CGAP Briefing.

Chen, G. (1997) 'The challenge of growth for microfinance institutions: the BancoSol experience', CGAP Focus Note no. 6.

Chen, G., S. Rasmussen and X. Reille (2010) 'Growth and vulnerabilities in microfinance', CGAP Focus Note no. 61.

Churchill, C. (ed.) (2006) *Protecting the Poor: A Microinsurance Compendium*, Geneva: ILO.

Dichter, T. and M. Harper (2007) *What's Wrong with Microfinance?* London: Practical Action.

Doligez, F., F. Seck Fall and M. Oualy (2012) *Expériences de microfinance au Sénégal*, Paris: CRES – Khartala.

Fernando, N. A. (2006) 'Understanding and dealing with high interest rates on microcredit', Technical Report, Asian Development Bank.

Gonzalez-Vega, C. and M. Villafani-Ibarnegaray (2011) 'Microfinance in Bolivia: foundation of the growth, outreach and stability of the financial system', in B. Armendáriz and M. Labie (eds), *The Handbook of Microfinance*, London/Singapore: World Scientific Publishing/Imperial College Press.

Guérin, I. and M. Roesch (2012) 'Les fondements d'une crise exemplaire: la microfinance indienne', *Techniques Financières du Développement*, March, pp. 121–34.

Guérin, I., S. Morvant-Roux and J.-M. Servet (2011) 'Understanding the diversity and complexity of demand for microfinance services: lessons from informal finance', in B. Armendáriz and M. Labie (eds), *The Handbook of Microfinance*, London/Singapore: World Scientific Publishing/Imperial College Press.

Hudon, M. (2011) 'Ethics in microfinance', in B. Armendáriz and M. Labie (eds), *The Handbook of Microfinance*, London/Singapore: World Scientific Publishing/Imperial College Press.

Johnson, S., N. Mule, R. Hickson and W. Mwangi (2003) 'The managed ASCA model innovation in Kenya's microfinance industry', in M. Harper (ed.), *Microfinance: Evolution, Achievements and Challenges*, London: ITDG Publishing, pp. 159–71.

Kai, H. (2009) 'Competition and wide outreach of microfinance institutions', *Economics Bulletin*, 29: 2628–39.

Labie, M. (2005) 'Comprendre et améliorer la gouvernance des organisations à but non lucratif: vers un apport des tableaux de bord?', *Gestion*, 30(1), HEC Montreal, pp. 78–86.

Labie, M. and R. Mersland (2011) 'Corporate governance challenges in microfinance', in B. Armendariz and M. Labie (eds), *The Handbook of Microfinance*, London/Singapore: World Scientific Publishing/Imperial College Press.

Ledgerwood, J. and J. White (2006) *Transforming Microfinance Institutions. Providing Full Financial Services to the Poor*, Washington, DC: World Bank.

Lelart, M. (2002) 'L'évolution de la finance informelle et ses conséquences sur l'évolution des systèmes financiers', *Mondes en Développement*, 30(119): 9–21.

Longman (2003) *Longman Dictionary of Contemporary English*, London: Longman.

Maes, J. P. and L. R. Reed (2011) 'State of the microcredit summit campaign report 2012', Technical report, Washington, DC: Microfinance Summit Campaign.

MicroRate (2013) 'The state of microfinance investment 2013 – survey and analysis of MIVs – 8th edition'.

Mix Market (2014) 'Microfinance Information Exchange', Washington, DC.

Morduch, J. (2000) 'The microfinance schism', *World Development*, 28: 617–29.

Morvant-Roux, S., M. Roesch and I. Guérin (2012) 'Les impayés de la crise marocaine: un phénomène complexe', *Techniques Financières du Développement*, March, pp. 107–20.

Osmani, S. R. and M. A. Baqui Khalily (eds) (2011) *Readings in Microfinance: Reach and Impact*, Institute of Microfinance, Dhaka: The University Press.

Ouedrago, A. and D. Gentil (2008) *La microfinance en Afrique de l'Ouest: histoire et innovations*, Paris: CIF – Khartala.

Périlleux, A. (2011) 'Governance and growth of cooperatives in microfinance', PhD thesis, University of Mons.

Reille, X., S. Forster and D. Rozas (2010) 'Foreign capital investment in microfinance: reassessing financial and social returns', *CGAP Focus Note* no. 71, Washington, DC.

Rhyne, E. and M. Otero (2006) 'Microfinance through the next decade: visioning the who, what, where, when and how', *ACCION International*, paper commissioned by the Global Microcredit Summit 2006.

Robinson, M. (2001) *The Microfinance Revolution, Sustainable Finance for the Poor*, Washington, DC: World Bank.

— (2009) 'Supply and demand in microfinance: the case for a financial systems approach', in D. Hulme and T. Arun (eds), *Microfinance, a Reader*, Routledge Studies in Development Economics, New York: Routledge.

Rutherford, S. and S. Arora (2009) *The Poor and Their Money*, London: Practical Action.

Sapundzhieva, R. (2011) 'Funding microfinance: a focus on debt financing', *MicroBanking Bulletin*.

Servet, J.-M. (2011) 'La crise du microcrédit en Andhra Pradesh (Inde)', *Revue Tiers Monde*, 207: 43–59.

— (2012) 'Un facteur externe de crise de microcrédit: la concentration des investissements étrangers dans un nombre restreint d'institutions de microfinance', *Techniques Financières et développement*, 106: 23–34.

Stearns, K. E. (1991) 'El enemigo oculto: morosidad en programas de micro-credito', Discussion Document no. 5, March.

Urgeghe, L. (2013) 'Funding of microfinance institutions and double bottom line objectives: essays on microfinance investment vehicles', PhD thesis, UMONS, Mons.

Vogelgesang, U. (2003) 'Microfinance in times of crisis: the effects of competition, rising indebtedness, and economic crisis on repayment behavior', *World Development*, 31(12): 2085–114.

Woller, G. M. (2002) 'The promise and peril of microfinance commercialization', *Small Enterprise Development*, 13: 12–21.

Woller, G. M., C. Dunford and W. Woodworth (1999) 'Where to microfinance', *International Journal of Economic Development*, 1: 29–64.

Year of Microcredit 2005 (2012) 'International Year of Microcredit', www.yearofmicrocredit.org.

2 | ESTIMATING LEVELS OF CREDIT MARKET SATURATION[1]

Emmanuelle Javoy and Daniel Rozas

Cycles of boom and bust, especially in credit markets, have existed for centuries. Thus, the emergence of loan repayment crises in several microcredit markets since 2009 should surprise no one. Nevertheless, the sector's claims to serve a social mission as well as a financial one raise the stakes.

One of the key elements in most of the post-2009 microcredit crises was the high level of liquidity fuelling rapidly growing markets. In many cases, this influx of funding came from social investors and development finance institutions who were at the time largely unaware of the risks these funding flows were creating. That experience has resulted in far greater focus on risk management generally, and a focus on market overheating in particular, with microcredit funders and investors having invested considerable efforts to be able to predict, and thus avoid, saturation-induced crises in the future. Closely related to this are efforts to reduce the risk of client over-indebtedness, which is one of the core components of widely adopted Client Protection Principles promoted by the Smart Campaign.[2]

To date, the best tool to credibly evaluate market saturation is an over-indebtedness survey using either information from MFI clients or data from credit bureaus. Such surveys have by now been carried out in a number of markets that have either gone through a repayment crisis (Bosnia), or where there have been concerns about potential over-saturation (Table 2.1).

However, these surveys have also proved to be too time intensive and overly costly to be broadly deployed and sustained. Since 2008, to our knowledge, only nine have been conducted. Moreover, markets are rarely static, and the applicability of such studies declines rapidly. In most markets, surveys that are two or more years old are unlikely to be of much value in assessing the current state of these markets, and in more dynamic markets even a single year may render them out of date. Thus, an individual – whether an investor, ratings analyst or researcher – looking to assess the saturation levels of markets in mid-2014 would at best have current information on only two countries, Mexico and Cambodia.

The other means for assessing market saturation rely mainly on a mix of heuristic frameworks and rules of thumb, or on a handful of prototype

TABLE 2.1 List of over-indebtedness surveys, by country

Country	Date	Source
Mexico	2014	MF CEO Working Group
Cambodia	2012	Incofin/BO/Oikocredit
Azerbaijan	2011	MFC/EFSE
Kyrgyzstan	2011	MFC/ICCO
Ghana	2011	CERMi
Kosovo	2010	MFC/EFSE
India (Kolar)	2010	CGAP
India (Andhra Pradesh)	2010	IFMR-CMF
Bosnia	2008–09	MFC/EFSE

Source: Authors' research

quantitative models. Over the past few years, these quantitative models have been developed by several researchers, applying different methodologies, each building upon the success of earlier works. Some of these models have been deployed by risk managers of different microcredit investment funds. The most recent prototype – the MIMOSA – was developed by the authors.

This chapter reviews the evolution of these different approaches for estimating market saturation and over-indebtedness, takes an in-depth look at the MIMOSA model, and considers current and likely future developments in this area.

Box 2.1 Supply, demand and credit bubbles

It's a basic tenet of economics: for a given level of supply, there is a price point at which demand and supply will be in equilibrium. If the supply is too great, the price will drop, pushing the least efficient producers out of the market and bringing supply back into balance with demand. Yet this law doesn't work well in credit markets.

Consider the example of a common consumer good – the television. When buying one, purchase decisions are driven mainly by need and the amount of money one can spend. The need is somewhat flexible – low prices may induce a household to buy more TVs, say for different rooms or to replace older models, but generally speaking, there is an upper limit. As for affordability, the TV purchase has to compete with other household demands, thus its affordability is inherently limited by budget.

Now, consider the case of credit. Credit has no current budget limit – in fact, it increases the budget available for spending. The demand limit rests on some future budget – something people often overestimate, and in some cases fail to consider at all. Credit repayments can even exceed available incomes, a situation that can be sustained for some time by borrowing from one lender to repay another.

Unlike with standard goods, the constraint on borrowing does not come from the demand side. It is lenders who ultimately decide whether a loan will be granted. Imagine going to a retailer with money in your pocket and being told that you are not a reliable customer and they won't sell you the TV! Yet this is exactly how credit works. And since lenders are also the providers of supply, as they become more willing to lend, they also increase credit supply, encountering relatively little resistance from the demand side. The price of credit thus need not necessarily drop when supply increases.

This isn't to say that increased competition – i.e. greater supply – does not result in declining prices. It often does. But this effect works only when lenders use generally similar lending standards in their credit decisions. Clients who would normally qualify for loans from different lenders could then shop for the lowest-priced product.

But what happens when aggressive lenders broaden their standards, for example by lending to individuals who already have loans, or by lending to individuals with less reliable incomes? In the long run, such lenders may be placing themselves on shaky ground, but in the short run they are likely to gain market share. Incumbents then face the choice of maintaining their standards and watching their market share erode, or loosening their standards in an effort to compete.

Ironically, throughout this process, lenders will often see their profits grow. Those providers who try to resist the siren call of market share will also be sacrificing substantial profits in the short run. It's a decision that only a hardened few are able to make. Most will seek some way of maintaining market share, and in the process inflate a bubble.

This is a dynamic that is in many respects unique to credit markets, and understanding it is key to recognizing bubbles as they develop and acting in time to prevent a crisis.

Heuristic models

The first efforts to recognize microcredit markets at risk of over-saturation were based on prior experience and qualitative observations. An example is the crisis in Bolivia in 1999, brought on partly through aggressive competition from consumer lenders seeking to capitalize on the apparent success of the country's MFIs, but also in part by competition among the MFIs themselves. This was also perhaps the first documented case of multiple borrowing leading to over-indebtedness (Rhyne 2001). Since then, aggressive competition has become one of the foundational components of markets at risk of over-saturation.

Nearly ten years later, a landmark study by CGAP deepened the analysis. Analysing four recent crises – in Bosnia, Morocco, Nicaragua and Pakistan – it not only found aggressive competition to be one of the core indicators, but also overstretched systems and controls, as well as erosion of MFI lending discipline (Chen et al. 2010). It also added additional refinements: competition was important, but more relevant was the level of concentration among the competitors, often in large cities or select regions. It mattered also that the growth which accompanied the rise in competition was fuelled by the influx of (mostly) debt funding. Growth also entailed a rapid increase in inexperienced personnel, both at field and middle-management levels, and it also strained internal control systems that had been designed for much smaller operations. Finally, an emphasis on growth and competition also contributed to erosion of credit discipline, as loan officers were encouraged to focus on volume, resulting in more cursory client evaluations. All this was accompanied by a glaring absence of information sharing, notably the lack of an effective credit bureau.

It's notable that the latter study by CGAP, published in February 2010, included a separate section on the risks facing India, which exhibited many of the warning signs noted by the authors. Eight months later, the Indian microcredit market exploded into the largest microcredit crisis to date. And yet, the authors' warnings were not sufficiently heeded, perhaps demonstrating the weakness of heuristic models – while they can identify the risks, such models find it difficult to quantify the extent of over-saturation, and thus cannot effectively communicate the level of urgency required to avert a crisis. They are also nearly impossible to deploy on a multi-country basis in a way that is comparable across borders.

Demand estimation models

The simplest models for saturation essentially look at two indicators: the number of outstanding loans and population. In this way, they allow basic comparison of microcredit penetration in different countries. However, large differences between countries in terms of levels of urbanization, economic development, the regulatory and institutional infrastructure underpinning the formal financial sector, and countless other factors make cross-market comparisons more difficult. This, coupled with the absence of useful benchmarks for sustainable penetration rates, limit the value of such models in predicting over-indebtedness and over-saturation.

A more refined version of this approach is to compare outstanding loans not just to the population itself, but specifically to the target population of microcredit customers. This naturally entails significant assumptions and estimates, but has the advantage of providing some metric of both demand and supply. A model of this type was employed by Daniel Rozas in late 2009 to compare saturation levels in Andhra Pradesh and Bangladesh, finding that the former had already exceeded its realistic level of demand, since the number of loans exceeded the entire number of potential borrowers in the state. Noting that the only plausible explanation for this ratio was extensive multiple borrowing, Rozas suggested that the sector was already in a state of a 'microfinance bubble' (Rozas 2009).

The model was effective in identifying a market at risk of over-saturation, and its clearer indicators support cross-border comparisons. However, the model has a major downside – identifying the target population of MFIs is a highly inaccurate exercise. The inaccuracies come from two sources: uncertainty over who exactly comprises the population served by MFIs (a figure that can also change substantially across different institutions), and lack of reliable data in many countries on the population's socio-economic stratification. In some countries, the target market may be the bottom quintile of the income scale, whereas in others that same quintile may be too poor to qualify even for microfinance. Similarly, an absolute measure – such as individuals living on between one to five dollars a day and deriving most of their income from informal sources – would not apply in many middle-income markets.

The result is that the model is highly sensitive to assumptions and data quality. An elaboration on the same model developed by Rozas in 2010 had its penetration-to-capacity ratio vary by a factor of two, depending on whether a national or state-wide poverty survey data was used (Rozas and Sinha 2010).

Multi-indicator models

One of the first attempts to develop a predictive model using multiple indicators was the Early-Warning Index (EWI) of Overindebtedness, developed by a team at the University of Zurich in 2010 (Kappel et al. 2011). The model included fourteen separate indicators, including at the macro level (remittances), the sector level (growth rate, intensity of competition, presence of credit bureau, etc.) and the MFI level (loan sizes, productivity, growth targets, multiple lending, etc.). This wide range required the use of a broad set of data sources, including the Mix Market and publicly available indexes (e.g. Global Microscope), as well as a survey of industry practitioners in each market.

These variables were lagged by a year and used to predict the incidence of delinquency and default. The result was an index applied to thirteen markets, scoring them according to the predicted probability of an over-indebtedness crisis. Notably, the output placed Bosnia (at the time in the midst of a repayment crisis), along with Cambodia and Peru, at the top of the risk ranking – a result that was consistent with expert perceptions of market risks at the time (India was not one of the countries sampled).

The methodology showed substantial promise, and many of the indicators suggested by the model were commonly included in rating analyst templates and investor due diligence scorecards. However, the degree of effort to collect the data and the narrow number of countries covered limited the effectiveness of the model as a tool for day-to-day assessment of market saturation.

Moreover, the exercise suffered from the same challenge as the earlier demand estimation models. To estimate the size of the potential microcredit market in each country, the team relied on various measures of poverty, using both international and national poverty lines. Unfortunately, this introduced substantial volatility into the model, which fell short of being able to assess market capacity and penetration. Instead, the model emphasized reliance on other indicators, especially qualitative assessments of lending practices captured from a survey of market participants.

MIMOSA: Microfinance Index of Market Outreach and Saturation[3]

The model developed by the MIMOSA team is an outgrowth of these three strands of work. Like the EWI, MIMOSA employs an easy-to-use scoring system that allows comparison between different markets. However, MIMOSA's market coverage is global, encompassing 109 countries – a scale that is more practicable for implementation on the ground. Not surprisingly, MIMOSA scores have been incorporated in the due diligence process of a substantial number of fund managers, often as a component of scoring country-level risk.

The ability to reach this scale is largely the result of two factors. First, MIMOSA was developed following the release of the Global Findex database,[4] a World Bank data set that measures the use of formal and informal financial services (bank accounts, savings, credit, payments, etc.), based on population surveys of 148 countries. That provides a level of geographic coverage unavailable to the earlier efforts. Second, MIMOSA bypassed the problems of volatility that plagued earlier efforts to estimate target markets, simply by avoiding defining the target market altogether.

Findex reports most indicators at both the overall country level and according to several different breakdowns, including the bottom 40 per cent of earners. Unfortunately, like poverty rates, this measure does not apply equally to all microcredit markets. In wealthier countries, such as in eastern Europe, the threshold may be too high, with microcredit focusing on perhaps the bottom 20 or 30 per cent of earners. Meanwhile, in the poorest countries, this threshold may be too low, with most microcredit customers fitting mainly in the 40–80 per cent income range. As it happens, borrowing frequency at different income levels tends to closely track overall national figures, so that by relying on data for the full population, we avoid the problems of estimating the potential market, without sacrificing model accuracy.

The MIMOSA model also differs in its simplicity. It is based entirely on regressing the Findex figure for the share of population that use formal borrowing against two other Findex indicators: formal savings, and semi-formal borrowing (e.g. private moneylenders, employer and store credit), as well as the country's Human Development Index (HDI).

Credit capacity and HDI The single largest predictor of formal borrowing levels found in Findex is the country's HDI, an index developed by the UNDP (United Nations Development Programme), incorporating per capita GNI (gross national income, at purchasing power parity) as well as indicators for education and health.[5] HDI shows a strong positive correlation with formal credit use, with developed countries reporting much higher levels of formal credit than less developed ones. Perhaps more noteworthy is the strong upper bound of this trend, with only a small handful of countries exceeding the apparent limit, with the least-developed countries showing a limit below 10 per cent penetration, while most developed ones approach 30 per cent (Figure 2.1).

As a predictive factor for credit utilization and capacity, HDI works because it explains much of what we observe in reality. Widespread and persistent concern in the sector about over-indebtedness,[6] and especially for countries that breach the implied upper bound in Figure 2.1, suggests that the natural credit absorption limit in these markets is lower than previously thought. A major factor for this is that low and irregular incomes and the absence of reliable social supports such as pensions and health insurance increase borrowers' risk of taking on formal debt, thus reducing credit demand, or at least the level of demand that is sustainable (see chapters on demand in India and Dominican Republic).

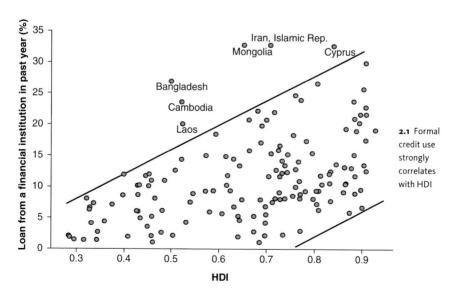

2.1 Formal credit use strongly correlates with HDI

Note: Lines represent visual approximations of upper and lower boundaries of borrowing rates

Sources: Adapted from Findex data

But what about the most obvious argument against HDI: doesn't such a metric go against the stated objectives of expanding financial inclusion, which is to increase access to financial services in developing markets? Are we not turning the notion of financial access expansion on its head by suggesting that financial access (or at least, use of credit) should be lower in developing countries than developed ones? After all, part of the reason developing countries have less formal credit is exactly because they also have fewer and less developed financial institutions,[7] with weak supervision, absence of centralized credit reporting, limited outreach to remote areas, and limited offerings of well-designed credit products that fully suit the needs of low-income populations. So why would we want to still take this route?

Rate of saving at financial institutions In fact, we don't. The second key predictor in MIMOSA is the reported savings rate at financial institutions, which is positively correlated with the use of formal credit. By including formal savings rates in the MIMOSA model, we can correct for the weakness of using HDI alone. A low-HDI country that stands out by having a more developed financial sector than its peers would feature higher levels of formal savings and would thus be modelled at a higher level of credit market capacity than suggested by its level of economic development.

There are two main reasons why saving at financial institutions is an important factor for predicting credit capacity. First, saving serves as an indication of client financial capability and also reflects the nature of their relationships with financial institutions. Second, savings rates are a strong indication of financial access, in terms of both financial sector development and the level of institutional presence in the market.[8]

Savings also help clients to borrow. They reduce the risk assumed by the client – in the event of a cash-flow shock, savings can be tapped to make repayments, thus cushioning the negative impact of the shock. Moreover, a client who saves is probably a better financial manager, and thus more likely to take on debt with a better understanding of the attendant risks and commitments.

We don't want to overstate our case here. The hypothesis that the presence of greater savings outreach can be a positive factor in increasing client borrowing capacity requires additional research to validate it. And even if this effect does get validated, the use of formal credit will still be to a large extent bounded by the country's level of development. Nevertheless, it does suggest that promotion of savings is something that MFIs, regulators and donors should consider not just in the context of improving financial inclusion generally, but also in the context of stabilizing and strengthening credit markets.

Semi-formal credit The third and final leg of the MIMOSA model is what we call 'semi-formal credit', which we define as the average rate of borrowing from private lenders (e.g. moneylenders), employer loans and store credit. In

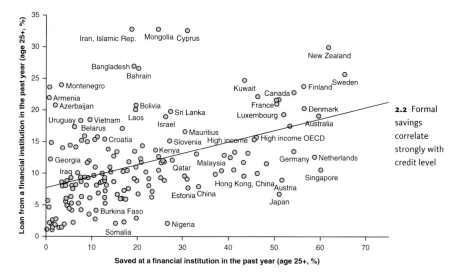

2.2 Formal savings correlate strongly with credit level

Source: Adapted from Findex data

evaluating credit penetration, one key area to recognize is the level of intrinsic demand, i.e. what is the credit culture in a given country? As the chapters on demand in Morocco and India demonstrate, the demand for credit can vary greatly. And even in countries with similar levels of HDI and savings frequency, some societies seem inherently more predisposed to credit than others. Use of semi-formal credit, which has a positive correlation with financial sector borrowing (Figure 2.3), is the proxy by which we measure this credit culture.

An important reason why we believe semi-formal borrowing is an effective proxy for credit demand is that such credit tends to develop organically, without

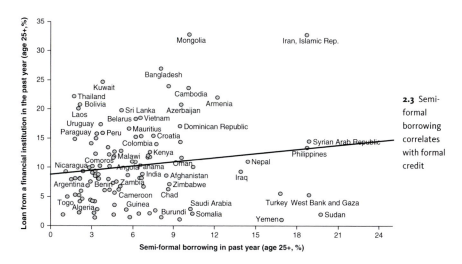

2.3 Semi-formal borrowing correlates with formal credit

Source: Adapted from Findex data

requiring infrastructure or external support. It is rarely, if ever, regulated, and is largely independent of the quality level of the country's governing institutions (in some more developed countries these types of loans may be formally registered and reported to credit bureaus, which distinguishes them from completely informal transactions). Likewise, from the borrower perspective, because semi-formal loans are sourced outside the home and outside of immediate kinship circles, they retain some of the same qualities as formal credit.

There is, however, a risk in relying on semi-formal lending as a proxy for credit demand. While its impact is indeed substantial and statistically significant, there are several countries that appear to buck the trend: Bolivia, Laos and Thailand all have low rates of semi-formal and high rates of formal lending – a disparity that cannot be explained by HDI. The resulting output of the model shows a lower credit capacity than would be the case if semi-formal lending were more commonplace. But that conclusion is not necessarily right. To take the most prominent example, Bolivia is a market where microcredit has been active for well over two decades, during which time it has become fully integrated into the broader financial sector. It is reasonable to postulate that over the decades in which MFIs have been active, they may have had a strong influence in shaping the population's perception of credit, thus raising credit utilization via these formal channels, even if semi-formal channels remain little used.

Constructing the MIMOSA model

The three indicators above – HDI, formal savings rate and use of semi-formal credit – are combined in a simple linear regression model to estimate a country's formal credit usage. The result is a set of predicted credit usage rates that generally follow the pattern set by the observed rates. However, there is another, more notable outcome that leads to significant policy implications: the slope of the upper bound is shallower than for the observed rates. Thus, for the least developed countries (HDI below 50), the predicted output tends towards the higher end of observed credit usage rates. This implies that the financial sectors in a significant number of these countries are underdeveloped, even after accounting for their lower level of overall human development.

This pattern can be seen in Figure 2.4. A strict argument for financial access would imply that the upper horizontal line should be the ideal representation, with the upper limit for credit usage remaining the same regardless of the level of development. Our estimation is that the market potential for formal credit is more like the second line from the top in that same figure: by focusing on strengthening the financial and microfinance sectors, increasing savings rates and improving credit offerings to include longer maturities and more flexible terms, market potential can be raised above the currently observed limits. However, all these improvements combined still cannot fully balance out the lower market potential for formal credit in countries with low HDI.

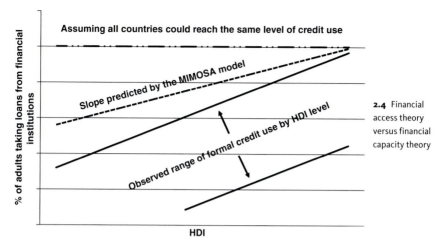

2.4 Financial access theory versus financial capacity theory

Source: Adapted from Planetrating

Using the predicted usage rates generated by the model, we score current penetration levels on a five-point scale, with 1 being least penetrated and 5 being most penetrated. We set the boundary between categories 2 and 3 at the neutral point, where the predicted score equals the observed value. The other thresholds are set at the limits denoted in Table 2.2.

The boundaries of these thresholds are guided by two understandings of credit use. First, we recognize that the estimation provided by the model is not necessarily a specific target that ought to be reached and maintained. Variation around this level is normal and should be expected. Thus, we view both categories 2 and 3 as normally functioning markets, with the main difference being that the former displays greater capacity for growth.

The outside categories seek to define more significant deviations from this normal target level. At the bottom of the scale, category 1 denotes a country where retail credit appears to be substantially below what its potential demand would suggest, which might argue for a stronger focus on developing financial institutions and their outreach. The highest category of 5, where credit utilization rates are at least double their predicted value, presents a significant risk.

TABLE 2.2 MIMOSA market scorecard

Category	Market penetration	Number (share) of countries (HDI<80)
5	>100% above predicted level	6 (6%)
4	50–100% above predicted level	14 (13%)
3	0–50% above predicted level	29 (27%)
2	0–30% below predicted level	32 (29%)
1	>30% below predicted level	28 (26%)

Source: Adapted from Planetrating calculations

Results from MIMOSA

The output from MIMOSA demonstrates just how strongly the modelled borrowing capacity is affected by HDI (Figure 2.5). Nearly all the countries that are outside the implied capacity limit (Laos, Cambodia, Bangladesh, Mongolia) are scored at the highest level, while the remaining high-risk markets, Kyrgyzstan and Bolivia, are close to the implied ceiling.

Equally interesting is how closely the result matches up with the implied scores of the EWI (Table 2.3).

However, there are also differences that need explaining: six markets (Armenia, Bolivia, Bosnia, Ecuador, Georgia and Paraguay) have score

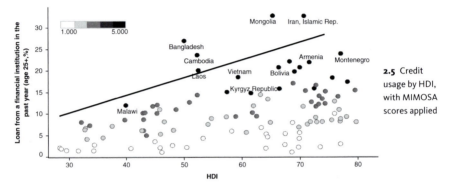

2.5 Credit usage by HDI, with MIMOSA scores applied

Source: Adapted from Findex and UNDP data, and from Planetrating calculations

TABLE 2.3 Comparing MIMOSA with EWI

	MIMOSA	EWI*
El Salvador	1	1
Tajikistan	2	2
Ghana	2	3
Kosovo	2	3
Ecuador	3	1
Georgia	3	1
Colombia	3	3
Bosnia	3	4
Armenia	4	2
Paraguay	4	2
Peru	4	4
Bolivia	5	1
Cambodia	5	4

Source: Adapted from Planetrating, Early Warning Index

* Scores derived from EWI colour bands

differences greater than 2 points. For Bolivia, this is likely due to the above-discussed weakness of MIMOSA in applying semi-formal borrowing as an indicator of loan demand, even in countries where it may not be applicable. But at the same time, it's probable that the EWI is not successfully capturing the existing saturation levels in Bolivia, thus under-counting the true risk of over-indebtedness. Most likely, Bolivia should be placed somewhere in the middle to high range of the spectrum.

The difference in Bosnia, on the other hand, can be attributed mainly to the timing of the underlying data, with the EWI reflecting a market still deep in the midst of crisis (2009), while MIMOSA data is from 2011 – well after the crisis had passed. Naturally, the MIMOSA score is lower.

The four remaining countries reflect a combination of factors. In all cases, MIMOSA scored these as being at greater risk of over-indebtedness than did EWI. In part, this is due to the timing of data – as with Bosnia, the two additional years between the two models mean that these markets have seen further growth and increased competition. Moreover, all four of these markets have significant competition from banks and consumer lenders, and MIMOSA captures these behaviours directly, whereas EWI includes them only as one of fourteen indicators.

Meanwhile, both Cambodia and Peru are both scored at or near the top of the list by both MIMOSA and EWI, to which MIMOSA also adds Kyrgyzstan, Laos, Bangladesh and Mongolia. Of these, Kyrgyzstan sparked sufficient concern to warrant an over-indebtedness survey conducted in 2011. Meanwhile, Bangladesh was noted as having come to the brink of crisis in 2008, with concerted efforts by the MFIs averting one just in time (Chen and Rutherford 2013).

For a basic regression model featuring only three predictor variables, this is quite an effective outcome.

Next steps for MIMOSA

Nevertheless, given its simplicity, it's not surprising that MIMOSA has a number of gaps. Chief among them is the fact that its view is limited to the country level, without adjusting for differences between regions or between certain sub-segments of the population. Thus, for Mexico – a market that features the highest rate of multiple borrowing to date (Rozas 2014) – MIMOSA gives a score of just 2, or below the level of predicted demand. The problem in that case is that, unlike in most markets, the incidence of borrowing among microcredit clients in Mexico is highly divergent from borrowing patterns among the rest of the population. This was a failure recognized already at the time of the original publication of MIMOSA.

Another example is Nigeria. Any person familiar with microcredit in Lagos will affirm that it is a highly competitive microcredit market, yet Nigeria has a MIMOSA score of just 1. This is the result of a large country whose microcredit sector is concentrated in a handful of areas – Lagos and a couple of other cities – where competition is high. The remainder of the country has little or no microcredit activity.

As both Mexico and Nigeria demonstrate, MIMOSA's green light can mislead. It is with that in mind that we are currently embarking on the second phase of the project, MIMOSA 2.0, which will combine three levels of data: Findex and other macro-level indicators, microfinance-specific indicators such as regulation and market infrastructure, and field-level observations of institutions and clients. The goal is to retain the broad multi-country coverage that MIMOSA provides, while for select markets, adding additional evaluation to fine-tune the results and provide capacity and penetration scores also at the in-country regional level. In some respects, this combines the approaches of the EWI and the original MIMOSA in a way that is cost effective and cross-comparable between different countries.

Conclusion

The multiple strands of work to develop an accurate and effective assessment of market capacity and over-indebtedness levels have come a long way. Whereas just a few years ago market analysts were limited entirely to heuristic assessments or highly simplistic estimations, we are now closer to having a workable and sufficiently reliable tool that the microfinance sector can use to reduce the boom-and-bust cyclicality inherent to credit markets.

As always, this comes with potential downsides. For one, if the MIMOSA scores trigger similar behaviour among investors and other parties, this may in theory increase the volatility of funding flows, with funds flowing into markets scored below capacity, and flowing out of markets scored above capacity. For the former, an over-rapid influx of funds may cause destabilization. Meanwhile, an over-rapid outflow of funds could trigger a liquidity crisis, even in otherwise stable (if saturated) markets.

However, these are just suppositions. It seems unlikely that MIMOSA scores would trigger a rapid and uniform response. More likely, investors will weigh the input from MIMOSA as part of their internal risk assessment, and the result will likely be multifaceted, reflecting the large variety of risk preferences and strategies among different investors. There is also the fact that, like any model, MIMOSA can never be perfect, and those with greater knowledge of specific markets should be able to arbitrage those weaknesses to their favour, thus facilitating more optimal allocation of capital.

At the end of the day, MIMOSA is a tool that can help investors understand markets and help lower the risk of market overheating. However, its value is limited by how well it is applied, with the full recognition that its prediction of overheating markets could never be perfect.

Notes

1 This chapter is adapted from Javoy and Rozas (2013).

2 The Smart Campaign (smartcampaign. org) is an industry-wide initiative launched in 2009 to promote improved focus on client protection practices for microfinance institutions worldwide.

3 Adapted from Javoy and Rozas (2013).

4 World Bank, datatopics.worldbank. org/financialinclusion.

5 Annual publication of the United Nations Development Programme, hdr.undp. org/en/statistics/hdi.

6 Lascelles et al. (2012, 2014). The survey found over-indebtedness to be the topmost concern of microfinance practitioners in both 2012 and 2014 (there is no 2013 version). The topmost risk in the two prior surveys (2009 and 2011) was credit risk, which implies similar concerns, given its close relationship with over-indebtedness and the fact that over-indebtedness specifically was not included among the list of possible risks in those years.

7 Formal institutions in Findex include not only banks and non-banking financial institutions (NBFIs), but also NGOs, credit cooperatives and other formal organizations, regardless of their regulatory status.

8 Presumably, one could use the number of bank accounts for the same purpose. However, because saving is an ongoing activity and requires a significant level of trust in financial institutions, it provides a more meaningful measure of financial access than simply counting the number of bank accounts.

References

Chen, G. and S. Rutherford (2013) 'A microcredit crisis averted: the case of Bangladesh', CGAP Note no. 87, Washington, DC: CGAP.

Chen, G., S. Rasmussen and X. Reille (2010) 'Growth and vulnerabilities in microfinance', Focus Note no. 61, Washington, DC: CGAP, February.

Javoy, E. and D. Rozas (2013) *MIMOSA: Microfinance Index of Market Outreach and Saturation; Part 1 – Total Credit Market Capacity*, Paris: Planetrating and Fondation PlanetFinance, March.

Kappel, V., A. Krauss and L. Lontzek (2011) *Over-Indebtedness and Microfinance: Constructing an Early Warning Index*, Zurich: Centre for Microfinance/University of Zurich and responsAbility, CMEF, Triodos.

Lascelles, D. and S. Mendelson (2012) *Microfinance Banana Skins: The CSFI Survey of Microfinance Risk*, New York: Center for the Study of Financial Innovation.

Lascelles, D., S. Mendelson and D. Rozas (2014) *Microfinance Banana Skins: The CSFI Survey of Microfinance Risk*, New York: Center for the Study of Financial Innovation.

Rhyne, E. (2001) *Commercialization and Crisis in Bolivian Microfinance*, DAI.

Rozas, D. (2009) 'Is there a microfinance bubble in South India?', microfinance focus, Blog, www.microfinancefocus.com/content/there-microfinance-bubble-south-india, November.

— (2014) 'Microfinance in Mexico: beyond the brink', European Microfinance Platform, Blog, www.e-mfp.eu/blog/microfinance-mexico-beyond-brink, 19 June.

Rozas, D. and S. Sinha (2010) 'Avoiding a microfinance bubble in India: is self-regulation the answer?', Blog, www.microfinancefocus.com, January.

3 | MICROCREDIT CRISES AND THE ABSORPTION CAPACITY OF LOCAL ECONOMIES

Isabelle Guérin and Jean-Michel Servet

Introduction

Many of microcredit's promoters believe that it still has considerable growth potential. The argument runs that microcredit helps very small businesses and informal self-employed workers develop and expand. Self-employment accounts for a huge share of employment today: the International Labour Organization estimates it at approximately one third of the world's non-agricultural employment (53 per cent in sub-Saharan Africa, 44 per cent in Latin America, 32 per cent in Asia and 31 per cent in North Africa) (ILO 2009: 6–7). Estimates of this potential market for small loans vary widely depending on the criteria used, but the number most often put forward is 1.5 billion people.

We believe, however, that this figure is clearly overestimated and raises risks of huge cash injections for people and countries that cannot absorb them, especially given the concentration of supply within these countries. As D'Espallier et al. point out in this volume, too much growth too soon is harmful to MFIs, some of which are incapable of adjusting to the demands of this growth. This line of thinking could be taken further by exploring how too sharp a growth curve affects the absorption capacities of economies and local populations. Javoy and Rozas' chapter in this volume considers the risks of national saturation (see also Hes and Poledňáková 2013). We focus here on the risks of *local* saturation.

The main argument developed in this chapter is that microcredit crises may be indicative of saturation on local markets unable to absorb any further liquid assets above a certain point. There are three main reasons for this: not enough outlets for the goods and services produced by the influx of microcredit, competition from informal supplies of financial services, and frequent use of microcredit for consumption with its potential repercussion of over-indebtedness. In this chapter, we describe the mechanisms underlying this saturation process, but do not attempt to quantify them. As explained in the conclusion, the next step would be to find ways to identify saturation thresholds in given environments.

What outlets are there for the goods and services produced by the influx of microcredit?

In microeconomic terms, a microloan will have a positive effect on the borrower's income provided the borrower invests in a business for which there is a market. Either outlets already exist or the investment creates them by means of a knock-on effect in a local economy. Yet there is a major stumbling block here, since outlets in underdeveloped economies are few and far between. This puts quite a brake on the positive income-raising impacts of microcredit.

In the case of new lines of business, a copycat effect is often found to be at work among borrowers. This shrinks each borrower's prospective outlets and undermines the loan's potential to generate new additional resources owing to greater local competition in the business sector in question.

Monographs on villages in southern India point to a string of failures due largely to a shortfall in local demand (Guérin and Palier 2005).[1] In many cases – ranging from the production of washing powder, joss sticks, candles, paper cups and mushrooms through local craft trades and fish farming to cattle breeding – not one of the businesses took off, more often than not for want of buyers. Either the products were new and met with zero uptake (mushrooms and paper cups), or they faced competition from better-quality and/or better-priced manufactured products (washing powder, candles and local craft trades). Or they called for conditions beyond the borrower's means: fish farming and stock breeding require a minimum of technical skills, available manpower and access to certain common resources (ponds and grazing land) if they are to be profitable. A number of studies in Senegal describe high-speed saturation in certain sectors such as market gardening, small-scale stock breeding and street food stalls (Guérin 2003; see also Touré 2013).

In Bolivia, a jewel of microcredit, women in the slums of La Paz began borrowing to start up craft trade businesses in the early 2000s. They all set about selling the same thing to a thin, cash-strapped customer base – the country was reeling from structural adjustment programmes and the subsequent privatizations and massive unemployment. The women barely broke even, did not pay themselves, needed friends and family to help pay back their loans, and regularly had to take out new loans with the microfinance organizations in a vicious cycle of debt (Brett 2006). In Egypt, Julie Elyachar (2006) describes the many downfalls of those who embarked upon ventures in Cairo, and found themselves drowning in unsold merchandise, up to their necks in debt and harassed by their lenders. Not only does microcredit generally not create a new business, but those who already have well-established businesses of a certain size use the artifice of bogus micro-enterprises to be eligible for microcredit.

Lamia Karim provides a detailed account of the discontents of the 'chicken' project in Bangladesh set up by the Bangladesh Rural Advancement Committee (BRAC), the country's number-two microcredit organization

(Karim 2011: 123–9). Although BRAC's activity reports present chicken farming as undisputed proof of the success of its loans, the author paints quite a different picture. BRAC's profitability calculations do not take account of either the animals' actual death rate – one in two chickens does not live more than two months – or certain costs, such as special premises run on electricity and kept at the right temperature. In addition, there is a lack of demand: the local people do not eat much meat and do not intend to increase their intake, while the export sectors selling mainly to Gulf countries are not connected to the production sector.

Poor returns on investment The poor profitability of very small businesses compared with the cost of microcredit can also be a restrictive factor. Microcredit's credibility is based partly on the assumption that very small businesses have high profit rates. Evidence, however, is very scarce (Morduch 2008), and we believe that this is far from true. In many situations, the estimates made are misleading since they do not include remuneration for the work (Karnani 2011: 37). A number of large-scale surveys show just how micro-entrepreneurs scrape by on paltry earnings with little prospects of growth.[2] A study conducted in Accra in Ghana shows that almost 60 per cent of borrowers do not make enough from their work to pay back their loans and three-quarters of them have to scrimp in order to repay their debt: they work more, they sell goods or dip into their savings, they eat less, they ask friends and family to help and so on (Schicks 2014). A survey by Edoé Agbodjan (2012) in the prefecture of Ogou in Togo shows that borrowers who take out a loan to fund an income-generating activity sometimes have to put in so much in terms of working hours and using family workers and especially child labour to cut operating costs that the business has a limited lifespan once the loan has been repaid. Few studies can compare the cost of microcredit to borrowers (estimated at around 30 per cent on average per year, although figures vary widely) with the profitability of the activities financed, but it is highly probable that the former is higher than the latter in many (albeit not all) cases.

The argument put forward by some microcredit organizations and promoters is that the financial cost is but a fraction of the total product cost. This same argument could be put regarding the burden a consumer loan places on income compared with other constraints such as housing and food. Yet the danger of this financial burden can be seen at local level when considering the macro rather than the micro picture.

The interest paid to microcredit organizations and banks puts a brake on the potential multiplier effects that an injection of money might have. In so doing, it places a drain on the locally available money supply and income generated by production and trade, if not impoverishing the area or sector altogether.[3]

The survival rate of very small businesses is low in all cases. Now this is hardly surprising, but it does put a squeeze on the increase in volume borrowed per household and even growth in the loan renewal rate (see Morvant-Roux and Roesch on Morocco this volume).

What are the knock-on effects? Over and above specific goods and service markets, an assessment of the extent of local economic saturation calls for an exploration of any income multiplier or knock-on effects generated by goods and service purchases and wages paid *locally*. If traders and craftspeople taking out microloans buy in locally produced resources, they will step up local demand for this type of resource and hence drive forward trade and the production of local goods and services. This observation is in keeping with the model pioneered by J. M. Keynes (and well known by economists) on the demand-driven income multiplier effect, which may tend upwards or downwards. Take the case of a grocer's shop. Knock-on effects are few and far between when most of the products sold are foodstuffs produced, processed and packaged abroad. However, knock-on effects are higher when a large share of the products comes in the form of foodstuffs produced, transformed and packaged locally.

Exploration of spillover effects on local economies also sheds a different light on the consumption/production debate. For a Senegalese family, taking out a loan to trade in American second-hand clothes or ready-to-wear imported from China or Bangladesh probably has less effect on local employment than buying goods and services produced locally on credit. The most conclusive example is found in housing. The principle of progressive housing states that the poor rarely buy finished housing, but build gradually over time as and when income and loan opportunities permit. It is not unusual to find microcredit used to add a room, floor, balcony, toilet, shower or similar. This does not generate direct income for the borrower, but the expenditure can boost the local economy by means of a multiplier effect since the borrower will often have to pay a builder and buy materials, at least some of which are not imported.

Frequent displacement effects Any microeconomic analysis focused solely on borrowers will be misleading owing to *displacement* effects, as also suggested by Bateman (2010). These effects are hard to measure, but are probably highly frequent. A displacement effect occurs when a new or expanding business on a local goods or service market replaces another or forces it to cut its margins by capturing part of its customer base. For example, where craftspeople and traders use microcredit to buy larger quantities of inputs or the goods they sell, thereby enabling them to cut their prices, they will probably attract more customers at the expense of their competitors if they do reduce their prices. Basically, as the microloan recipient's profit margin grows, some will get richer at the cost of others.[4] The same effect can be found where borrowers use microloans to tide them over such events as the end of a harvest, when prices are low, so that they can sell at a higher price when the glut is over. This is also the case where producers use microloans to hold off selling their field crops before they are harvested to traders who give them advances during the lean period and then have the monopoly over their sales. Therefore, although microcredit raises the income of part of the population, no additional wealth is created for the local economy as a whole. All that happens is that income is transferred to the microcredit recipients away from other very small businesses and traders. What we have here, then, is a zero-sum game that does nothing to drive up demand, supply or income by means of a positive multiplier effect.

Concentration of supply In some cases, the concentration of MFIs in given geographic areas, and sometimes in certain sectors, accelerates this local economic saturation. Competing microcredit structures often target the same customers. They therefore tend to be concentrated in the same areas. A large number of microcredit agencies can sometimes be found in one and the same street. This has been observed in Andhra Pradesh (Fouillet 2009), in Bamenda in Cameroon (Ojong 2013: 208), in Peru (Vanroose 2014) and in cities in Benin (Martinez 2007), the Dominican Republic (see Morvant-Roux et al. this volume) and Senegal (see Baumann et al. this volume). A social impact statement from the Réseau des Caisses Populaires du Burkina Faso reports that fewer than 5 per cent of their credit agencies are established in areas where there are no other microcredit organizations or bank branches (Coulibaly and Servais 2009: 8). In India, not only is the supply of microcredit still highly concentrated in the south of the country, but detailed spatial analyses of self-help groups[5] have found huge differences between and within districts (Fouillet 2009).

This concentration model can be explained by two factors. Some MFIs target priority customers and areas usually expected to be profitable, such as urban centres, neighbourhoods near markets and large corporations, since a growing proportion of the customer base is made up of wage earners. Again for reasons of profitability, some MFIs set up shop in the same place as their competitors to take advantage of the learning effects in these areas: the local people are already familiar with microcredit, making the initial awareness-building stage cheaper. This spatial concentration of the credit supply forms a further factor for saturation, which cannot be seen from counting the number of borrowers nationwide.

Competition and complementarity between microcredit and other informal supplies of financial services (credit and savings)

Assessment of the extent of local economic saturation also calls for a focus on already existing financial practices. The expression 'financial inclusion', which has gradually taken over from the term 'microcredit' or 'microfinance', is defined as access to the full range of financial services by the people,[6] as clearly identified by field studies such as *Portfolios of the Poor* (Collins et al. 2009). These practices have a potentially double-edged saturation effect: either by being complementary, but fostering over-indebtedness, or by competing and therefore holding back expansion capacities.

How microfinance complements informal practices and risks of over-indebtedness We now know that microfinance (whether microcredit or saving services) rarely replaces informal finance and that local populations rather tend to juggle difference sources of funds (Collins et al. 2009; Guérin et al. 2011; Guérin et al. 2013).These juggling practices come in a range of different strategies. People may combine informal loans with microcredit. This combination can amass the sum needed when each type of loan does not raise enough separately. The combination can also be used to play off different repayment schedules and timelines against each other. Most microloans have to be paid back at regular intervals and there is little tolerance of late payment, while informal loans are generally flexible and negotiable, albeit with the possibility of being staggered over time, which raises the risk of dependence and extra cost (see Guérin et al. on Tamil Nadu, India and Morvant-Roux et al. on the Dominican Republic this volume). Loan combinations are also quite simply a way of spreading risk by avoiding too much dependence on one lender, whoever that lender may be.

Another form of juggling is to take out a new loan to pay off a previous debt. These juggling practices are routine to the poor and are not necessarily a sign of over-indebtedness. They are not always forced upon them, but are driven by different financial strategies (the lenders' cash constraints, the high, dissuasive cost of loans over long time periods, etc.) and social strategies (diversifying relations) (Guérin et al. 2013).

Sometimes, however, a greater borrowing capacity can foster over-indebtedness (owing particularly to the weight of consumer loans, as we will see later). Initially, this raises the demand for loans. Yet it can more or less quickly trigger a saturation effect owing to the inability of borrowers to pay off their debts.

At times, microcredit can even drive up the supply of informal finance (see the case of Tamil Nadu by Guérin et al. this volume).

Competition between microcredit and informal practices and limited growth for microcredit In certain situations, microcredit and informal finance compete with one another. Informal finance curbs the growth of formal microcredit as it is generally much more suited to the needs of the people and its actual total cost can prove lower than that generally found when comparing all the costs generated by microcredit services.

There are a number of reasons for this competition. It may be due to social and moral considerations. In some regions of Kenya, where the relationship to the land is inextricably linked with the relationship to the society and ancestors, attempts to introduce rural credit requiring that farmers mortgage their land have met with fierce resistance. Local practices such as peer-to-peer lending, borrowing from moneylenders and buying on credit from shopkeepers have much more social credibility (Shipton 2010). This can also be seen in certain Moroccan regions where microcredit has few takers among the people owing to their particular interpretation of Islam, local standards of honour and status, and confusion as to the origins of microcredit often wrongly associated with *Makhzen* (the king) (Morvant-Roux et al. 2014; see also Morvant-Roux and Roesch this volume). The survey by Morvant-Roux et al. concludes that reluctance to take on debt is endemic and that the people borrow very little on the whole. However, the amount owed is probably largely underestimated. Moral disapproval of credit is such that these practices may well be hidden as much from survey interviewers from outside these regions as from the neighbourhood and even friends and family. The people living here are believed to have no choice but to take out loans to make ends meet, but they are not prepared to wash their dirty laundry in public or for an unknown interviewer to see.[7]

There is also the possibility that people do not perceive as debts certain practices that constitute a form of indebtedness from an economic point of view. This concerns particular credit from suppliers and advances on harvests, which are apparently extremely widespread among businesses and producers irrespective of size and activity sector. It also relates to late payments. If they are seen as debts from a financial perspective, then the total sum of indebtedness is much higher than is usually estimated.

Another comparative advantage of informal finance is found in its capacity to manage risk. Credit granted by suppliers, and found in many situations, comes under this category. Such credit can form a source of dependence and consequent hidden costs, but this is far from systematic. It often has the advantage of guaranteeing a regular supply of merchandise or raw materials, and the business also benefits from the time lag before payment during which it can itself sell on credit. It often implies a relationship of trust and a social network, which some businesses do not have. Microcredit can therefore play a role here, but one that might appear limited over time. This is what we have observed in Morocco. Traders and craftspeople starting up who are not known by their suppliers take out a microloan to be able to place their orders. Yet once they have established a relationship with their suppliers, they prefer to buy from them on credit for the above-mentioned reasons. As the microcredit bodies lose these borrowers to the informal slate system, they have to constantly seek out new borrowers. If not, microcredit would structurally become consumer microcredit. So this is not a system in which productive microcredit replaces informal credit, but totally the opposite. Senegalese examples of the fishing sector and the cereals and retail trade (Touré 2013) also show the informal weight of pre-financing, credit to consumers and producer advances, which cover the risks of poor sales, supply fluctuations and the immorality of interest-bearing loans in a Muslim culture.

The predominance of informal savings practices can also explain low microcredit growth in certain circumstances (see the chapter by Morvant-Roux and Roesch this volume).

The limitations of the documentation available today prevent any real exhaustive list of informal financial practices, calculation of their weight or assessment of any interaction they may have with microcredit. Needless to say, an estimation of the microcredit institutions' growth prospects, including the risks of cross-formal/informal borrowing, can in no way choose to overlook this type of investigation any more than can the estimation of the expansion potential of microcredit in terms of the number of borrowers and volume borrowed. The fact that neither microfinance organizations nor monetary and banking regulatory institutions have systematically conducted surveys in this area reflects the sector's dominant top-down nature. There is an imbalance between the bottom and the top such that, no matter how much goodwill and benevolence there is towards the people (not necessarily poor, but financially excluded), the institutions reason more in terms of product marketing, impact and product uptake[8] than a bottom-up approach to product design based on solvent demand, expressed needs and, beyond those, latent and diversified needs, and on their consideration of the wide range of local alternatives to their loans and microcredit subversion and misuse practices.

Producer microcredit saturation, consumer credit and over-indebtedness

We have seen that the local goods and service markets in which microcredit customers are supposed to invest have limited growth potential and therefore quickly become saturated. This in turn triggers producer microcredit saturation, which comes all the sooner where competing informal practices are found. Two scenarios are consequently possible: either low demand for producer credit gives rise to microcredit saturation or the people need credit to consume, but with not inconsiderable risks of over-indebtedness should their actual earnings not rise enough or, worse still, suddenly drop.

Microcredit saturation Poor local opportunities for income-generating activities may prompt local populations to steer clear of microcredit. This is the case, for example, with farmers in the Red River Delta in northern Vietnam who refrain from borrowing to diversify their crop-growing systems because there is no guarantee that they will sell enough on urban markets (Gironde 2007). It is also the case in some rural areas of Morocco (see the chapter by Morvant-Roux and Roesch this volume). A number of studies assessing the microcredit take-up rate show that it ranges from 5 to 25 per cent (Hes and Poledňáková 2013).[9]

In addition to the above-mentioned factors, individual and family strategies need to be explored in the context of how they are perceived by society. There is a widespread misconception that all borrowers want loans to constantly boost to the maximum their economic capacities to accumulate and generate additional income. A proportion of the clientele, to which a figure cannot as yet be put, borrow to serve household welfare and satisfy a given number of needs. Surveys conducted in Morocco also find a household strategy based on savings in the form of investment in livestock (see Morvant-Roux and Roesch this volume). In general, then, a straightforward householding rationale prevails over any idea of accumulation. This reasoning clearly holds much more currency in rural areas and among urban populations with close family ties with the countryside. Here, microcredit serves to build vital stock to be sold on, processed in a craft trade activity or used in agricultural production. Self-sufficiency hence prevails over accumulation. This is found in particular in the north-east of Morocco among those who procure contraband to sell it on, whether motor fuel bought in Algeria or consumer goods (such as clothing) acquired in the two Spanish enclaves on the Mediterranean coast. Once the stock level is such that a certain level of income can be earned within a given period, credit no longer serves any purpose. This suggests that people maintain their relationship with the microcredit organization more for a 'rainy day' (which can be partially dealt with by savings in the form of investment in livestock) than as part of an ongoing capital accumulation strategy. This explains why a proportion of the clientele do not gradually increase their borrowing and do not even systematically renew their loan application. As we have seen, this proves to be demotivating when it comes to personal pressure to repay. Insurance would then be a better solution to meet needs than credit.

Consumer microcredit and over-indebtedness The question of microcredit supply saturation has been addressed here mainly on the assumption that these loans are designed to increase the production capacity or turnover of a business in the form of working capital. Firstly, however, very small businesses and self-employed workers use part of the funds secured by their microloan to manage their consumer expenditure. Secondly, microcredit customers are by no means all business people. We now know that there are a huge number of cases in which microloans are used for consumer expenditure. Estimates vary depending on the environments, social groups and methods used. Accurate calculation of the use of these loans is further complicated by monetary fungibility, but we could reasonably posit that, on the whole, over half of all microloans are taken out for social purposes.[10] These cover expenditure on regular food outlays, healthcare, education, social and religious ceremonies, durable goods, housing and even paying off old debts.

The supply of small loans can improve the intertemporal management of incomings and outgoings by households and their members. This is precisely what Solène Morvant-Roux (2006) shows in Mexican villages in the state of Oaxaca. And it is also found by the financial diary surveys conducted by the *Portfolios of the Poor* in South Africa, northern India and Bangladesh. Stuart Rutherford (2004: 277–83) explains that the success of the small *Safe*Save organization he launched in Dhaka's slums in Bangladesh was due to its good match with the continuously fluctuating cash flows of its customers, who constantly alternate between cash needs and surpluses. Beyond the informal very small businesses, households of semi-waged workers and low-wage workers also have to cope with constantly fluctuating cash flows. A lot of people use microcredit in the same way as households in the 'developed' countries use their credit cards. In many African countries, for example, the use of credit cards is restricted to a tiny percentage of the population. In Central and West Africa, only 16 per cent of adults have a debit card (64 per cent have a bank account), and this percentage plunges to a mere 3 per cent when it comes to actual credit cards. It even falls below 2 per cent in Senegal (Demirguc-Kunt and Klapper 2012a: 36, 2012b: 8, 12).

Although this boost to household budgets (often rolled into one with business accounts for those who have a business) can prove extremely useful, budget management remains a day-to-day process. As such, any budget increase can be but a very short-term improvement and can raise the fraction of resources spent on productive investment only in exceptional circumstances (Bateman 2010). These budget boosts make for better household budget management without necessarily having any direct positive growth effect (in volume or number) on income-generating activities. An indirect positive income effect is found where loans are spent on buying medicinal products or covering school fees, owing to the increase in the population's general well-being and the subsequent improvement in labour productivity. Yet the positive impact in terms of raising incomes can only in exceptional circumstances be immediate. The use of loans can therefore turn into an addiction to credit with an attendant slide into over-indebtedness and, for some, impoverishment.

Over-indebtedness occurs when a growing share of income is absorbed by the cost of the debt (Guérin et al. 2013) and/or borrowers and their families make greater sacrifices to save face and pay their dues (Schicks 2013). This triggers a vicious circle in which families have no choice but to borrow again to pay off old debts. This vicious circle has been observed in areas of Bangladesh (Huq 2004; Karim 2011), Pakistan (Burki 2009), Tamil Nadu (Roesch and Héliès 2007; Guérin et al. 2009), Andhra Pradesh (Taylor 2011), Karnataka (Joseph 2013), Indonesia (Lont and Hospes 2004: 197–212), Morocco (Morvant-Roux et al. 2014), Mexico (Angulo 2013; Hummel 2013), Bolivia (Brett 2006), Ghana (Schicks 2013), Bosnia and South Africa (Bateman 2010, 2012).

As in Europe, note that over-indebtedness is not specific to the poorest populations. In some countries and for some microcredit organizations, the majority are found to be low-wage workers, especially civil servants, as found in Cameroon and Senegal, and miners in South Africa. The miners' over-indebtedness actually sparked their uprising, which was crushed, in the summer of 2012. Refusing to endure the shame of being in too much debt, they did not point the finger at the microcredit organizations, but took on their employers. They demanded better pay to repay their debts, which were automatically paid out of their bank accounts by monthly debit (Bateman 2012; James 2013).

As mentioned above, it is important to study the dynamics of consumer credit not just at individual and household level, but also in terms of impacts on local economies (which in turn influence individual and household incomes). Although effects vary depending on the nature of the local economies, calling for specific studies to be conducted on this issue, the income multiplier and use of consumer credit effects are probably moderate in a large number of cases in that a large proportion of consumed goods are imported into the local economy. The local economy captures at best nothing more than the traders' margins, with consequently limited knock-on effects.

Conclusion

Access to capital can definitely be a way for many small businesses to improve their production quality and broaden their range of products and services, whether by securing working capital or the means to invest in capital expenditure. There is no end of examples: a little eatery buys a refrigerator to offer its customers chilled drinks; a grocer or small restaurant installs audio equipment or a television to attract clientele; a greengrocer diversifies its patronage; a fabric merchant expands her stock to offer more choice; a carpenter switches from working solely to order and displays his creations, expanding his customer base; a tailor buys better machines to increase quality and speed; an embroiderer offers new designs, and so on.

Nevertheless, it would be a mistake to believe that the potential for productive credit is unlimited, as so many microcredit industry players seem to think. The pressure exerted to grant a growing volume of microcredit (see, for example, the chapter by Morvant-Roux et al. on the Dominican Republic this volume) – pressure found right the way along the supply chain from investors to field agents – is based on the conviction that financial institutions systematically lack the lending resources to meet the supposedly virtually unlimited demand from their potential clientele. On the basis that there are allegedly few microcredit market saturation effects and limited risks of over-indebtedness, instantly profitable microcredit organizations and programmes could be set up for 'poor', if not very poor, customers provided that the structures were well managed and could bring to bear the pressure they need to ensure repayment with the help of the local authorities.

As we have seen in this chapter, low local purchasing power, competition from often imported manufactured products, problems sourcing raw materials, poor infrastructures, no property rights over local resources, low business profitability, crowding-out effects when knock-on effects are small, and a sometimes disproportionate concentration of supply all combine in varying ways depending on sector and geographic area to saturate local goods and service markets and consequently saturate the demand for microcredit.

Many studies on the dynamics of employment areas and sectors, agricultural and non-agricultural, stress the extent to which financing is just one condition among others. Considerations over and above financing are product quality and qualification, production know-how and techniques, organization of sales networks and infrastructures, infrastructure quality, and regulatory measures at the different levels – from local through to global – which themselves determine the distribution of value-added among the chain players (Requier-Desjardins 2010). Private initiatives cannot stand up on their own in this environment. Strong public intervention is needed to address all the elements.

Where the demand for productive microcredit is relatively low, there is much more demand for consumer microcredit. We now know that a large proportion of microloans are used to deal with pressing needs and for consumption. This observation, unthinkable just a few years ago, has now been at least partly acknowledged as the line that microcredit makes a huge contribution to poverty reduction has been dropped in favour of the promotion of broad financial inclusion for the people. Some take bottom-of-the-pyramid approaches to hold up consumer credit as a source of economic growth and wealth, including for the poor by means of a trickle-down effect. The history of the industrialized countries shows that consumer credit, especially during the post-war economic boom period, did indeed fuel the demand for mass-produced consumer durables and hence drive the development of productive fabrics. To a certain extent, it also played a social inclusion role. Yet it was coupled with redistribution and social protection measures at the time, and its cost was partially cushioned by inflation. These conditions are far from present today. So it is highly likely that consumer credit – microloans or others – triggers or speeds up impoverishment and rising inequalities while maintaining the illusion of growth or non-recession.

The symptoms of microcredit market saturation are manifest in many countries and areas where supply is concentrated within these countries. Yet does this mean that a saturation threshold can be quickly and easily calculated? Building national saturation indicators is a first and doubtless very useful step (see the chapter by Javoy and Rozas this volume). However, the data are not available for indicators to go any deeper than the national level, whereas the microcredit supply often tends to be concentrated in certain regions, certain social classes and sometimes certain activity sectors. Note also that national saturation indicators can make investors suddenly withdraw from markets potentially risky to profit-making investments. Such indicators therefore bear the risk of social irresponsibility since 'good' microcredit players can end up suffering the same fate as ruthless local players (as shown by the collapse of Basix in Andhra Pradesh owing to a crisis provoked by another microcredit institution, SKS).

A clear picture of the 'microcredit market' therefore calls for a regional, if not local, level of analysis and the development of special measurement tools. One option could be to use local social accounting matrices designed to represent all the economic flows in a given area. This type of mesoeconomic analysis is often made complicated by a lack of available data, problems identifying suitable boundaries, and so on. This complexity is part of the reason for the preference for microeconomic and macroeconomic analyses. Yet the mesoeconomic level is vital if we are to understand the real – not supposed – effects of microcredit and its growth potential and possibilities.

Notes

1 See also Mader (2015).

2 See, for example, NCEUS (2007) on India and Beck et al. (2003) on Kenya. For an overview, see Cling et al. (2014).

3 Hence the relevance of initiatives such as that in Brazil with the Las Palmas bank replications designed to couple microcredit with additional local currency (Servet 2013).

4 See Bateman (2010: 64–8, 137). Another example can be found in Adams and Vogel (2013: 47) in South Africa, based on a paper with the eloquent title of *Lying about Borrowing* (New Haven, Innovations for Poverty Action, 2007) by D. Karlan and J. Zinman; the paper has the merit of showing how customer surveys under-report their consumer microloans.

5 Self-help groups are still the major form of supply today in India (see the article of Guérin *et al.* on the subject in this volume).

6 See Guérin et al. (2011). See also Servet (1995).

7 A parallel can be found here with the case in Mauritania presented by Diop (2010).

8 Which may well have (especially if the comparison is made with other countries) a high profile, good brand image and high level of customer satisfaction, as in the case of Al Amana (2009: 21–2).

9 The authors base their findings on different studies conducted in Indonesia, Peru, Mexico, Ghana, Morocco, the Philippines, India and Ecuador.

10 For specific examples, see the chapters on the analysis of demand in the Dominican Republic, India and Morocco in this volume. For an overview of the studies available, see Morduch (2013), Bateman (2010: 137) and Guérin (2015). See also Demirguc-Kunt and Klapper (2012a: 5).

References

Adams, D. A. and R. C. Vogel (2013) 'Through the thicket of credit impact assessments', in J.-P. Gueyie, R. Manos and J. Yaron, *Microfinance in Developing Countries*, Basingstoke: Palgrave Macmillan, pp. 36–61.

Agbodjann, E. (2012) 'Déterminants monétaires de la performance sociale des institutions de microfinance: une analyse à partir du cas de la région de l'Ogou (Togo)', Doctoral thesis in Development Studies, Geneva; IHEID.

Al Amana (2009) *Rapport d'activité*, Rabat: Al Amana.

Angulo, L. (2013) 'The social costs of microfinance and over-indebtedness for women', in I. Guérin, S. Morvant-Roux and

M. Villarreal (eds), *Microfinance, Debt and Over-indebtedness: Juggling with Money*, London: Routledge, pp. 232–52.

Bateman, M. (2010) *Why Doesn't Microfinance Work? The Destructive Rise of Local Neoliberalism*, London: Zed Books.

— (2012) 'The rise and fall of microcredit in post apartheid South Africa', *Le Monde Diplomatique*, English edn, 14 November, mondediplo.com/blogs/the-rise-and-fall-of-microcredit-in-post, accessed 12 July 2014.

— (2013) 'The age of microfinance: destroying Latin American economies from the bottom up', ÖFSE Working Paper 39, Vienna: Österreichische Forschungsstiftung für Internationale Entwicklung – ÖFSE.

Beck, T. et al. (2003) 'Small and medium enterprises, growth and poverty: cross country evidence', Policy Research Working Paper 3178, Washington, DC: World Bank.

Brett, J. A. (2006) 'We sacrifice and eat less: the structural complexities of microfinance participation', *Human Organization*, 65(1): 8–19.

Burki, H.-B. (2009) 'Unraveling the delinquency problem (2008–2009) in Punjab-Pakistan', *Micronote*, 10, Microfinance Pakistan Network.

Cling, J.-P., S. Lagrée, M. Razafindrakoto and F. Roubaud (eds) (2014) *The Informal Economy in Developing Countries*, London: Routledge.

Collins, D., J. Morduch, S. Rutherford and O. Ruthven (2009) *Portfolios of the Poor: How the World's Poor Live on $2 a Day*, Princeton, NJ: Princeton University Press.

Coulibaly, M. and K. Servais (2009) *Rapport social Evaluation SPI du RCPB-Burkina Faso*, Bilan social de la Confédération des Institutions Financières et de ses membres 2008–2009.

Demirguc-Kunt, A. and L. F. Klapper (2012a) *Measuring Financial Inclusion: The Global Findex Database*, World Bank Development Research Group, Finance and Private Sector Development Team, April.

— (2012b) 'Financial inclusion in Africa: an overview', World Bank Policy Research Working Paper no. 6088, June.

Diop, A. (2010) 'Institutions de microfinance et inégalités sociales en milieu urbain mauritanien', Doctoral thesis in Development Studies, University of Geneva /IHEID.

Elyachar, J. (2006) *Markets of Dispossession: NGOs, economic development and the state in Cairo*, Durham, NC: Duke University Press.

Fouillet, C. (2009) 'La construction spatiale de la microfinance en Inde', Doctoral thesis, Brussels: Université Libre de Bruxelles.

Gironde, C. (2007) 'Manque de crédit ou manque de profit. L'économie familiale au Vietnam', in *Annuaire suisse des politiques de développement 2007*, 26(2): 157–72, Geneva: IUED.

Guérin, I. (2003) *Femmes et économie solidaire*, Paris: La Découverte.

— (2015) *La microfinance et ses dérives. Emanciper, exploiter ou discipliner?*, Paris: Demopolis/IRD.

Guérin, I. and J. Palier (eds) (2005) *Microfinance Challenges: Empowerment or Disempowerment of the Poor?*, Pondicherry: French Institute of Pondicherry Editions.

Guérin, I., S. Morvant-Roux and J.-M. Servet (2011) 'Understanding the diversity and complexity of demand for microfinance services: lessons from informal finance', in B. Armendáriz and M. Labie (eds), *Handbook of Microfinance*, Washington, DC: World Scientific Publishing, pp. 101–22.

Guérin, I., S. Morvant-Roux and M. Villarreal (eds) (2013) *Microfinance, Debt and Over-indebtedness: Juggling with Money*, London: Routledge.

Guérin, I., M. Roesch, G. Venkatasubramanian and O. Héliès (2009) 'Microfinance, endettement et surendettement', *Revue Tiers Monde*, 197: 131–46.

Hes, T. and A. Poledňáková (2013) 'Correction of the claim for microfinance market of 1.5 billion clients', *International Letters of Social and Humanistic Sciences*, 2: 18–31.

Hummel, A. (2013) 'The commercialisation of microcredits and local consumerism. Examples of over-indebtedness from indigenous Mexico', in I. Guérin, S. Morvant-Roux and M. Villarreal (eds), *Microfinance, Debt and Over-indebtedness: Juggling with Money*, London: Routledge, pp. 253–71.

Huq, H. (2004) 'Surviving in the world of microdebt: a case from rural Bangladesh', in H. Lont and O. Hospes (eds), *Livelihood and Microfinance. Anthropological and Sociological Perspectives on Savings and Debt*, Delft: Eburon Academic Publishers, pp. 43–54.

ILO (International Labour Office, Employment Sector and Social Protection Sector) (2009) *The Informal Economy in Africa: Promoting Transition to Formality: Challenges and Strategies*, Geneva: ILO.

James, D. (2013) 'Regulating credit: tackling the redistribution of neoliberalism', Paper for presentation at ECAS, Lisbon, June.

Joseph, N. (2013) 'Mortgaging used saree-skirts, spear-heading resistance: narratives from the microfinance repayment standoff in Ramanagaram, India, 2008–2010', in I. Guérin, S. Morvant-Roux and M. Villarreal (eds), *Microfinance, Debt and Over-indebtedness: Juggling with Money*, London: Routledge, pp. 272–95.

Karim, L. (2011) *Microfinance and Its Discontents. Women in Debt in Bangladesh*, Minneapolis/London: University of Minnesota Press.

Karnani, A. (2011) *Fighting Poverty Together: Rethinking Strategies for Business, Governments, and Civil Society to Reduce Poverty*, New York: Palgrave Macmillan.

Lont, H. and O. Hospes (eds) (2004) *Livelihood and Microfinance. Anthropological and Sociological Perspectives on Savings and Debt*, Delft: Eburon Academic Publishers.

Mader, P. (2013) 'Study of an alternative to microcredit points to the failure of micrenterprises strategies', Blog, 12 September, governancexborders. com/2013/09/12/study-of-an-alternative-to-microcredit-points-to-the-failure-of-microenterprise-strategies/, accessed 2 November 2014.

— (2015) *The Political Economy of Microfinance: Financialising Poverty*, London: Palgrave.

Martinez, O. (2007) 'Microfinance et territoires dans le Sud-est béninois', *Autrepart*, 4(44): 67–90.

Morduch, J. (2008) 'Can the poor afford microcredit?', Financial Access Initiative, Wagner Graduate School, New York University.

— (2013) 'How microfinance really works? (What new research tells us)', CERMi's 5th birthday celebration, Brussels, 18 March.

Morvant-Roux, S. (2006) 'Processus d'appropriation des dispositifs de microfinance: un exemple en milieu rural mexicain', Doctoral thesis in Economic Science, Lyons: Université Lumière Lyon 2.

— (2013) 'International migration and over-indebtedness in rural Mexico', in I. Guérin, S. Morvant-Roux and M. Villarreal (eds), *Microfinance, Debt and Over-indebtedness: Juggling with Money*, London: Routledge, pp. 170–91.

Morvant-Roux, S., I. Guérin, M. Roesch and J.-M. Moisseron (2014) 'Adding value to randomization with qualitative analysis: the case of microcredit in rural Morocco', *World Development*, LVI: 302–12.

NCEUS (National Commission for Enterprises in the Unorganized Sector) (2007) *Report on Conditions of Work and Promotion of Livelihoods in the Unorganized Sector*, New Delhi: NCEUS.

Ojong, N. D. (2013) 'Microfinance, informal financial mechanisms and low-income populations: an analysis of the life-styles of low-income populations in the North West Region of Cameroon', PhD dissertation in Development Studies, Geneva: IHEID.

Requier-Desjardins, D. (2010) 'L'évolution du débat sur les SYAL: le regard d'un économiste', *Revue d'Economie Régionale et Urbaine*, 4: 651–68.

Roesch, M. and O. Héliès (2007) 'La microfinance: outil de gestion du risque ou de mise en danger par surendettement? Le cas de l'Inde du Sud', *Autrepart*, 44(4): 119–40.

Rutherford, S. (2004) 'The microfinance market: huge, diverse – and waiting for you', in H. Lont and O. Hospes (eds), *Livelihood and Microfinance. Anthropological and Sociological Perspectives on Savings and Debt*, Delft: Eburon Academic Publishers, pp. 263–89.

Schicks, J. (2013) 'The definition and causes of microfinance over-indebtedness: a customer protection point of view', *Oxford Development Studies*, 41(Supplement 1): S95–S116.

— (2014) 'Over-indebtedness in microfinance – an empirical analysis of related factors on the borrower level', *World Development*, 54: 301–24.

Servet, J.-M. (ed.) (1995) *Épargne et liens sociaux*, Paris: CDC/AUF.

— (2010) 'Microcredit', in H. Keith, J.-L. Laville and A. D. Cattani (eds), *The Human Economy*, Boston, MA, and Oxford: Polity Press, pp. 130–41.

— (2013) 'Le Chicago plan revisité par les monnaies complémentaires, le microcrédit solidaire et les tontines', in B. Hours and P. Ould-Ahmed (eds), *Dette de qui, dette de quoi? Une économie anthropologique de la dette*, Paris: L'Harmattan, pp. 45–72.

— (2015) *La vrai révolution du microcrédit*, Paris: Odile Jacob.

Servet, J.-M. and H. Saiag (2013) 'Household over-indebtedness in northern and southern countries: a macro-perspective', in I. Guérin, S. Morvant-Roux and M. Villarreal (eds), *Microfinance, Debt and Over-indebtedness: Juggling with Money*, London: Routledge, pp. 24–45.

Shipton, P. (2010) *Credit between Cultures. Farmers, Financiers and Misunderstandings in Africa*, New Haven, CT, and London: Yale University Press.

Taylor, M. (2011) 'Freedom from poverty is not for free: rural development and the microfinance crisis in Andhra Pradesh, India', *Journal of Agrarian Change*, 11(4): 484–504.

Touré K. (2013) 'Socio-économie de la microfinance au Sénégal. Une approche en termes de filière, de territoire et de proximité', Doctoral thesis in Economics, Univesity of Toulouse-le-Mirail.

Vanroose, A. (2014) 'Factors that explain the regional expansion of microfinance institutions in Peru', CEB Working Paper no. 14/030 2014, Brussels: Université Libre de Bruxelles.

Part II
DEMAND

4 | IS THE DEMAND FOR MICROCREDIT IN RURAL TAMIL NADU SUSTAINABLE?[1]

Isabelle Guérin, Cyril Fouillet, Santosh Kumar, Marc Roesch and G. Venkatasubramanian

Introduction

The Andhra Pradesh microcredit crisis became global news owing to intense media coverage. While microcredit had long been considered the gold standard for poverty reduction, the events made people wonder whether it could in fact be a new form of usury, an insidious means of pushing women into destitution, prostitution and suicide, or India's version of the United States' subprime mortgage debacle.[2] Its neighbouring state, Tamil Nadu, has the second-highest share of borrowers and loan portfolios after Andhra Pradesh, with around 10.7 million active borrowers in 2012[3] for a total population of 72.1 million. At first glance, it might seem that Tamil Nadu has been spared the microcredit crisis. Not only does it have a better macroeconomic climate, especially in rural areas, but its state policies have been much more interventionist over the past decade than in Andhra Pradesh. Tamil Nadu state and its successive governments have always closely monitored the microcredit sector. Over the past fifteen years, there has been constant expansion in supply, but not the soaring growth observed in Andhra Pradesh just before the crisis.

This does not mean, however, that the situation is an optimal one. As reported by the latest available official data, active borrower numbers have been decreasing and repayment rates falling severely since 2012 (Nabard 2014: 50). Until recently, repayment rates have been reported as excellent, but there have been widespread renewal practices among a number of microcredit providers in our fieldwork regions (four districts in the north and north-east of the state), which have often hidden repayment difficulties. As long as credit providers are refinanced and grow, the problem is covered up. Moreover, good repayments do not necessarily mean that clients are happy or financially secure (Schicks 2014; see also Morvant-Roux et al. on the Dominican Republic this volume). But conversely, microcredit is not necessarily the root cause where people are financially vulnerable or even over-indebted.

This chapter draws on a twelve-year research programme based at the French Institute of Pondicherry, for which several household surveys and a large number of case studies (see Box 4.1 for a description of the method) were carried out, to shed light on the complexities and ambiguities of microcredit on households' financial vulnerability. Various specific results emerged from this research programme and have been published elsewhere. This chapter is an attempt to offer a global perspective on the role of microcredit in financial vulnerability and over-indebtedness processes.

Box 4.1 Method and data collection

The results in this paper are part of a of long-term research programme on labour and finance in various districts of north and coastal rural Tamil Nadu. It was begun in 2002 and still continues today. It has brought together researchers of various origins and backgrounds, some of whom live on site. It has drawn on a wide range of methods, including semi-directive interviews, case studies, informal discussions and observation, detailed analysis of villages, value chains and markets, and four household surveys, as detailed in Table 4.1. Our informal discussions and observation involved spending time with women borrowers (who make up around 90 per cent of the clientele), sharing parts of their daily lives, both at home and in their neighbourhoods. We also spent time at the headquarters of microcredit providers to observe their day-to-day activities, and had many discussions with founders, managers and some of their partners and allies, such as public officials, donors, local associations and informal networks. We also spent time with microcredit officers, both during their field visits and outside their work.

In a climate where there is a strong propensity to get into debt, rising aspirations for consumerism and upward mobility, and booming credit supply (far beyond microcredit), our analyses indicate that microcredit contributes to an increase in debt of questionable sustainability. It is related to many other forms of debt and often constitutes only a small proportion of total household debt, but its modalities – rigid instalments that are ill suited to irregular incomes, and growth targets leading to unbridled supply – make it particularly dangerous.

Our chapter makes three main arguments. Firstly, microcredit hasn't been the first opportunity for rural Tamil households to borrow. Over-indebtedness goes far beyond microcredit, which is not solely responsible for households' financial fragility. To pinpoint only microcredit would ignore the fact that rural households are in desperate need of borrowing (as was also found for the Dominican Republic; see Morvant-Roux et al. this volume). Secondly, microcredit has very mixed effects on over-indebtedness mechanisms. As it is mostly used for consumption, it has had a negligible direct effect on income creation. Moreover, compared to the other sources of debt rural households juggle, microcredit's strong unique feature – its rigidity – works as a double-edged sword. It can help people to get out from lengthy (and expensive) loans, but because it does not mix well with the irregular incomes that are far more the rule than the exception, it can also push people farther into debt. Thirdly, weaknesses and deficiencies in selection procedures and microcredit providers' growth constraints are a further risk factor. These can encourage some clients to engage in risky investments, the most common being for social and religious rituals, housing and sometimes small businesses or private education. In other words, credit itself isn't necessarily a problem, but its distribution procedures are.

Context

Microcredit and its effects must be put in context, as they cannot be separated from broader economic, social, cultural and political dynamics. In the villages we studied, as with many other Tamil villages, non-farm labour is on the rise. Agriculture has not gone away – it is still a source of income and social status – but it is increasingly dependent on non-farm labour, which is mostly casual (and informal) via various forms of migration. Around 93 per cent of all labour is informal, a figure which has held steady over time. While 68.5 per cent of total employment in India was in agriculture in 1983, this had fallen to 56.5 per cent in 2004/05 and to 53.2 per cent in 2010/11.[4] Tamil Nadu, one of the most industrialized and urbanized states, has seen an even greater decline (in 2009/10, 44.2 per cent of total employment was in agriculture). Rural, mostly male labourers, are thus increasingly commuting workers who shift between workplaces and occupations, moving according to their needs, indebtedness and employment opportunities. The increasing importance of non-farm labour and male seasonal migration has had a variety of consequences. It has firstly led to increasing monetarization in social relationships, as self-consumption and payments in kind are now very rare. Along with the electricity supply for the countryside and the widespread development of television (encouraged by governmental schemes), exposure to urban life is leading to the adoption of urban living standards. Ten years ago, buying consumer durable goods such as mass-produced clothing, mobile phones, motorbikes, hi-fi equipment or household appliances was the privilege of the upper classes (and often upper castes). It is now increasingly common.[5] Some such products are supplied through governmental schemes (televisions, grinders, fans) but the rest is through private consumption. Consumption demand has exploded not only for consumer durable goods but also for private healthcare access, private education and improved housing (Wilhite 2008). We found that expenses for ceremonies and rituals are also continuing to rise, probably as an indicator of a need for identity assessment. Wedding costs, in particular, commonly add up to two to four years of annual household wages.[6] Even if inequalities remain remarkably intractable, the poorest and lowest castes are expressing a growing desire for social mobility or at least integration: consumerism is integral to this.

Through this we observed that new or growing needs have been emerging, including among the poorest people. This is feeding into strong demand for credit, because most casual workers' real incomes have been declining on average (Kundu and Mohanan 2010: 28). Demand for credit is all the higher given that debt is widely accepted culturally. History and anthropology have shown that attitudes towards debt vary greatly between and within cultures, and that Hinduism is notably tolerant towards both lenders and debtors (Graeber 2011). Many references to debt can be found in Hindu religious texts such as the Dharmasastra (Pandurang 1941). This includes various kinds of debts, be these to ancestors, divinities, kin or society as a whole, which are honoured through ceremonial and ritual expenses. It also includes debt to relatives, one's neighbourhood or private lenders, some of whom are from specific castes with century-old professional networks (Hardiman 1996). Religious texts set out the rights and obligations of lenders and borrowers, interest rate rules, repayment modalities, etc. (Pandurang 1941; Malamoud 1988). In India, 'every being is born as a debt' and debt echoes human beings' mortal condition, writes Charles Malamoud, drawing on the Sanskrit vocabulary of Brahmanic thought (Malamoud 1988: 13–27). Far beyond ancient texts, daily uses and experiences of debt in contemporary rural southern India reflect its pervasiveness: debt is an integral part of the human condition and even if it is often a source of exploitation and hierarchy, it would seem very strange to get out of it. Common expressions such as 'I borrow like I breathe' and 'a life without debt is like a meal without salt' reflect the importance of debt in daily life. Not all debt is equally valued: some is a source of honour while some is degrading (Guérin et al. 2013), but the fact is that economic and social life is organized around debt.

Over-indebtedness as a structural phenomenon

Various surveys carried out from 2004 to 2010 in north and north-east Tamil Nadu by the French Institute of Pondicherry (see the survey details in Table 4.1) indicate that around 90 per cent of households are in debt, to an average outstanding amount of roughly one year's household income. Microcredit has quite a high penetration rate (around 40 per cent of households have access to it) but it constitutes only a small proportion of outstanding debt (around 10–25 per cent on average).[7] Most debt is from other, frequently (but not always) informal sources: pawnbrokers, local moneylenders (such as members of the local elite and landowners), labour intermediaries, relatives

TABLE 4.1 Household surveys

	Sampling[a]	Main focus
2010 survey Villipuram and Cuddalore districts	407 households Representative sample of the local population	Labour and financial practices
2008 survey Tiruvallur and Vellore districts	170 households Representative sample of microcredit clientele	The gender of financial practices (an analysis of women and their financial practices)
2006 survey Villipuram and Cuddalore districts	344 households Representative sample of the local population	Over-indebtedness and microcredit
2004/06/09 survey (longitudinal analysis) Tiruvallur district	395 households Representative sample of microcredit clientele	Over-indebtedness and microcredit

Source: Authors

[a] For all our household surveys, sampling was stratified by caste and location (dry/irrigated, and proximity to urban centres)

and friends, and private financial companies. Many households can already access various, chiefly informal, sources of credit, which they patch together according to their needs and preferences, but also according to the facilities available to them.

The financial market is not just diverse, but highly active. Besides microcredit organizations, an increasing number of credit providers have emerged in the countryside. Some landowners have shifted from agriculture to moneylending. Most of them were used to lending money in the past, especially to their own labourers, but some have left agriculture to focus intensively and solely on moneylending. Vendors of various items (containers, clothes) have begun door-to-door selling with credit facilities. Door-to-door moneylenders are nothing new, but the number and the frequency of their visits have clearly increased: in many villages moneylending on doorsteps is offered daily. Commuting to urban areas has also opened up new opportunities: workers can obtain loans from their workplace, especially from their colleagues, bosses or contractors. Pawnbroking is booming. While this was long the preserve of specific communities, it is now easily accessible to anyone with the capital, whatever their caste (although the supply is highly segmented along caste lines). Powerful urban-based pawnbroker networks such as Muthoot Finance now have branches in the countryside and large billboards can be found in any small town and along all major roads. In various sectors wage advances are the rule, and act both as a job guarantee and as a way to tide over labourers. Private banks are also showing a renewed interest in rural areas. Though they don't target the poor yet (except a few of them through self-help groups – SHGs), they may do so in the near future.[8] And as we shall see in the final section, microcredit can create or boost new prospects: loan officers and SHG leaders are often moneylenders themselves. Very few loans are free of cost, even to relatives and friends. The prices are difficult to estimate precisely, as they are often negotiable and not always paid regularly (especially to informal private moneylenders), but rough estimates range from 1 to 5 per cent monthly. We shall come back later to a price comparison.

People not only borrow but save, but there are almost no monetary savings. Saving accounts have been developed a lot over the last decade, strongly incentivized by 'financial inclusion' policies, but many of the accounts are dormant. People worry that they won't be able to access their funds when they need them, and prefer to invest or circulate any surplus they have, either through onward lending or counter-gifts (Guérin et al. 2011). They are also concerned about the lack of anonymity and don't want their wealth to be made public, relatively modest as it might be. Using gold or rotating savings and credit associations (ROSCAs) remains the most common means of saving for many households, whatever their social standing, as seems to have long been the case.

Such ready access to credit can create opportunities and mitigate dependency on local patrons, but it can also push households into excessive debt: notwithstanding microcredit, many households are heavily indebted and are arguably over-indebted in the sense that they are experiencing a process of pauperization through debt.

Who are the over-indebted?

Out of the four surveys discussed above, two specifically focused on over-indebtedness. The first was carried out in 2006 on 305 randomly selected households from two districts (Villupuram and Cuddalore). We saw that indebtedness was quite high and ought to be explored in more depth, so we conducted a further detailed survey of the 20 per cent most indebted households. Their average household debt was 4.5 times higher than their annual income, and 1.4 times the monetary value of their assets. Clearly, all of them were over-indebted (on average only 6 per cent of the total debt volume was microcredit, which made up 17 per cent of the loans). On average, half their monthly income was spent on debt repayment (Guérin et al. 2013).

The second survey was a longitudinal survey of another district (Tiruvallur) in collaboration with a local microcredit non-governmental organization (NGO). We compared the debts and assets of 400 microcredit borrowers in 2004, 2006 and 2009. The increase in debt over five years was extremely striking (increasing by a factor of 2.5 in constant prices). This was driven both by microcredit and informal debt (which accounted respectively for 25 and 75 per cent of outstanding debt in 2009). On average, assets increased slightly (partly driven by the rise in gold value) over the period but with wide disparities. Net wealth (assets minus debt) was negative (and the decrease was significant) over the whole period. For a quarter of the households, the loss was more than the equivalent of a year's household income (Guérin et al. 2015).

Both surveys included case studies of over-indebted households – i.e. ones that had been sucked into chronic debt, which had lost assets with little or no chances of recovery from high debt. Two typical scenarios emerged. In the first, over-indebtedness was the outcome of successive shocks (most often illness, death, unexpected ceremonies, job loss), which gradually weakened the households' asset portfolio such that tangible assets dwindled (gold or land was sold), social networks were exhausted, and loan repayments took up a growing proportion of income. The speed and violence of this process depend both on the initial strength of the households' asset portfolio and the intensity of the shocks. The second typical case is the outcome of risk-taking, be this through livelihood diversification, marriages, housing or education. Both scenarios may of course coincide.

It is easy to understand households' vulnerability to shocks. Despite the Tamil Nadu government's recent efforts to develop social protection schemes such as microinsurance, very few households have coverage and health expenses are a heavy burden.[9] Such high vulnerability does not necessarily deter them from risk-taking. As discussed above, in rural communities, including their lower hierarchical echelons, there are growing aspirations to upward mobility, and great willingness to take risks in these bids. Some people, sometimes with microfinance providers' encouragement, may start up new businesses that go on to fail. But ceremonies, housing and education are by far the biggest forms of investment.[10]

Prestigious festivities are a source of honour and esteem: weddings are used as indicators of the quality and status of the family. People also stated that weddings are a way to extend social relationships. Marriages have a self-insurance function, both for the couple and their parents, who expect to be supported in their old age by their children and their spouses. But this is a long-term and risky investment: returns sometimes come too late, or are too small to offset the initial costs. A few examples can illustrate this. One couple was having difficulties because of false promises: a groom was meant to pay back the loan contracted for the ceremony, but in the end refused to do so. In another case, the parents and the bride had found out that the groom only had a temporary job as a teacher, rather than the permanent position he had claimed to have before the marriage (which was supposed to help with repaying the loan taken on for the ceremony). In yet another case, the scale of the ceremony sparked conflicts and jealousy with the household's circle of relatives, who then refused to help with repayments ('if you can organize such big ceremonies, then you can manage on your own').

Housing and education are also used as investment strategies. People talk about housing as security from environmental hazards (flood, fire) and as an asset. They also saw housing as a source of status and a means to get a better deal for the marriage of their children. They highlighted that the perceived 'standing' of the house could allow them to look for someone better off. Housing is also seen as a means to increase creditworthiness and thus borrowing capacity. Here again, some households turned out to be under stress, because their housing investment exceeded their repayment capacities.

We also saw that a growing number of households wanted their children to get out of agriculture and manual work and have an education as a matter of status and 'profit' – a qualified young person is expected to get a skilled and possibly permanent job. But this too is a very risky strategy. The Tamil Nadu job market for graduates and diploma holders is already saturated and getting a job often depends on paying a bribe.[11] The amounts are such that families are sometimes unable to pay. In one of the cases we encountered, the parents had borrowed more than INR 400,000[12] from various local informal sources to educate their three daughters, with an annual income of around INR 45,000. They used both pawnbroking and microcredit at the same time to pay the interest, but most of their jewels had already gone. They were expecting the elder daughter to pay back the capital once she got a job as a nurse. The main source of uncertainty was the bribe she would have to pay to get the job.

What we want to highlight here is that over-indebtedness, in the sense of pauperization through debt, goes far beyond microcredit and reflects structural problems that also go far beyond microcredit (this in echo of Morvant-Roux et al. on the Dominican Republic this volume). This said, it is important not to underestimate microcredit's potential contribution, to which we will now return in greater depth.

What is microcredit's role?

Microcredit as consumption credit A very clear observation is that in the regions studied, microcredit is mostly used for non-income-generative purposes. The four surveys from the past ten years indicate that the percentage of microcredit used for generating direct income ranges from almost zero to a quarter of usage at most, depending on location and microfinance organization profile. As is shown in Table 4.2, microcredit is primarily used for food security, health, ceremonies, paying off past debts and investments in statutory expenses such as ceremonies. Owing to the fungibility of monetary flows and the fact that loans are usually used for a variety of purposes, sticking to this type of indicator is restrictive. What is, however, clear is that there is only a marginal direct impact on job creation.[13]

TABLE 4.2 Microcredit use

	Average microcredit amount (INR)	Income-generating activities as primary use	Other uses
2010 survey	10,000	9.9%	Family expenses (57%), loan repayment (9.3%), housing (7.3%), health (6%), ceremonies (5.9%), education (4.6%)
2008 survey	6,100	4%	Ceremonies (24%), housing (22%), loan repayment (15%), health (11%), education (7%), other (7%)
2006 survey	12,800	26%	Ceremonies (14%), daily life (23%), loan repayment (6%), health (10%), education (11%), housing (4%), other (6%)
2004 survey	5,000	19%	Loan repayment (26%), health (19%), daily life (14%), education (10%), ceremonies (5%), other (7%)

Source: Own surveys

Note that the distinction between 'social' and 'productive' purposes is partly artificial. Using microcredit to buy medicine, finance children's education or renovate housing – in a context where small businesses are often run from home – can boost the households' working capacity in the medium or long term. But there is no guarantee of this, and loans have to be repaid in the short term.

In the face of official rhetoric – the great majority of MFIs and NGOs operating in the surveyed areas claim that their microcredits are for productive purposes – how can we explain that microcredits are mostly used for non-income generative purposes?

Firstly, and as stated above, people's needs have been constantly increasing over the past decades. Our own data indicate that consumer durable goods acquisition mostly took off from 2005. Microcredit arrived at just at the right time to meet this emerging demand (or to stimulate it, one might speculate).

Secondly, there is much less potential for business creation or expansion than microcredit promoters advocate. Our surveys indicated that around 10 per cent of total employment is in non-farm self-employment, and that the potential for expansion is extremely limited, as we have shown elsewhere (Guérin et al. forthcoming).

Thirdly, where there is the potential for business creation and growth, informal loans are a much more suitable option. None of the male or female entrepreneurs we spoke to in our 2010 study mentioned microcredit as a means of microfunding their activity (ibid.). Microcredit sums are often too low – on average around INR 10,000 – while the average amount invested is INR 70,000. But more importantly, it is too inflexible for financing a sustainable income-generating activity (i.e. monthly instalments do not adapt to the irregularity and seasonality of many businesses). Most businesses, whether created by men or women, are partly funded though savings and inheritances, and in part through debt from more flexible sources. These include relatives, providers, local private moneylenders and, in some rare cases, banks or financial companies. The very inflexibility of microcredit distinguishes it from other sources of borrowing, as we shall now see.

Microcredit as a double-edged sword How does microcredit work in conjunction with other sources of borrowing, and how does it affect over-indebtedness patterns? As we have already discussed, households juggle a wide range of borrowing sources and microcredit represents only a small proportion of their debt. As has been observed elsewhere (see Morvant-Roux 2006; also Roesch and Héliès 2007 and Morvant-Roux et al. this volume), adjustable repayment schedules (weekly, monthly or negotiated; interest-only or capital plus interest) give households some room for manoeuvre when managing their budgets.[14] As people are frequently constrained by a calendar mismatch between their income and expenses and they are very much used to being in debt, any additional cash source is welcome. This is all the more so in that microcredit is often cheaper than other sources, although this all depends on how costs are calculated (as discussed later on). For many households, microcredit is another source among many and does not dramatically change their budget management. Under certain conditions, however, which depend both on the amounts borrowed and the ups and downs of household daily life, it can either help households to escape lengthy and expensive informal debts, or conversely push them farther into debt. We shall discuss these two scenarios.

One feature distinguishes microcredit from other sources of credit: its inflexible repayment modalities. Not only are a lot of microloans used to pay off past debt, as discussed above, but the repayment structure (regular and rigid instalments, short fixed duration) also incentivizes faster repayments. Though microcredit amounts are on average similar to those of other borrowing sources such as pawnbroking or family and friends, the average duration is shorter (according to our 2006 survey, 246 days for microcredit as opposed to 291 days for pawnbrokers and 423 days for relatives and friends).

The observations of Collins et al. (2009) partially hold true here: regular repayments function as a form of 'self-discipline' that some people appreciate. By contrast, most other sources (informal moneylending, pawnbroking, sale on credit, advances, etc.) often (but not always) rely on 'negotiability'.

Repayment modalities and duration can be debated, bargained and revised throughout the duration of the loan.[15] In some cases, moreover, and particularly for loans from local private moneylenders, only the interest is paid regularly while the capital is paid at the end. But the duration is not always predefined and may depend on the constraints of the borrower or of the lender. Not only is the effective interest rate much lower (i.e. the borrower can use the regular instalment money for other purposes and then save money) but the capital may never be repaid, especially when the interest exceeds a certain amount, which is usually twice or three times the capital. Such negotiability is well suited to irregular cash flows and helps to sustain social networks. But on the other side of the coin, such negotiability is likely to keep people in long-standing and sometimes costly debt, not only financially, but socially too.

Various case studies confirm that microcredit can be used to avoid or complement sources of debt that are expensive or socially degrading. One woman used her microcredit to pay her daughter's school fees, whereas she may otherwise have borrowed from her sister-in-law. This would have been a source of social pressure and she preferred not to owe her anything (although it was possible she would have to approach her for something else in the near future). Another man borrowed almost INR 140,000 for his son's wedding from four sources, including a INR 20,000 microcredit. Multiple lenders were unavoidable, as he would never have been able to borrow such a lump sum from a single lender. But it was also a way to limit pressure from lenders at the time of repayment and to diversify payment deadlines. He opted for microcredit because it was a good opportunity – his wife was able to get a loan at the time – and he was sure of paying off the microcredit debt quickly because of the regular instalment obligations.

The social meaning of debt is often notably instrumental in these juggling processes: notwithstanding the financial cost, some debts, such as when the lender has a lower status, are socially degrading and borrowers try to get free of them as quickly as possible (Guérin et al. 2013).

But microcredit's comparative advantage in terms of regular repayments and 'discipline' remains very abstract (Roesch and Héliès 2007). Firstly, even for households that prefer regular repayments, the self-discipline principle may not be compatible with their financial constraints and incoming cash flows. It is quite common to borrow from informal sources to pay back microcredit instalments, and vice versa:[16] ultimately, the cost and duration of the loan repayment may be much higher than planned on paper. Box 4.2 gives an example to illustrate this.

Some households juggle multiple sources easily and without trouble, while for others such juggling practices lead to a spiral of increasing debt that is sometimes difficult to stop. 'It's like a spider web,' one person commented: 'once you are in, you cannot get out of it.'

Box 4.2 Comparing the cost of debt

Let's take the hypothetical case of a woman who borrows INR 10,000 for one year at a 2 per cent (constant) monthly interest rate. She will have to pay back INR 1,033 monthly, and the final cost of microcredit will be INR 2,400 (24 per cent), with an effective interest rate of 41.7 per cent. Monthly repayments are often complicated by irregular sources of income. We can now suppose that she borrows from a mobile lender to pay back most of her microcredit instalment (INR 1,000). Usually, this sort of repayment takes ten weeks, with a weekly repayment of INR 100 and a further instalment for the interest (i.e. 10 per cent for ten weeks). If she does this every month, the total cost of her microcredit will be INR 3,600, with an effective interest rate of 88.6 per cent.

If she had borrowed the same amount from a private local moneylender, the rates would have ranged from 2 to 5 per cent monthly, but the big difference is that the repayment of the capital would have occurred at the end. The total cost would range from INR 2,400 to 6,000, given that the repayment of regular interest is negotiable and can easily be postponed without additional cost, and the effective interest rate would thus range from 24 to 60 per cent.

Ultimately, the best option depends not only on the interest rate (which varies greatly among informal lenders) but also the compatibility between the repayment modalities and the frequency and regularity of the borrower's income flows. If these are irregular and dependent on migration, as is often the case, repaying at the end of the period might be much cheaper and avoid the psychological stress of looking for the money every month. In our example here, with microcredit, the borrower would have to find INR 1,000 a month, while for an informal loan she would have to find INR 200 to 500 per month (and a bulk amount at some point).

Furthermore, not all borrowers are looking for a self-discipline mechanism. When we asked them whether they thought they might be able to get out of debt more quickly with microcredit, many answered that it was more a way to get additional loans. Economic textbooks define borrowing as a temporary strategy for people whose needs exceed their income, but this does not apply here: many households organize their livelihoods around debt, seeing it as a permanent and unavoidable practice. Rather than replacing pre-existing debt, we saw microcredit working as leverage for people to access other sources of cash.

This leverage effect works through various channels. Firstly, repaying past debts allows borrowers to maintain their reputation and/or to recover pledged jewels, and to then borrow from the same creditor again at a later point. Being a microcredit borrower is also a source of creditworthiness. Creditworthiness in local financial markets involves various considerations: assets and income sources (amount and regularity), but also questions of trust, reputation, notoriety, credit history and personal references. Borrowers' abilities to access other sources of finance to make repayments also come into the frame. ROSCAs, for instance, are very commonly used as a form of guarantee. ROSCA membership is a sign of creditworthiness as the share can be used to make repayments. Microcredit is used in a similar way. As one woman summed up: 'microcredit makes us trustworthy'. Door-to-door moneylenders are clear that microcredit borrowers are favoured clients. Some tie in their visits to villages according to microcredit repayment schedules, knowing that many women will need their services. Conversely, moneylenders also know microcredit borrowers will be able to rely on microcredit if they have a repayment problem. Some informal private lenders ask SHG leaders to act as guarantors for their peers. The women themselves use their SHG membership to convince private lenders. Our 2010 survey found that 35 per cent of SHG members use their membership as a guarantee, committing themselves to taking out microcredit to be given to the lender in the event of non-repayment, while 65 per cent of them pledge their membership to lenders as a moral guarantee of their creditworthiness.

The weakness of screening procedures Unlike what is observed in other countries (such as the Dominican Republic, as shown in this volume by Morvant-Roux et al.), there is very little standardization of procedures in the area, even with the most professional MFIs (of those we studied, one regularly got excellent ratings from notation agencies). Even if there are such procedures, loan officers may not have the time or opportunity to apply them (though this is a crucial condition for a healthy supply; see D'Espallier et al. this volume). Most loans are delivered through SHGs, which are selected on their bookkeeping ability, but also on their commitment to taking part in a lot of the events organized by NGOs or MFIs or their allies. Microcredit does not escape the complicated rules of local networks of patronage (Guérin and Kumar 2007; see also Picherit's chapter this volume). This means that, ultimately, selection criteria may have very little to do with women's actual solvency.[17] Even where microcredits are paid out individually, as is increasingly the case in the areas studied here, groups and their leaders in particular still play an informal role in screening and enforcement, and here too there is no proper evaluation of borrowers' true creditworthiness. If people struggle to repay, they may resort to various strategies: juggling informal loans (or other microcredits), renewing their microcredit from the same NGO or MFI, or through migration.[18] It is very difficult to get precise renewal figures, but discussions with borrowers and loan officers both suggested that it was common practice.

As long as supply keeps increasing and getting funding, the system can appear to be healthy. Here as elsewhere, microcredit providers of all statuses have specific growth targets.[19] Rather than finding new clients, it is easier to focus on existing good clients and to encourage them to borrow increasing amounts. Macro data illustrate this process well. As indicated in the figure below, the number of SHGs for all of India has considerably declined since the Andhra Pradesh crisis (dropping from around 1.6 million to around 1.2 million) but the average amount of loan per group is still growing strongly: over the past six years (2007–13), the average amount of loan per group multiplied by a factor of almost (from INR 60,000 to 180,000).

Even taking inflation into account, this is a considerable increase. This trend was largely confirmed in our fieldwork areas. Women talked about how difficult it was ten or fifteen years ago to access a few thousand rupees, and how easy it now is to get credit for tens or even hundreds of thousands of rupees. Larger amounts are meant to be exclusively for income-generating activities, but this, as before, remains an illusion. On the supply side, the bank branch managers we met were also very clear: the media coverage of the microcredit crisis in Andhra Pradesh was an opportunity for them to reduce the number of grant loans to focus on the most efficient and powerful SHGs; the concern was to reduce the number of loans granted while increasing the amounts allocated to each of these loans.

By contrast, informal lenders cannot afford to cover what looks like a headlong rush. Their portfolios are usually small (the largest one we encountered was for a few hundred clients) and have limited prospects of expansion, both because of funding constraints and the challenges of

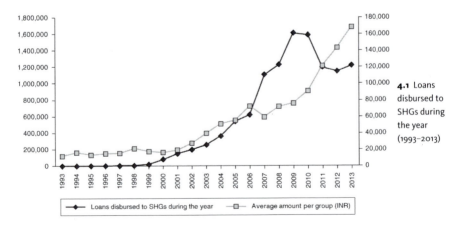

4.1 Loans disbursed to SHGs during the year (1993–2013)

Source: Compiled from Nabard annual reports and Nabard publications (various years).

screening clients and enforcing repayments on a larger scale. They have many disadvantages (cost, dependency, etc.) but their means of operation are less of a hazard as regards client over-indebtedness.[20]

Conclusion

By drawing on the case of rural Tamil Nadu, our purpose was to shed light on the mixed impact of microcredit on household budget management. The amounts borrowed are of course important, but so are microcredit operational procedures. On the one hand, microcredit is far from the first opportunity Indian villagers have had to borrow, and our understanding of microcredit's effects should be situated in a broader context of strong attachment to debt (for social and cultural reasons), growing dependence on urban wage labour (highly irregular, precarious and poorly paid), the pursuit of social status (mainly through consumption and social investments), and an increasingly large credit supply. On the other hand, microcredit's specific procedures – inflexibility, partial disconnection from village realities and its growth constraints – present new dangers.

Two of our surveys showed that a fifth to a quarter of our samples were caught in a vicious cycle of over-indebtedness in which debt is impoverishing rather than a source of accumulation or stability. How many people are pushed farther into debt because of microcredit? We don't honestly know. Complicated chains of causality and multiple interactions between various factors make it very difficult to establish the precise role of microcredit. Though it is far from being the only factor, we can reasonably assume that it is a contributing one. Credit delivery procedures are strongly disconnected from borrowers' actual solvency. In group lending, members mostly rely on households' reputations and moral attributes in their selection process. In individual lending, which is increasingly common, loan officers simply have no time to carry out a proper assessment of clients' creditworthiness. Loan officers often have performance targets based on factors such as portfolio volume, growth and quality. Growth targets encourage loan officers to continue lending ever larger amounts; as these officers are often authorized to renew loans before their terms, repayment defaults remain low.

Clearly, the MFIs in our survey area fail to adhere to 'good practices' such as those designed by the microcredit industry (see D'Espallier et al. this volume). Since 2011, in the wake of the Andhra Pradesh crisis and in line with these 'good practices', legislation has imposed a number of restrictions on MFIs, such as loan ceilings based on borrower income, strong restrictions on consumption use (less than 30 per cent of the loan should be used on consumption), reporting to a credit bureau and greater repayment flexibility. In our field area in 2011 and 2012, a number of microcredit providers, and more frequently NGOs, stopped their activity because their funds were drying up. But newcomers have emerged. Some are NGOs which have turned into financial entities, while others are financial companies that have set up microcredit services. In our field area, except for multiple lending (borrowers should not borrow from more than two microcredit organizations), none of them adhere to the legislative regulation. Further work would be needed to explore this in more depth, but we can reasonably assume that these rules are poorly suited to the true nature of demand (consumption rather than running a business or production), to working constraints (as before, staff fall short in conducting proper evaluations) and to growth targets. 'Good practices' are certainly worthy, but in our view, and as has also been observed in other contexts studied in this volume (see Morvant-Roux and Roesch on Morocco and Morvant-Roux et al. on the Dominican Republic), what should first and foremost be queried is the general framework within which microcredit providers operate, and especially the illusion of a large and sustainable demand for productive purposes.

How long can this headlong flight into debt last? The system is sustainable as long as economic growth continues and allows debt repayment to be absorbed. Short-term and short-distance migration is the most common strategy for repaying debt and is driven by the expansion of both major and medium-sized towns. Economic growth has seriously slowed down over the past five years (with a rate of 3–4 per cent as opposed to the 9–10 per cent of the previous decade).[21] It is clear that the labour market in the coming years will be utterly unable to absorb the mass of young people (Mitra and Verick 2013). Weakened by the slowdown in economic growth, employers in Tamil Nadu increasingly resort to northern Indian workers, especially in the construction sector (which is still the major driver of job creation). They accept much lower wages and poorer working conditions. The labour market is thus likely to be increasingly squeezed in the coming years. It is therefore urgent to question the development model behind microcredit. It has certainly been successful in fighting financial exclusion from the formal system, but in the absence of social protection mechanisms and with a labour market that remains highly unsecure, it contributes to a debt economy that does not look to be very sustainable.

Notes

1 We sincerely thank Bryan Hock and Margaux Teuliere for their data analysis assistance.

2 The microcredit crisis has been widely covered by the media, both in India and abroad, and in the USA in particular. Several articles were written, for instance, in the *Wall Street Journal* (Bellman and Chang 2010; Gokhale 2009; Evans 2010) and the *New York Times* (Bajaj 2011; Polgreen and Bajaj 2010).

3 Sa Dhan data are available on www.sa-dhan.net/Others/Microfinance%20Heat%20Map%202013.htm, accessed 21 July 2014.

4 According to the latest official data (National Sample Survey Office). See Lerche (2015). It is also worth noting that the share of agriculture in the country's gross domestic product (GDP) declined faster. It was 51.9 per cent in 1950/51, which came down to 13.7 per cent in 2012/13 at 2004/05 prices.

5 In our 2010 survey, 53.3 per cent of households had a motorbike, 93.8 per cent a mobile phone, 41 per cent a gas cooker and 35.6 per cent a television. Among low castes, these percentages had more than doubled in three years.

6 Marriage expenses include ceremony costs and, for women, frequently (but not always) the dowry. Social and religious rituals also include puberty ceremonies for young girls, contributions to temple-building projects and religious festivals.

7 Official data also shed light on the prevalence of debt in rural areas. The latest available official data from the 59th All India Debt and Investment Survey (NSSO 2005) report that almost three-quarters (73.5 per cent) of farmer households are in debt.

8 Between 2007 and 2011 significant changes were made in banking legislation, and private banks are now investing and expanding their presence in unbanked areas. An example is ICICI Bank, which was the first private commercial bank and known in the 2000s as a bank of the new urban Indian middle class, and which is now looking to the countryside. In 2014, its network in the state of Tamil Nadu had over 363 branches, including 127 called 'Gramin' branches in villages without any other banking entities. Although public commercial banks are still largely the most important players in rural areas, they are no longer alone. The number of rural branches increased by 141 per cent between March 2006 and March 2014 for private commercial banks (from 982 to 2,362). Data compiled from from the Reserve Bank of India quarterly statistics on deposits and credit of scheduled commercial banks (RBI various years).

9 Health was one of the most important financial stresses raised in the two surveys. In another survey looking at labour contracts in greater depth (survey 1), we found that less than 2 per cent of households had health insurance while 4.4 per cent were eligible for a pension.

10 In the 2006 survey, the most common sources of high debt among the 20 per cent most indebted households were ceremonies (42.7 per cent of households), housing and health (25 and 23.5 per cent). These were followed by economic investments (17.7 per cent) and private education expenses (16.2 per cent). In the 2004/06/09 survey, people were

asked to list the big expenses they had made over the past decade. Ceremonies came out first (48.35 per cent), followed by housing (17.5 per cent) and health (16.2 per cent), economic investment (10.9 per cent) and education (9.4 per cent). In the 2010 survey, health, education and ceremony expenses amounted on average to 54 per cent of annual expenses.

11 For a detailed analysis of this topic in a different Indian state, see Jeffrey (2010).

12 In October 2014, 1 INR = €0,013.

13 For similar results in other contexts, see Bateman (2010) and Van Rooyen et al. (2012).

14 Most microcredit institutions ask for monthly repayments while many door-to-door moneylending repayments are made weekly, and local informal lenders ask for regular interest (often monthly but this is highly negotiable) and the capital is paid at the end.

15 Our 2010 survey indicated that, globally, 46.1 per cent have a fixed and predetermined term, 43.4 per cent are paid when the borrower has the money, and 10.5 per cent when asked by the lender.

16 In our 2010 survey 1, 69.6 per cent of the households said they struggle to meet their repayments; 26.6 per cent of them had borrowed from elsewhere to pay off their debt.

17 Similar observations were made in Andhra Pradesh (Rao 2005).

18 Migration patterns are mostly internal (within India and most often within Tamil Nadu state). Other factors, such as over-indebtedness problems partly caused by microcredits, contribute to international migration flows, as has been observed in Mexico (Morvant-Roux 2013) and Cambodia (Bylander 2014).

19 The most prominent example of this is SKS. In March 2006, Kosha Ventures and other venture capitalists invested 2.1 million euro in this MFI. At that time, it was the largest ever investment in the Indian microfinance private sector. It led to a portfolio explosion: in the 2007 fiscal year, the number of clients rose from 200,000 to 700,000.

20 We are not referring here to specific forms of debt that are a source of bondage and exploitation, which are still widespread but are on no equal footing with microcredit, as they act as a job guarantee.

21 According to the Central Statistical Office, Ministry of Statistics and Programme Implementation.

References

Bajaj, V. (2011) 'Microlenders, honored with Nobel, are struggling', *New York Times*, 5 January.

Bateman, M. (2010) *Why Doesn't Microfinance Work? The Destructive Rise of Local Neoliberalism*, London: Zed Books.

Bellman, E. and A. Chang (2010) 'India's major crisis in microlending', *Wall Street Journal*, 28 October.

Bylander, M. (2014) 'Borrowing across borders: migration and microcredit in rural Cambodia', *Development and Change*, XLV(2): 284–307.

Collins, D., J. Morduch, S. Rutherford and O. Ruthven (2009) *Portfolios of the Poor: How the World's Poor live on $2 a Day*, Princeton, NJ: Princeton University Press.

Evans, J. (2010) 'Microfinance's midlife crisis', *Wall Street Journal*, 1 March.

Gokhale, K. (2009) 'A global surge in tiny loans spurs credit bubble in a slum', *Wall Street Journal*, 13 August.

Graeber, D. (2011) *Debt: The First 5,000 Years*, Brooklyn, NY: Melville House.

Guérin, I. and S. Kumar (2007) 'Clientélisme, courtage et gestion des risques en microfinance. Etude de cas en Inde du Sud', *Autrepart*, XLIV: 13–26.

Guérin, I., B. D'Espallier and G. Venkatasubramanian (forthcoming) 'The social regulation of self-employment. Why does microfinance fail in rural South-India?', *Development and Change*.

Guérin, I., S. Morvant and J.-M. Servet (2011) 'Understanding the diversity and complexity of demand for microfinance services: lessons from informal finance', in B. Armendariz and M. Labie (eds), *Handbook of Microfinance*, London and Singapore: World Scientific Publishing, pp. 101–22

Guérin, I., M. Roesch, G. Venkatasubramanian and S. Kumar (2013) 'The social meaning of over-indebtedness and creditworthiness in the context of poor rural South India households (Tamil Nadu)', in I. Guérin, S. Morvant-Roux and M. Villarreal (eds), *Microfinance, Debt and Over-indebtedness: Juggling with Money*, London: Routledge, pp. 125–50.

Guérin, I., M. Roesch, S. Kumar, G. Venkatasubramanian and M. Sangare (2015) 'Microfinance and the dynamics of financial vulnerability', in T. Nair (ed.), *Microfinance in India: Approaches, Outcomes, Challenges*, New Delhi: Routledge, pp. 114–41.

Hardiman, D. (1996) *Feeding the Baniya: Peasants and Usurers in Western India*, New Delhi: Oxford University Press.

Jeffrey, C. (2010) *Timepass: Youth, class and the politics of waiting*, Stanford, CA: Stanford University Press.

Kundu, A. and P. C. Mohanan (2010) 'Employment and inequality outcomes in India', Unpublished document, Paris: Organisation for Economic Co-operation and Development, www.oecd.org/els/emp/42546020.pdf, accessed 21 July 2014.

Lerche, J. (2015) 'Regional patterns of agrarian accumulation in India', in J. Heyer and B. Harriss-White (eds), *Capitalism in Development*, London: Routledge, pp. 46–66.

Malamoud, C. (ed.) (1988) *La dette*, coll. Purushartha vol. IV, Paris: Éditions de l'École des Hautes Etudes en Sciences Sociales (EHESS).

Mitra, A. and S. Verick (2013) 'Youth employment and unemployment: an Indian perspective', ILO Asia-Pacific Working Paper Series, Delhi and Geneva: DWT for South Asia and Country Office for India, International Labour Organization.

Morvant-Roux, S. (2006) 'Processus d'appropriation des dispositifs de microfinance: un exemple en milieu rural mexicain', PhD thesis, Lyons: Université Lumière Lyon 2.

— (2013) 'International migration and over-indebtedness in rural Mexico', in I. Guérin, S. Morvant-Roux and M. Villarreal (eds), *Microfinance, Debt and Over-indebtedness: Juggling with Money*, London: Routledge, pp. 171–86.

Nabard (2014) *Status of Microfinance in India, 2012–2013*, Mumbai: National Bank for Agriculture and Rural Development.

— (various years) *Progress of SHG-Bank Linkage in India*, Mumbai: National Bank for Agriculture and Rural Development.

NSSO (2005) 'Indebtedness of farmer households', *NSSO 59th Round*, New Delhi: Government of India.

Pandurang, V. K. (1941) *History of Dharmasastra (Ancient and Medieval Religious and*

Civil Law), Poona: Bhandarkar Oriental
Research Institute

Polgreen, L. and V. Bajaj (2010) 'India
microcredit faces collapse from defaults',
New York Times, 17 November.

Rao, S. (2005) 'Women's self-help groups and
credit for the poor: a case study from
Andhra Pradesh', in V. K. Ramnachandran
and M. Swaminathan (eds), *Financial
Liberalization and Rural Credit in India*, New
Delhi: Tulika Books, pp. 204–37.

Roesch, M. and O. Héliès (2007) 'La
microfinance: outil de gestion du risque ou
de mise en danger par sur-endettement?

Le cas de l'Inde du Sud', *Autrepart*, XLIV:
119–40.

Schicks, J. (2014) 'Over-indebtedness in
microfinance. An empirical analysis of
related factors on the borrower level',
World Development, LIV(C): 301–24.

Van Rooyen, C., R. Stewart, R. and T. de Wet
(2012) 'The impact of microfinance in sub-
Saharan Africa: a systematic review of
the evidence', *World Development*, 40(11):
2249–62.

Wilhite, H. (2008) *Consumption and the
Transformation of Everyday Life. A view from
South India*, New York: Palgrave Macmillan.

5 | HOW GOOD REPAYMENT PERFORMANCES CAN HARM BORROWERS: EVIDENCE FROM THE DOMINICAN REPUBLIC

Solène Morvant-Roux, Joana Afonso, Davide Forcella and Isabelle Guérin

Introduction

Recent microcredit delinquency crises have raised awareness of the excesses and abuses of the microcredit system. They have drawn attention to household over-indebtedness and how microcredit can do more harm than good (Guérin et al. 2013). They have also pointed out the dangers of excessive, uncontrolled growth (Chen et al. 2010). This has helped reinforce the legitimacy of and need for initiatives to better protect clients, such as the Smart Campaign for client protection (which started in 2009) and financial education programmes. In the 2014 *Microfinance Banana Skins* survey, for instance (Lascelles et al. 2014),[1] practitioners, investors, regulators and observers ranked over-indebtedness as a top risk.

We believe, however, that lessons have still not been learnt, and that the case of the Dominican Republic is a good illustration of this. While indicators and practices point to the stability of the current situation, there are reasons to believe that some clientele, including some 'good' clients,[2] are struggling to make repayments and that microcredit is one of the explanatory factors.

As Gonzalez and Servet (2014) have discussed, various seemingly solid indicators of sound and prudent microcredit supply management are in evidence on all levels: growth and competition, screening procedures and risk management.[3] The sector has seen steady, but not massive, growth (less than 18 per cent a year on average from 2007 to 2012 for the five main MFIs in terms of portfolio volume, and around 21 per cent in clients from 2008 to 2011).[4]

The market leaders pay particular attention to the macroeconomic environment, arguing that microcredit growth is perfectly sustainable given relatively strong GDP growth (5 per cent on average from 2008 to 2012). As is often the case, the market is highly concentrated (Banco Adopem and Banco Ademi make up more than 50 per cent of the supply) but the competition seems to be fair and cooperative. For instance, Adopem organizes training sessions that are open to (and followed by) other MFIs. The average loan amounts issued by the leaders suggest that they operate among different segments of the population. There are two established private credit bureaus, which are widely used, including by some informal lenders, who usually report to one of the bureaus (Gonzalez and Servet 2014). For the largest MFIs at least, policies and procedures on the lending process (and particularly the screening process) adhere to international 'best practices'. This includes sophisticated techniques for assessing clients' indebtedness (including their informal indebtedness), repayment capacities and willingness to repay (Afonso 2013).[5] This cautious sector management has kept portfolio at risk (PAR) under control, if not perfectly (PAR at thirty days was 5 per cent in 2013).[6]

But our field observations on the basis of a sample of microcredit clients contrast with this positive picture. We have found that many clients in competitive areas of the country endure great financial hardship: they have relatively high debt/income ratios, regularly make sacrifices to keep up repayments, increase their numbers of loans, and have poor prospects of getting out from under high levels of debt in the near future. In light of this, we might wonder why and how they manage to repay. Firstly, they have little choice but to do so, given the powerful incentive role of the credit bureau (which, from what we have seen, works well for lenders but does little to protect borrowers). Secondly they juggle a variety of loan sources (including informal ones) to sustain their creditworthiness (but for how long?).

Although microcredit is far from the only factor, it certainly contributes to household financial fragility. Loan officers in competitive areas, constrained by high performance targets (which many cannot meet), are left with no choice but to focus on specific segments of clients (those who are creditworthy on paper), sometimes encouraging them to take on excessive risk. Our findings are based on qualitative analysis and make no claim for representativeness, but they do point out worrying trends that should be a matter of concern for the future of the sector.

Far beyond the particulars of this case study, our results contribute to current debates on the issue of microcredit repayment. Economic theory focuses primarily on motivations for repayment (why should people repay?) and enforcement mechanisms (how to make people repay?) (Armendáriz and Morduch 2005). From this perspective, the prospects of getting a new (and possibly larger) loan would be the major driver for repayment. The most common enforcement mechanisms would include frequent installments and repeated interactions with loan officers, financial penalties, social pressure and collateral seizure. But sociological and anthropological approaches can shed light on alternative (and complementary) repayment motives (the social and cultural norms of debt and debt repayment) which vary across contexts.[7] In some particular cases, such as Bangladesh (Karim 2011) and Andhra Pradesh (Servet 2011), coercion also plays a role. Peer pressure is so strong that people are obliged to pay if they want to avoid social stigma or exclusion.

Sociologists and anthropologists have also looked at *how* people repay. It seems that in some contexts, people have no choice but to sell assets, juggle informal debt or resort to migration to pay off their microcredit (Guérin et al. 2013). Our case study shows how these various motives and strategies come together. It also highlights another subtle, indirect form of coercion – the credit bureau – insofar as being blacklisted has dramatic consequences for defaulters. Though these credit bureaus are currently considered by the microcredit industry as efficient tools for consumer protection, we have found that they can act as very powerful instruments for protecting lenders. Far beyond this case, our observations raise a number of fundamental issues for microcredit regulation and highlight the perverse effects of market rules.

Context

With a GNI per capita of US$5,470, the Dominican Republic is classified as a middle-income country, with the largest economy in Central America and the Caribbean. It has been through rapid economic growth, with average GDP growth of 5.8 per cent from 1991 to 2012 (with a 2014 forecast of around 3.6 per cent). This growth has, however, been job-weak, and the relatively few jobs created have mainly been low skilled or in the informal sector. As the World Bank has reported, real wages have declined by 27 per cent over the last ten years.

Thirty-seven per cent of the labour force is viewed as vulnerable and lives without any social protection.[8] Despite recent efforts to tackle this, out-of-pocket health expenditure accounts for 38.7 per cent of total health expenses. Infrastructures are still highly inadequate (in 2012, for instance, there were 17.7 electrical outages in an average month, in contrast to 2.5 for the subcontinent). Poverty is higher today (40 per cent) than in 2000 (32 per cent), although this is declining from a 50 per cent peak in the immediate aftermath of the local economic and financial crisis in 2003.[9] Growth has equally slowed down in the wake of the global economic crisis of 2008, in reflection of a strong dependency on the United States economy.

Over the same period, urbanization increased and almost half the population (45 per cent) now lives in the two biggest cities (Santo Domingo and Santiago de los Caballeros). Consumerism also increased, as is reflected in the percentage of households with a mobile phone subscription (88 per cent), an internet connection (45 per cent) or a motor vehicle (13.2 per cent).[10] These figures are lower than the average for the subcontinent, but much higher than those of middle-income countries.

As far as financial supply is concerned, twelve MFIs with a variety of legal statuses providing financial services to around 314,000 clients reported to the Mix Market.[11] As the introduction discussed, two institutions dominate the market – Ademi and Adopem. Both started out as NGOs and then turned into banks in 1997 and 2004, respectively.[12]

The microcredit landscape is much larger and more diversified, however. There are firstly public programmes with the declared aim of improving poor households' financial inclusion. These include Promipyme and Banca Solidaria, which are both partners with BanReservas (a public bank), and provide credit at lower interest rates than the private sector. Standard banks willing to downscale their activities (especially through credit cards) to low-income populations also work with microcredit clients. Banco BHD and ScotiaBank are particularly active on this level and have set up separate microcredit units – 'Crédito Amigo' and 'Scotia Soluciones'.

There are various other formal and semi-formal providers of credit to low-income households, including local cooperatives, non-profit organizations and many small to medium-sized companies. They usually offer credit at a higher interest rate[13] than MFIs, and have shorter terms and more frequent instalments.

Beyond semi-formal and formal credit providers, various recent studies have shown that looking at informal financial landscapes can help to understand how people perceive and use different formal financial services such as microcredit (Morvant-Roux 2006; Collins et al. 2009; Guérin et al. 2011). The linkages between microcredit and informal credit sources will be discussed further below, but here we will highlight some salient features of the financial landscape in these regards.

The Dominican Republic's informal financial sector is highly developed and dynamic. Ortiz-Medina and De Garcia-Perez (2012) point out that 30 per cent of the loans taken out by low-income populations in 2009 came from informal providers. Lending money is perceived as a lucrative activity and many microcredit officers accordingly start their own moneylending businesses (after leaving their MFIs), while, as we will see later, some microcredit borrowers are themselves moneylenders.[14] The informal sector also includes pawnbrokers, ROSCAs, informal loans from relatives, friends or neighbours, and credit purchases for durable goods.

MFIs are thus part of a highly dynamic and interrelated financial landscape.

Over-indebtedness and household financial fragility

Assessing over-indebtedness Financial fragility and over-indebtedness can be measured in various ways, including through financial indicators such as debt/income ratios, chronic debt and number of loans (Guérin et al. 2013) or subjective factors such as the sacrifices experienced by the borrower (Schick 2013). We used various indicators in our study, all of which confirmed that a large proportion of our sample is highly financially vulnerable.

We calculated the debt/income ratio (monthly debt repayment compared to monthly income) of forty-two households (Figure 5.1). In Europe, a

---

Box 5.1 Research method

This research uses qualitative analysis, which is best suited to unravel the cognitive and social processes underlying observed effects, i.e. how a given intervention sets off events that ultimately lead to an observed outcome. Eighty-five interviews with diverse actors were conducted, with the aim of better understanding demand and the role of microcredit in clients' trajectories. We focused on specific neighbourhoods[15] in the two largest cities, Santo Domingo and Santiago, where competition is greatest and which account for around 40 per cent of the microcredit portfolio.[16] We followed the basic rigour criteria for qualitative analysis. Diversifying cases was the first principle adhered to. We met forty-seven clients from six MFIs (Ademi, Adopem, ASPIRE, FDD, Fime and FONDESA) and fourteen non-clients. We selected for diverse client repayment behaviours (using information from MFI staff) – clients who always pay on time, those who are sometimes late, and those who are regularly late – while also ensuring we included the most common types of employment. Triangulation was another basic principle and took two forms: comparing and contrasting the observations of different researchers (most interviews were conducted jointly by two of us), as well as observations from various sources. Clients and non-clients were our main focus, but we also met eleven loan officers, five branch managers, four heads of six MFIs in our sample and four moneylenders. As far as possible, discourses – what people say – were compared and contrasted with practices – what people really do – by asking our interviewees to be very concrete. For more in-depth analysis, we carried out forty-nine interviews with forty-five MFI clients and four non-clients. The socioeconomic characteristics of our sample were as follows: thirty-four women (69 per cent), of whom fourteen were single (plus two unspecified), who accounted for 29 per cent of the total sample. In terms of age group, younger clients were less well represented (two were under thirty); but other age groups were well represented, with 37, 33 and 26 per cent in their thirties, forties and over fifty respectively.

---

common threshold for over-indebtedness is where households spend over 30 per cent (or one third) of their gross monthly income on total loan repayments (secured or unsecured).[17] Repayment-to-debt ratios have their limitations in that they fail to take relative income disparities (higher levels of debt affect low- and high-income households differently) and household assets into account, but these seem to be more significant limitations for high-income households, who are not microfinance institutions' focus. We therefore use

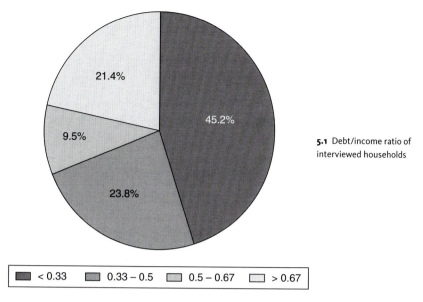

5.1 Debt/income ratio of interviewed households

< 0.33   0.33 – 0.5   0.5 – 0.67   > 0.67

Source: Authors' survey

this ratio as our indicator of reference, which places twenty-three of the forty-two Dominican households as over-indebted. For nine of our cases (21 per cent), debt repayment accounted for over two-thirds of their monthly income.[18]

Looking at the two extreme groups (those with a debt/income ratio of below 0.33 and those over 0.67) it is key to note that only two out of the nineteen less indebted households used microcredit to repay other debts, but this was microcredit's primary use for the most indebted (seven out of nine). By contrast, only three over-indebted households partly used credit for running a business, while in the other group seven used the whole loan to invest in a business, and another five partly did so. Four of the least indebted group had applied for the money in order to help others.

Financial vulnerability can also be assessed in terms of other criteria. These include short-term sacrifice (mainly on daily consumption) and long-term sacrifice (on housing and other investments), people's prospects of getting out of over-indebtedness (whether they have workable strategies for doing so over the coming years), and family support (which can be a deliberate repayment strategy, minimizing over-indebtedness).

Table 5.1 shows that there are fewer households making daily or long-term sacrifices (43 and 38 per cent, respectively) than the 55 per cent with a debt/income ratio of over a third. This is in line with the argument that poorer and marginalized populations are highly skilled at adapting and tolerating sacrifices. For the other two criteria, the figures are very close to the debt indicator (55 per cent have no exit prospects from high indebtedness and 60 per cent lack

TABLE 5.1 A broader approach to over-indebtedness

	Daily sacrifice		Long-term sacrifice		Prospects of getting out of high debt		Family support	
42 households	Yes	18	Yes	16	No	23	No	25
	No	24	No	26	Yes	19	Yes	17
9 households with debt/income > 0.67	Yes	9	Yes	8	No	9	No	5
	No	0	No	1	Yes	0	Yes	4

Source: Authors' survey

family support as part of their repayment strategies). These factors increase the gravity of the nine highly over-indebted households' situations, leaving them trapped in a vicious cycle of debt and impoverishment. They make short- and long-term sacrifices and have no prospects of breaking out of debt, despite four of them also having some form of family support.

Furthermore, it is important to stress that many households accumulate various sources of borrowing. Our forty-nine cases had an average of 2.85 sources of debt. Twelve households (24 per cent) had one source, twenty-two (45 per cent) two or three and twelve (29 per cent) four or more sources.[19] This went up to 4.3 for the nine most fragile households, some of which had as many as six or seven active debts. Most also resort to formal and informal financial suppliers. These borrowers constantly need informal loans to pay off formal loan instalments (or vice versa).

These various indicators allow us to see that some MFI clients are financially vulnerable. It is interesting to note that six out of the nine most indebted households (in terms of income) were introduced to us by MFIs, and that loan officers considered four of them 'normal' or 'good' clients who always or often repaid on time. But these indebted clients were all open in interviews that they struggled to repay their loans. A fifty-year-old married man selling fruit and vegetables at the market (a very small business) told us that he was always struggling and that he had no way out (‘*siempre vivo con apuro y no hay forma de pararlo*’). Like others, he keeps struggling and 'finding' the money somehow (‘*cojo aqui, cojo ahí*’). But as most of them stressed, it is better to make sacrifices such as only eating rice and bananas than to lose the asset of being a good payer. A sixty-one-year-old married man, a municipal employee and former small entrepreneur, told us that failing to pay is a source of shame (*verguenza*) so he always returns to the lenders even without the money to pay them. He began to struggle after one of his businesses, into which he had invested savings and for which he had borrowed from a commercial bank, had gone out of business. It's important to consider the origins of such financial fragility. We would argue that it stems from employment vulnerability, particular sets of household characteristics, inadequate infrastructure, and preferences for debt and easy access to it, all of which is putting some households into a very difficult situation.

Key factors for financial vulnerability and over-indebtedness As in other developing countries, the households have diverse portfolios of economic activity and sources of income. Twenty-six per cent of the interviewees had a single source of income, while 20 per cent had four or more. Of these various sources, eleven households raised income by both renting out housing and moneylending (22 per cent), while a further three interviewees had plans to rent out houses in the future; seventeen (35 per cent) of the interviewees had their own or family members' wage earnings to contribute to their standard of living; remittances, while essential for those receiving them, were rare (four cases).

Men do most of the wage labour, for instance as municipal workers, security guards, drivers, factory and warehouse employees at private companies, and some in *zonas francas*.[20] Opportunities seem to be more restricted for women, who mainly work in *zonas francas* or lottery shops. It is difficult to find a job and wage jobs are low-paid so a significant proportion of the population (around 40 per cent) is self-employed.[21]

Self-employed men mostly work in the following sectors: trade (grocery shops, products to enhance well-being and pharmaceuticals, iron), craft (furniture making and renovation) and services (mechanics). Some men also sell small goods in the street, such as phone cards and various gadgets. Self-employed women often work from home, or do small-scale trade in fruit and vegetables, flowers, second-hand clothes, underwear or cosmetics. Some also offer services such as small restaurants, cafeterias and beauty salons. We also came across one case of handicraft (furniture renovation). Moneylending is apparently quite a frequent source of income, both for men and women, and is usually done alongside other activities.

These entrepreneurs usually have low education levels. Their businesses are too small to thrive, being a poorly organized mix of domestic and professional budgets, while failing to differentiate themselves from other similar businesses, which leads to cash-flow problems, and in some cases project failure.[22] This is epitomized in second-hand clothing businesses, which usually sell on packages of clothes from the United States and were everywhere to be found in the two main cities. While being a source of income for over a quarter of our sample, it is a highly competitive and saturated market. There are few success stories, and most often households can at best survive on this unreliable source of income.

Jobs are no guarantee of financial stability, however, as contracts are often insecure and wages very low. Wages can equally be a double-edged sword inasmuch as they facilitate very easy access to formal credit (to credit cards in particular), and may also encourage unrealistic aspirations (for instance, for housing) and expectations among close family and friends.

A common feature of our nine highly indebted households is how they only had one or two sources of income. One to two members of three of the households surveyed were wage workers, but their incomes were not regular enough to solve their financial problems. None of the indebted families rented out accommodation or lent money, which are apparently the most secure income-generating activities.

Both individual and household characteristics and trajectories can also contribute to financial vulnerability. Disadvantageous situations can include disability and chronic health problems, single motherhood and cash-flow uncertainty. Households have a variety of structures, from individuals living alone, to single mothers with children from different partners, and extended families of up to eight parties. Households had four members on average, with thirty-two cases consisting of three to five members. The households we looked at were very diverse and levels of kinship solidarity varied a lot. A number of single mothers were struggling a great deal, but others were doing well thanks to sophisticated coping strategies, which makes it difficult to draw firm conclusions as to the impact of this factor.

It is easier to confirm the significant impact of inadequate infrastructure on various levels. Although there has been recent progress in improving access to basic services and health insurance,[23] many households still have social security and face maternity-related health expenses, which frequently contribute to financial vulnerability. Almost 60 per cent of the households (twenty-nine) can be considered as house owners, while eight owned more than one (and up to four) houses. But many households have no ownership deeds, or only have one in a relative's name, while the term 'house' covers a wide range of homes, from large concrete houses to small rooms with iron roofs. The problems of absent or high-cost property deeds, as with the country's other problems, are offset by the lack of regulation. This has several drawbacks, including a lack of collateral to guarantee cheaper loans at traditional banks. It does, however, allow people to get hold of land at no or very low cost, and to rent houses as a business (in several cases this proved an important source of income, if not in terms of value, then in terms of regularity).

Finally, we're often told that Dominicans 'like' getting into debt and that they are strongly encouraged to do so by an abundant (and high-profile)[24] credit supply. There seem to be little by way of saving practices, perhaps for cultural but also security reasons, which limits saving options. While some people keep savings at home (particularly those who were also lenders), most people said that they did not do so, for fear of being robbed. Safety concerns have been growing in recent years and have compounded a lack of appropriate saving solutions for poor clients, since only some MFIs offer savings products.

The challenges of accumulating sufficiently large sums to invest, buy assets (houses, furniture, etc.), or to cope with emergencies (notably health-related costs and death), high consumption aspirations among the younger generations in particular, and the need to build a credit history (as we shall see below) are strong borrowing incentives. Though it is difficult to be admitted to traditional commercial banks, poor people have other, largely informal or semi-formal, solutions. These are usually financially costly but allow people to obtain and accumulate different types of loans. This raises the question of the capacity of households and local economies to absorb the growth of the credit supply.

As a final note on the nine highly indebted households, we can point to various typical scenarios. Some of the households plunge into debt after a specific crisis, most often owing to health problems or project failure (these may be business-related or the result of projects such as migration). Some people live with high debt for a long time, owing either to very high poverty (as with an old widow we interviewed) or to chronic cash-flow problems in their business. This latter category includes wage earners who have unrealistic aspirations, and/or who face high expectations from their close family and friends.

Why and how do people repay?

As we have already highlighted above, both poor and non-poor segments of the population of the Dominican Republic have a strong demand for and use of credit (in contrast to Morocco, for instance; see the chapter by Morvant-Roux and Roesch this volume). Credit sources currently serve a wide range of purposes in Dominicans' daily lives. But surprisingly, the ready availability of credit and strong cross-borrowing potential are not correlated to repayment defaults. This is due firstly to social norms on debt. Debt has a central place in everyday life, and this, secondly, results in a strong commitment to maintaining creditworthiness (which is heavily reliant on a clean credit history) to keep credit options open. This feeds into the third factor: caring about a good repayment record is based on the powerful incentive role of the credit bureaus.

Credit provider hierarchies, social norms and credit history Field testimonies indicate that paying off debt is a strong social norm for Dominicans. Several interviewees regularly skip meals (including their children's) or cut down on food in order to pay what they owe (as with a mother who gave her children sugar water rather than milk to drink, or an old single lady who adjusted her meals according to what she owed). Many people talked about the social stigma of defaulting on payments. We were once told that delaying by over a week was shameful. As has been highlighted elsewhere, borrowers have their own hierarchies of credit sources, and not all debts have the same social and economic roles and meanings. We found in our fieldwork that people prioritized repaying what they referred to as the 'bank' (namely formal credit providers). This held particularly true for marginalized people, as with two of our highly indebted interviewees: 'the bank is sacred' or 'the bank doesn't play'. People allow themselves some leeway with repayments, but still observe strict limits. For those in desperate need of borrowing options, ensuring access to future loans is key: *'credit, es eso que hace uno caminar'*. Notwithstanding social norms, therefore, our interviews found that their greatest motive was to secure further loans in the future. Moneylenders are also central to total indebtedness (51 per cent of our sample borrows from informal sources) but, as we will see, informal lending is frequently used to maintain creditworthiness with formal lenders.[25] Maintaining one's creditworthiness and a clean credit history heavily depends on the power of the credit bureau.

The powerful role of the credit bureau ('el diablo') Credit reporting has recently attracted much attention from microcredit practitioners and policy-makers in the face of high growth, competition and a growing risk of cross-borrowing and borrower over-indebtedness. Credit bureaus are seen as one of the most effective means of protecting clients, for their role in preventing over-indebtedness caused by cross-borrowing practices.

As a recent CGAP focus note pointed out, all the lenders involved in a given market are meant to issue reports for the process to be effective (Chen et al. 2010). In recent credit bureau experience at the base of the pyramid, most have failed to do so. Not only do they fail to include all the regulated financial institutions, but they also ignore other credit sources, despite their importance in people's financial practices. Here again, the Dominican Republic is a typical case. The two privately run credit bureaus (DataCred and TransUnion) do have a large share of the credit provision for low-income populations, because they also include telecommunication companies, electricity, etc. As mentioned above, it is also interesting to note that some informal moneylenders (even if only a small percentage, estimated at around 10 per cent) report to one of the credit bureaus (Gonzalez and Servet 2014).

Beyond the issue of coverage, the consequences of being blacklisted and how far this incentivizes borrowers' repayment behaviours also matter. Our field observations suggest that credit bureaus are a very strong enforcement mechanism. They are *'el diablo'*, as we were once told, for various reasons. Firstly, borrowers who default are barred from future loans: borrowers are well aware of this and talk about it in interview. As they know they will regularly need credit, they are very careful to maintain a good standing. This incentive is all the greater in that the information exchanged does not just concern the credit bureaus: local lenders share information with one another (be these formal, semi-formal or sometimes even informal lenders), as well as regularly sharing information through loan officers (and possibly moneylenders) who know one another personally. A wide range of lenders may thus exclude people blacklisted by the credit bureaus, including those who don't issue reports, leaving them with access only to very small informal loans. Secondly, blacklisting can have dire consequences far beyond credit access: losing one's bank account or monthly mobile phone subscription, or even difficulties getting a formal job or a visa. Some large companies apparently request the credit history of job applicants, as do embassies (the United Sates embassy in particular) for migration applicants. We met a security guard who had been confined to the informal economy and excluded from entering the United States because he had been blacklisted.

Finally, this information remains in the credit history for several years (seven, according to a branch manager). This all makes the credit bureau an extremely efficient means of enforcing repayment, while validating clients' worries and drive to maintain a clean credit history.

We will now turn to the question of how, in the face of high debt, people manage to meet repayments.

Repayments: juggling practices with informal borrowing and various temporalities
Sixty per cent of the households in our sample reported having two or more debts, while 46 per cent of the households borrowed from formal and informal sources at the same time (whereas 48 per cent borrowed only from formal sources and 6 per cent only from informal). It seemed to be common to borrow from one source to repay another. For instance more than one third of households, as indicated above, used all or part of their microcredit to repay previous debts (this was the most frequent microcredit use after running a business).

An example of this is the case of a single forty-seven-year-old woman, 'Maria'. She lives alone with her seventeen-year-old son. She has been trapped in a persistent debt cycle ever since the economic shock of a failed migration project for which she sold her house: she repays 12,000 DOP per week to five different informal lenders plus a debit card, while she earns around 50,000 DOP per month (she owns a street food stall). According to the loan officer, Maria is a 'good client' since she repays well, but he had not realized at the time she asked for microcredit that she was already highly indebted. All these credits are used to finance her business, to pay the owner of her house and repay debts.

The dynamism of the financial landscape allows for juggling debt between various options (formal, informal, semi-formal) and time frames. While microcredit most often lasts one year (and possibly longer for some providers), semi-formal and informal lenders offer shorter-term loans (six to fifteen weeks), with very frequent instalments (daily or weekly). They also show some flexibility. As discussed above, a wide range of informal lenders all have their own strategies, but as one told us, and as was widely confirmed by the practices we observed, it is a 'demand-driven' market, and they adjust to their clients' needs. Our observations suggested that it is common for clients to set the frequency of instalments themselves, and moneylenders accept delays and reschedule loans without charging penalties (while MFIs charge for the slightest delay (one day) and start reporting to the credit bureau after thirty days).

Informal lenders' wide market coverage and highly flexible supply conditions allow vulnerable clients to repay formal loans and maintain their future borrowing capacity, and keeps the financial system sustainable, at least on the surface.

This partly explains why the different segments of the financial landscape (formal, semi-formal and informal credit suppliers) do not really fear competition, but instead cooperate and look for some degree of complementarity, as Gonzalez and Servet (2014) have discussed. Interviews with informal lenders confirm this: when moneylenders are approached by MFIs for information on their borrowers' creditworthiness, they do not worry about losing them. They know that if their clients take out microcredit, they may need their own services further in the future to make the microcredit repayment.

The role of microcredit in household financial fragility

The impact of microcredit on clients' financial strategies Out of the forty cases giving information on microcredit,[26] it accounts for over half of the household debt repayment of twenty-six households (65 per cent), while for 35 per cent it is less than half, so one can fairly argue that microcredit is quite decisive in clients' financial strategies. Table 5.2 shows that income-generating activities are the primary use. Twenty-six out of the forty-five MFI clients (57 per cent) used their microloan(s) (most often partly) for this purpose. We came across a number of cases where microcredit has been successfully used to maintain or consolidate a pre-existing small business (by raising or maintaining working

TABLE 5.2 Microcredit usage

Microcredit uses	No. of cases[a]	%
Business (working capital or equipment)	26	57.8
Debt repayments	17	37.8
Daily consumption	15	33.3
Housing	12	26.7
Emergencies + helping others	8	17.8
Moneylending	5	11.1

Source: Authors' survey

[a] Total exceeds 100% as loan usually serves various purposes

capital, sometimes by investing in fixed equipment), and more unusually to start a new activity (often together with other sources). As indicated, however, self-employed work is often small-scale and fragile, and many entrepreneurs operate in congested markets. 'Productive' uses are thus no guarantee of easy repayment. Furthermore, while running a business is the most frequent use, it is followed by (or combined with) debt repayment (seventeen cases, i.e. 37.8 per cent), daily consumption (fifteen cases, i.e. 33.3 per cent), housing (twelve cases), emergencies (which may include supporting relatives, eight cases) and moneylending (five cases).

As the companion chapter on India in this volume argues, in a situation where people draw on a wide range of debt sources, it is extremely difficult to directly assess the outcomes of MFIs' operations on clients' well-being. Moreover, we do not have the right data to try to do so. What we have done instead is to analyse MFI procedures, their current implementation by loan officers and branch managers, and attitudes within them that could contribute to their clients' financial fragility.

Assessing borrowers' creditworthiness in a context of strong concentration and competition As mentioned above, and despite cases where microcredit seems to be very useful, many of the clients in our sample are financially fragile, and we found elements to indicate partial MFI responsibility for this. They have highly standardized and professional official procedures, including very detailed analysis of borrowers' creditworthiness (including informal loans), personal visits to clients' workplaces, credit bureau consultation, etc. (Afonso 2013). However, our empirical data on six MFIs, at least in the most competitive areas we looked at, shows up concrete practices that may contribute to clients' financial fragility.

Most of the actors we met acknowledged that there was high competition between MFIs. Though some MFIs claim that the potential market is still very large – one internal study discusses unmet (and solvent) demand from 2 million people – they stick to the same geographical areas and activities. The two largest MFIs have very different average loan amounts (at Adopem it is lower than at Ademi by a factor of around 2.5):[27] while they do have very specific clientele at the two extremes of the spectrum, they heavily compete for the middle segment. Moreover, the MFI managers we interviewed regularly raised the point that specific areas of the market were saturated and that over-indebtedness was a risk. But there do not seem to be any concrete policies for preventing market saturation or over-indebtedness. While some MFIs discuss strategies for finding market niches (including private schools or *zonas francas*), most seem to keep competing for the same market segments.

It is difficult to give exact data on the extent of cross-credits between MFIs, but our interviews indicate that they are common. A manager at one

MFI's headquarters told us that on average their clients have two formal credits, while 15 per cent have more than two. The chief executive of another MFI told us that approximately 40 per cent of its portfolio is shared with other MFIs. In two branches of another MFI, we were told that 40–50 per cent of the clients are shared with others MFIs and that around 25 per cent of them have three or more formal loans.

The loan officer of another MFI explained that it is possible for clients to have five or six active loans. The details of his portfolio are an interesting example. He had 270 active clients at that time, of which 175 were also the clients of other MFIs, and he had 'stolen' 75 from other MFIs by offering a loan to refinance their previous debts. Refinancing other MFI debts seems to be commonplace. Most of the managers and loan officers we met deny it but argue that their competitors are doing it. We also met loan officers who were open about using this aggressive strategy to gain market share and meet targets.

There is also competition from government schemes, which are seen as unfair competitors and a potential risk (Gonzales and Servet 2014). Public intervention has grown quickly over the last two years with subsidized loans and, it seems, less attention to credit recovery.[28] MFIs cannot compete on price and so try to compete on service, especially for delivery speed (with the risk of lowering client selection standards). Some MFIs are afraid of losing clients because of this 'unfair' competition, but our fieldwork suggests that clients combine both sorts of credit, either for different or the same purposes.

Loan officers also have very specific performance targets. These relate both to portfolio growth and quality, and determine an important part of their monthly wages. In one of the two largest MFIs (the one for which we have precise data), incentives can represent around half of monthly wages for experienced loan officers, but only some are able to meet their fixed targets (Afonso 2013).[29] It is easy, then, to understand why they may stray from official procedures in competitive areas, sometimes with the complicity of the branch manager, who is also under a lot of pressure from performance targets.

In such a highly competitive market, it is easier to grow through existing clients than to find new ones. Indeed, it is many MFIs' policy to refinance clients once they have repaid without (too much) delay around three-quarters of the loan.[30] They also try to offer larger amounts. Some of the interviewed loan officers told us that if 'good' clients do not ask for a second credit, they try to stimulate the demand, 'creating the clients' necessities'. 'Creating the needs' seems almost to be an official policy at one of the MFIs we visited (at least at one branch in a competitive area). Loan officers making home visits to clients suggest possible ways to invest the credit, be it for consumption or running a business. Examples included buying a computer for the kids, buying or replacing a fridge, and home renovation. 'When people tell us they don't need a loan, we try to convince them it would be useful,' we were told. In this branch, a loan officer explained that all the loan officers behave like this and that they have weekly discussions on possible strategies to keep clients.

Another MFI sells appliances in its branches as a way of approaching potential clients and potentially combining the good's purchase with a consumption loan or another of the MFI's products. The client will have to regularly return to the branch for his/her instalments, which can be the opportunity to offer him/her a cash loan, as a loan officer explained to us. The MFI stores various kinds of appliances at its offices and headquarters.

Does the credit bureau help to prevent over-indebtedness?

The strong incentivizing effect of credit bureaus has been discussed above. The maximum number of active loans registered at the credit bureau for a client to be eligible at an MFI is an interesting proxy for the offer and competition of the microcredit market.[31] The MFIs we questioned have various policies regarding the number of loans their clients are allowed to have from other lenders. Some have fixed the maximum at three, while for others the amount is flexible and depends on case-by-case evaluations, while yet others have no limit. Taking into account that only a small number of informal lenders report to one of the credit bureaus, the total number of loans could be much higher. We indeed found clients with five, six or more active debts quite easily during our interviews (see above).

In some MFI branches, credit bureaus are used not only to assess the level of debt of their potential clients, but also as a source of information for stealing clients from other MFIs. This is claimed to be a competitive strategy whereby loan officers try to recruit new clients by offering to refinance their debts from up to three competitors, while also offering additional funding to meet the new client's needs. As we were told by one loan officer, 'when you see a client from another MFI, what do we do? We try to get them.' The two effective credit bureaus (in the sense that credit providers use them) are supposed to guarantee the sector's security; nonetheless, there are ways to get around them, as one branch manager and loan officer explained to us. Credit bureau information is not immediately updated (it can take up to a month). If a client applies for credit from more than one MFI at once, the request would not immediately register at the credit bureau and so the client might obtain multiple loans. We found such cases in our sample: a woman who had 20,000 and 15,000 DOP (around US$465 and 350, respectively) loans approved by two small MFIs, and another client who had applied for credit from three MFIs at once for 75,000, 75,000 and 50,000 DOP, and had managed to obtain a total of 200,000 DOP.

The picture we have painted in the previous sections shows that some clients with impeccable credit repayment records are in fact in a very fragile position. But we found no clear MFI strategies for offsetting this issue.

Moreover, some MFI head officers and branch managers claim that portfolio at risk (PAR) quality can measure over-indebtedness risks because over-indebted clients could never maintain a small PAR for longer than a couple of months. The empirical data given in the previous sections challenge this claim and highlight the excessive trust put in indicators such as the PAR to measure over-indebtedness, preventing MFIs from reacting to possible non-repayment crises in a timely fashion, or from simply avoiding furthering their clients' financial fragility.

Conclusion

High-standard microcredit service provision within a regulated, expanding industry with low portfolio at risk and widely used credit bureaus does not necessarily bring about positive social outcomes for clients. It may instead, in a highly dynamic microcredit industry, contribute to clients' financial fragility.

On the supply side, the market leaders have seen very good repayment performances mainly because of the effectiveness of credit bureaus, along with borrowers' needs to maintain a clean credit history in order to access future loans. In competitive areas, it seems that the most convenient choice for the MFIs is to concentrate on similar segments and geographical areas, and that targeting underserved or excluded populations is seen to be too costly. Even if there do turn out to be large niches with a lower concentration of formal financial services, the scale of actual market demand is much more limited than repayment performances would suggest. People still need to access adequate financial services, of course, but only when there is an investment opportunity or an emergency, and not all the time, as microcredit providers expect.

The anecdotal evidence from our sample suggests that once a household obtains its first credit, the door is open for debt accumulation through MFIs and informal actors. In short, it seems that the microcredit industry has shifted its paradigm from fighting credit rationing to facilitating 'too much debt' (for a specific segment of its clientele). The proportion of households able to continuously repay credits is limited, which could mean that growth targets should be revised. A wider study has confirmed some of our findings. A large-scale national survey on micro-, small and medium-sized businesses found that only 50 per cent of the 15,854 microentrepreneurs who were surveyed had been able to repay their loans while respecting the current loan conditions (Ortiz et al. 2014).

As such, the notion of a 'good client' (one who will not only repay but who will not be harmed by repayment) should be expanded in order to enable microcredit providers to fix their strategies and growth expectations in light of the real financial needs of the target population, the saturation of certain areas in terms of credit supply, and local absorption capacities.

More broadly, our case study raises the issues of risk-taking and the imbalance of power between creditors and debtors. As Graeber (2011) and

Lazzarato (2011) have argued, the current period is characterized by the predominant power of lenders. The global financial crisis has highlighted the imbalance between borrowers and lenders: the former should pay, whatever their situation, while the latter should get reimbursed, whatever their responsibilities for the troubles faced by borrowers. A more responsible microcredit industry has to rethink the issue of risk-taking. Borrowers cannot be the only ones to bear the risks. It has to rebalance the power between creditors and debtors. It should also rethink the role of competition, and design measures allowing for *sane* competition. Contrary to what mainstream economic theory often argues, competition does not necessarily feed into improved client well-being. Our case study is an illustration of this. Growth objectives and financial sustainability constraints lead MFIs to target only a small proportion of the excluded population, but also to concentrate on and accumulate through specific segments of their clientele, in specific geographic areas. This contributes to over-indebtedness and the saturation of local economies (see Guérin and Servet this volume). Far beyond the Dominican Republic case, several empirical studies have shown that adoption of market rules is likely to lead to the highly unequal spatial distribution of microcredit, as in Peru (Vanroose 2014) and India (Fouillet 2009). Growth objectives should be proportionate to *true* demand, in line with the absorption capacity of clients and local economies rather than MFIs' sustainability or profitability constraints, as is too often the case (Guérin 2015).

By thinking up sophisticated enforcement mechanisms without real concern for clients' well-being, it seems that, rather than helping the poor, the microcredit industry may be contributing to the 'making of the indebted man' (Lazzarato 2011) and the violence of contemporary debt (Graeber 2011). It is urgent to change perspective, and to take into account the limits and perverse effects of market rules in microcredit implementation.

Notes

1 The *Microfinance Banana Skins* survey has been carried out annually since 2008 to identify risks in the microfinance industry from the perspective of an international sample of practitioners, investors, regulators and observers. The 2014 survey was undertaken with 306 microfinance stakeholders from seventy countries.

2 From MFIs' perspective, good clients are those who regularly pay instalments, if perhaps sometimes with some small delays.

3 What follows draws heavily on Gonzalez and Servet (2014).

4 Figures calculated from Gonzalez and Servet (2014) data, drawing on the Mix Market. The numbers for 2013 are not available for all the indicators and MFIs, but the two larger MFIs notably saw portfolio growth rates of 7.4 and 13.4 per cent.

5 Afonso draws on an in-depth analysis of the practices of Adopem, one of the two market leaders.

6 Data from REDCAMIF Portfolio Quality Report, December 2013, available at www.redcamif.org/uploads/media/Presentacion_Calidad_de_Cartera_Diciembre_2013.pdf.

7 See Morvant-Roux and Roesch this volume; see also Guérin et al. (2013); Shipton (2010).

8 ILO source. 'Vulnerable' is defined as 'unpaid family workers and own-account workers as a percentage of total employment'.

9 World DataBank – *World Development Indicators: Poverty headcount ratio at national poverty line (% of population)*, available at databank.worldbank.org/ http://databank.worldbank.org/.

10 Ibid.

11 Penetration rate (2009): 16.7 per cent as compared to Nicaragua (47.7 per cent), Costa Rica (17.7 per cent), Panama (4 per cent) and Brazil (5 per cent (Pedrosa 2010). The sector growth rate over more recent years suggests that the penetration rate is also growing.

12 Other institutions are following this transformation pattern: ASPIRE became a cooperative in 2013 and FONDESA, the third-biggest MFI, is in the process of becoming a credit and savings bank.

13 Contact with clients and some moneylenders indicated a common interest rate of 20 per cent per month for informal loans, while one of the largest microcredit banks charged between 3 and 4.6 per cent per month for the different business loans. In some cases, the difference between interest rates was not as wide as one might expect. One private moneylender interviewed applied an average of 8 per cent per month.

14 The estimated number of moneylenders in the country appears to be between 8,000 and 11,500 (Gonzalez and Servet 2014).

15 In Santiago we focused on Cienfuegos, while in Santo Domingo we worked in three areas: West (Los Alcarrizos, Herrera and Las Palmas), East (Villa Faro, Alma Rosa, Los Minas) and National District (Cienaga and Villa Consuelo).

16 As of 31 December 2012, 34.4 per cent of microcredit clients, 33.1 per cent of portfolios and 35.7 per cent of branches were concentrated in the Santo Domingo area (including the National District). The figures were 7.4, 8.3 and 9.2 per cent for the same indicators in Santiago (Redcamif 2013). Note that 33.7 and 10.6 per cent respectively of the country's total population lived in these two areas in 2012 (Oficina Nacional Estadística).

17 There is no common European definition of household over-indebtedness. In 2008, the European Commission ordered a study entitled 'Towards a common operational European definition of over-indebtedness' that further highlighted various differences between countries as regards its definition and measurement, and policies for tackling it. Some common elements and measures are, however, used to assess over-indebtedness. These include debt-to-income ratios and arrears, number of loans and the subjective perception of debt (D'Alessio and Iezzi 2013; European Commission 2008).

18 Given the very small size of our sample, these figures are in no way generalizable. They do nevertheless help understand the research context. In particular, the very fact that 'good clients' (by the loan officers' criteria) are financially vulnerable is a worrying trend.

19 In one case the information is missing.

20 In *zonas francas* (free zones) one finds garment/clothing companies but also footwear, tobacco and some machinery/equipment companies.

21 40.3 per cent according to ILO sources, but is important to note that many wage workers need to complement their low wages with other activities, and that Dominicans are proactive and value their independence at work (see ILO *Key Indicators of the Labour Market* database available at World DataBank – *World Development Indicators* – databank.worldbank.org/).

22 Loan officer training stresses the need for businesses to differentiate themselves from their competitors, but this is hard to do in practice with this level of competition.

23 The 'Tarjeta Solidariedad' programme helps poorer families meet some of their basic needs by including them in the Social Protection Net and allowing access to different programmes (food, gas, electricity, education, etc.). In February 2014, the programme was supporting 990,704 beneficiaries (with 59,462 million DOP in subsidies, 52 per cent of which was for the food programme). See www.adess.gov.do/, accessed 20 October 2014.

24 Many providers, whatever their status, advertise their products and information is readily available everywhere (small advertisement boards, flyers, loudspeaker cars, etc.).

25 People on the margins of formal financial inclusion do, however, build close relationships with moneylenders, as we saw with some of our interviewees.

26 Microcredit is understood here as all small loans from formal financial institutions (MFIs, public banks and standard banks).

27 According to Mix data, the average loan at Adopem is 18,322 DOP = US$425 (2012), against 69,075 = US$1,605 for Ademi (2011) (US$1 = 43 DOP).

28 Banca Solidaria offers business loans with an annual interest rate of 12 per cent for individual loans. The programme targets people on low incomes and informal business owners. These are people with ideas and business experience, especially women (www. promipymes.gob.do/, accessed 20 October 2014).

29 Considering data from one of the MFIs for the first six months of 2013, out of 300 loan officers only eight managed to meet their targets every month for loan numbers, and only ninety-four did so for more than three months. The results were better for the arrears target, with 114 managing to comply with the objectives every month.

30 It is common policy for MFIs to renew loans, but some of them restrict this practice. One of the largest institutions encourages renewal for investment purposes but does not allow loans to be restructured in case of arrears problems.

31 It does not seem to be mandatory to check the credit bureau before every credit issue. At one MFI, we were told that it had been a year since branch managers had had to check n credit applications below 20,000 DOP. The branch managers nevertheless claim to continue to look to the credit bureau for all credit.

References

Afonso, J. (2013) 'Loan officers and preventing overindebtedness – the case of Banco ADOPEM', Research and Policy Brief Series no. 8, Microfinance in Crisis Research Project, Paris I University/Institute of Research for Development.

Armendáriz, B. and J. Morduch (2005) *The Economics of Microfinance*, Cambridge, MA, and London: MIT Press.

Chen, G., S. Rasmussen and X. Reille (2010) 'Growth and vulnerabilities in microfinance', Focus Note no. 61, CGAP.

Collins, D., J. Morduch, S. Rutherford and O. Ruthven (2009) *Portfolios of the Poor – How the World's Poor Live on $2 a Day*, Princeton, NJ: Princeton University Press.

D'Alessio, G. and S. Iezzi (2013) 'Household over-indebtedness: definition and measurement with Italian data', *Questioni di Economia e Finanza*, 149, Banca d'Italia.

European Commission (2008) 'Towards a common operational european definition of over-indebtedness', Brussels.

Fouillet, C. (2009) 'La construction spatiale de la microfinance en Inde', Doctoral thesis, Brussels: Université Libre de Bruxelles.

Gonzalez, C. and J.-M. Servet (2014) 'Pourquoi le microcrédit en République dominicaine a échappé à la crise?', Working document, Microfinance in Crisis.

Graeber, D. (2011) *Debt: The First 5,000 years*, Brooklyn, NY: Melville House.

Guérin, I. (2015) *La microfinance et ses dérives: émanciper, discipliner ou exploiter les pauvres?*, Paris/Marseille: Demopolis/IRD.

Guérin, I., S. Morvant-Roux and J.-M. Servet (2011) 'Understanding the diversity and complexity of demand for microfinance services: lessons from informal finance', in B. Armendariz and M. Labie (eds), *Handbook of Microfinance*, London and Singapore: World Scientific Publishing, pp. 101–22.

Guérin, I., S. Morvant-Roux and M. Villarreal (eds) (2013) *Microfinance, Debt and Over-indebtedness: Juggling with Money*, London: Routledge.

Karim, L. (2011) *Microfinance and Its Discontents. Women in Debt in Bangladesh*, Minneapolis: University of Minnesota Press.

Lascelles, D., S. Mendelson and D. Rozas (2014) *Microfinance Banana Skins 2014: Facing Reality*, New York: CSFI.

Lazzarato, M. (2011) *La fabrique de l'homme endetté. Essai sur la condition néolibérale*, Paris: Éditions Amsterdam.

Morvant-Roux, S. (2006) 'Processus d'appropriation des dispositifs de microfinance: un exemple en milieu rural mexicain', Doctoral thesis in Economics, Université Lumière Lyon 2.

Ortiz, M., M. Cabal and R. Mena (2014) *Micro, pequeñas y medianas empresas en la República Dominicana 2013*, Santo Domingo: FondoMicro.

Ortiz-Medina, M. and L. de Garcia-Perez (2012) 'Microcrédito como herramienta para la bancarización: un estudio empírico en República Dominicana', *Latin American Journal of International Affairs*, 4(1): 18–37.

Pedrosa, P. (2010) 'Microfinanzas en América Latina y el Caribe: el sector en cifras', New York: Banco Interamericano de Desarrollo.

Redcamif (2013) 'Memoria 2013. Red centroamericana y del Caribe de microfinanzas', www.redcamif.org/uploads/tx_rtgfiles/Memoria_Redcamif_2013_-_low.pdf.

Schicks, J. (2013) 'The definition and causes of microfinance over-indebtedness: a customer protection point of view', *Oxford Development Studies*, 41: S95–S116.

Servet J.-M. (2011) 'La crise du microcrédit en Andhra Pradesh (Inde)', *Revue Tiers Monde*, 207(3): 43–59.

Shipton, P. McD. (2010) *Credit between Cultures. Farmers, Financiers and Misunderstandings in Africa*, New Haven, CT, and London: Yale University Press.

Vanroose, A. (2014) 'Factors that explain the regional expansion of microfinance institutions in Peru', CEB Working Paper no. 14/030 2014, Brussels: Université Libre de Bruxelles.

6 | THE SOCIAL CREDIBILITY OF MICROCREDIT IN MOROCCO AFTER THE DEFAULT CRISIS

Solène Morvant-Roux and Marc Roesch

Introduction

Morocco, with its soaring growth rates and high repayment rates, has long stood as a model pupil, if not the jewel in the crown of the microcredit market. It is an internationally acclaimed success story, especially in 2008, when six of the twelve Moroccan microcredit associations (MCAs) rose to be among the hundred world leaders (Chehade and Nègre 2013). Yet, as in other environments, the country has strong regional disparities with most of the microcredit supply concentrated in urban areas.[1] This has given rise to a particularly high level of competition. Despite its reputation as a model microcredit sector, Morocco was hit by a credit delinquency crisis in 2009. The Zakoura Foundation, one of the top three Moroccan microcredit players nominated by Mix Market as one of the world's leading institutions in 2008, saw its portfolio at risk (thirty days) rise to over 30 per cent. This precipitated the foundation's bankruptcy and takeover by the Fondation Banque Populaire pour le Microcrédit (since renamed Attawfiq). At the same time, in Morocco as in other parts of the world, the microcredit sector suffered a wave of collective resistance in the form of massive credit delinquency by microcredit borrowers. The AVMC (Association des Victimes du Microcrédit), set up in Ouarzazate in southern Morocco in April 2011 following the local economic slowdown in tourism and film production, is a well-known and highly publicized illustration of the borrower backlash against microcredit providers worldwide (Bonzon 2012).

A CGAP analysis suggests that Morocco's credit delinquency crisis was due primarily to galloping growth, which drove up competition and multiple borrowing (Reille 2009).[2] Microcredit stakeholders responded in 2010 by switching tactics in a move to save the situation and fend off the crisis. The measures taken were designed to reduce cross-debts (informal credit bureaus for the leading MCAs and revised loan procedures) and to cut down the number of customers per loan officer to promote healthier growth. A map of the distribution of microcredit providers[3] was also produced to help improve the supply spread and prevent local saturation effects. Lastly, most of the Moroccan MCAs pledged to promote borrower protection as defined by the Smart Campaign.[4] Action taken to reduce cross-debts and exclude defaulters cut the number of borrowers from more than 1.2 million clients in 2007 to 800,000 borrowers in 2012. Yet the measures to improve portfolio quality did not do quite so well. PAR initially fell from 6.81 per cent in 2009 to 4.3 per cent in 2011, but bounced up again to 6.4 per cent in 2012, followed by a similar trend in 2013 (Mix Market country profile). Our argument, then, is that while strong growth, competition, reckless lending, cross-borrowing and a lack of credit reporting were definitely driving factors behind the credit delinquency crisis in Morocco, we also need to consider microcredit's social credibility. Here we focus on how loan officers dealt with microcredit's poor social credibility, what kind of creditor–debtor relationships were consequently built, and how far these relationships were reshaped following the credit delinquency crisis in Morocco.

We draw on in-depth fieldwork, considering loan officers and customers with different microcredit institutions in Morocco to analyse the strategies used by loan officers to meet the growth targets set by the Moroccan microcredit providers' senior managers (see Box 6.1). We show that, before the repayment

---

Box 6.1 Methodology: a qualitative approach combined with information from the management information system

This chapter is based on the findings of a number of studies of microcredit association customers in Morocco from December 2009 to January 2014.[5] The first study conducted in a number of the country's rural areas was not designed to understand credit delinquency, but to analyse the factors that determine microcredit programme uptake and rejection. However, it quickly became apparent to the research team that there were links between the determinants of demand and credit delinquency (Morvant-Roux et al. 2014). The second study was specifically tasked with gaining further insight into the causes of credit delinquency in the working-class neighbourhoods of Casablanca (Morvant-Roux and Roesch 2011). These two studies were rounded out by a study (whose material is used here) on the branches of a national MCA. We interviewed and field-monitored loan officers working for six urban MCA branches: two in Casablanca, two in Rabat and two in Fez. Our research also drew on detailed qualitative surveys to paint a picture of the 'life trajectories' of customers, local prominent figures, loan officers and branch managers. A total of nearly 150 interviews were conducted by these visits in four main areas of Morocco.[6] The branch analysis of an MCA was also supplemented by analyses of an original database built using information from the MCA's management information system over the 2008–12 period. This information covers a large number of variables at different levels and across the entire sample: branches, borrowers and loans.

crisis, loan officers faced great resistance from local populations to debt and credit. The upshot of this was either no or low microcredit uptake or high microcredit uptake with little willingness to repay. Loan officers hence turned to the use of local, personal relationships to meet demand and build market depth. We subsequently show how far these loan strategies were reshaped following the microcredit delinquency crisis. The post-crisis customer-learning process combined with fears of a new crisis among both field staff and senior managers made loan relations less personal and more formal. Yet although they now take a more professional approach, loan officers still rely on informal incentive mechanisms today, albeit opting for much more privacy-invasive techniques.

Building a sustainable microcredit market where there is reluctance to borrow money ...

A number of recent studies have shown that analysis of informal finance can help in understanding how people perceive microcredit and how this then influences debtor–creditor relationships between microcredit institutions and their borrowers (Guérin et al. 2012; Guérin et al. 2011). Moroccans are reluctant to borrow for religious and cultural reasons (Morvant-Roux et al. 2014). Credit is not a key component of financial management strategies and debt is seen as taboo and to be used only as a last resort. Pierre Bourdieu (1977) finds that Sharia prohibits the charging of interest on credit, with family assistance expected to play a strong role in this area. Two rural studies with totally different methodologies – a large-sample survey by the JPAL team (Duflo et al. 2008) versus a qualitative survey by the RUME team (Guérin et al. 2011) find extremely similar results regarding the demand for informal credit. The JPAL survey conducted from 2006 to 2010 shows that, although 26 per cent of households had an outstanding loan, a mere 6 per cent had access to informal credit over the period (Crépon et al. 2011). The RUME team's qualitative study comes to both similar and highly contrasting conclusions when compared with other environments such as India and the Dominican Republic (see elsewhere in this volume).

Informal loans are generally taken out with family, friends, the local grocer and suppliers in certain cases (male merchants and, to a lesser extent, female merchants). Amounts are small at some hundreds of dirhams (dhs, a few dozen euros) for short periods (weeks). The supply of informal financial services comes mainly from informal lenders, rotating savings and credit associations, grocers, and traders and craftspeople buying on credit from suppliers. It is hard to obtain information on moneylenders, who do not like to come out into the open.[7] Yet our interviews with people who have borrowed from this type of lender suggest that interest rates are incredibly high (people refer to it as 'renting money'). For example, on a loan of 10,000 dhs, the borrower pays

1,000 dhs per month in interest for twelve months, with the capital remaining due. This course of action also raises fears about repayment methods and collateral: pawning, IOUs and heavy-handed collection tactics. Here, borrowing from the moneylender is seen as a last resort and instead help from the family and different forms of savings (grain storage and livestock) play a central role. So there are financial needs (spending on festive, housing and health outlays and more 'productive' outlays for trading and craft businesses), but demand is expressed less automatically in credit form than in other environments. Business expenditure needs are more easily met by integrated debt forms such as a slate with a supplier, savings and to a lesser extent self-help (see Servet 2011). Taking out an interest-bearing loan for family needs (in rural more than urban areas) has negative social connotations since it is seen as a sign that the household head is unable to provide for the family's needs (Bourdieu 1977). In general, then, there is a demand for informal credit, but it is relatively small as people are not very willing to take out interest-bearing loans apparently for sociocultural and religious reasons. Although debt is uncommon, savings in kind (cereals and livestock) play a central role in smoothing dips in domestic and business cash flow and in preparations for important life events. This is borne out by the JPAL study, which finds that 72 per cent of households in the survey have at least one animal: 59 per cent have sheep and 50 per cent have cows (Crépon et al. 2011). Our study also looks into the role of the Islamic norm, mainly from the angle of the reprehensible if not prohibited nature (*haram*) of *riba*, i.e. interest. The interest rate does not appear to be a major factor of reticence. The religious texts only prohibits interest among Muslims. Interest may be charged on transactions between an individual and a commercial institution (Sami 2009). Some interviewees mentioned that interest was a problem, but more from the point of view of its cost than its prohibited or sinful nature. Ultimately, then, it would appear to be not so much the principle of paying interest to a microcredit institution that puts a major brake on the development of microcredit, but how debt is perceived locally (Morvant-Roux et al. 2014).

This scant use of credit is confirmed by the Global Financial inclusion database (Findex – also used by Javoy and Rozas in this volume). These data estimate that 39 per cent of the Moroccan population over fifteen years old had an account with a formal financial institution in 2011. This figure is close to the 38 per cent found for the Dominican Republic and not far off the 33 and 32 per cent reported for Algeria and Tunisia respectively. However, quite a different picture emerges when looking at the percentage of the population who took out a loan with a formal financial institution in the year before the survey (2010): 1, 3 and 4 per cent for Algeria, Tunisia and Morocco respectively and 14 per cent for the Dominican Republic. These data show that there is a wider gap between credit access and use in Morocco, Algeria and Tunisia (Findex data, 2011).

The growth in microcredit mentioned in the introduction might well seem paradoxical in light of this reluctance to take out credit, were it not for the following points. Firstly, the number of MCA financial intermediaries (twelve) in Morocco is very low compared with the country's size (32 million inhabitants). As a result the market penetration was one of the lowest in the world (4.3 loans per 100 population), as highlighted by Rozas et al. (2014). Secondly, there are no financial cooperatives in Morocco as there are, for example, in West Africa, Latin America and the Caribbean. The microcredit associations represent the one and only supply of formal credit available to the poor. Lastly, given the small size of the informal finance sector, any demand for financial services at the time inevitably fell at the door of these twelve MCAs. This gave microcredit a windfall gain, as it came to be seen as an open invitation to secure a loan, driven by reckless lending. If this source of credit were to start to dry up for any number of reasons, it would not dramatically disrupt households' financial management practices, as in Morocco not being able to obtain a new loan if you default on repayment is not seen as a problem, unlike the situation observed in other countries (here again, see the examples in this volume of India by Guérin et al. and the Dominican Republic by Morvant-Roux et al.). People might stop repayments because they do not intend to take out another loan after the one they have and decide to spend their resources on more pressing priorities. Borrowers withdraw from the market after taking out two or three microloans. The prospect of not taking out any further credit in the future reduces the incentive to repay the last outstanding loan.

... and weak repayment incentives

Microfinance institutions commonly apply two types of pressure to borrowers to honour their debts:

- Loss of access to future loans for the customer (or group) defaulting on repayment is one of the main microfinance incentive mechanisms. This mechanism is sometimes backed up by a credit bureau so that other loan entities can apply the same sanction.
- Legal sanctions based on the country's legal system and assisted by bailiffs, recovery agencies, threats of legal action, etc.

Low microcredit uptake due in part to the reluctance to get into debt means that the first option (access to credit in the future) carries little weight. As regards the second option, here too there are contextual differences. Work by the RUME team (Guérin et al. 2011; Morvant-Roux et al. 2014) finds an array of different perceptions of microcredit institutions in rural areas. These perceptions can be seen at work in feelings that range from defiance to fear, and dictate repayment behaviour. We draw on this rural/urban distinction for its ability to highlight major trends. Note, however, that there is no break, but a continuum between these two types of areas. In addition, in no way do these ideal types correspond to uniform, static realities.

In rural areas: from fear to impunity Two perceptions of microcredit are found in rural areas: intense fear (which drives low microcredit uptake, self-exclusion and restriction) and strong feelings of impunity (high microcredit uptake, but lower repayment rates). These two extremes are driven by the fact that microcredit is viewed as coming from village outsiders and very often from the *Makhzen* (the king). Basically, there are three configurations. They depend on both the perception of the MFI (is it a *Makhzen* body or not?) and the perception of the *Makhzen* (is it a legitimate entity or not?), and have direct repercussions on participation and incentive to repay. In a great many cases, the microcredit institution is purely and simply identified with the *Makhzen*. It is perceived as a body reaching from the capital (Rabat) into the villages whose loaned money comes from the king's coffers, the capital or the government. The identification of the MFI with the *Makhzen* makes for a huge amount of pressure to repay due to the imagined gravity of a default on payment. It clearly also plays a role in putting people off the idea of borrowing. In some cases, the MFI and microcredit repayment are used to directly challenge the authority of the state: the *Makhzen* may well inspire fear, but it is also seen as illegitimate. In this case, if the *Makhzen* is offering the loans, it becomes almost justifiable not to pay them back, and taking out loans is apparently seen as a game or an act of defiance. So different configurations can be found, depending on the nature of the relationship with the state. Lastly, MCA loans are also often confused with a gift. Despite the microcredit institutions' many communication efforts (such as where branches have put up posters plainly stating that microcredits are not gifts and that they absolutely must be paid back), the confusion is frequent. It is sometimes fuelled or channelled by local leaders, and some clients may well deliberately sustain the confusion to justify their own arrears.

In urban areas: legal action is not much of a deterrent In urban areas, although some borrowers do not think twice about opportunistically forming solidarity groups with no intention of repaying the loan, most borrowers do not make a calculated decision to default on payment. This raises the question of the potential role of the two sanction mechanisms. Our interviews found that the first sanction option (promise of access to a future loan) does not play the role it might in other circumstances. Many borrowers said they no longer wanted to use microcredit. Some said they wanted 'to sleep at night' in a clear display of the unease over interest-bearing loans in general and especially those that tie them to a foreign institution. Legal sanctions were found to be barely any more effective. Although surprise calls by loan officers intimidate borrowers with arrears (and meant that some people were reluctant to open the door to us for the interviews), few people fear real legal action. They are more worried about what the neighbours might think than the law.

Resistance to debt, which is behind the low microcredit uptake, and rather ineffectual legal sanctions considerably complicate the task of building a sustainable, lasting microcredit market. In this relatively hostile environment, loan officers opted for hybrid creditor–debtor relationships (not exclusively contractual and impersonal), with the emphasis on the quality of the relationship and mutual trust, to be able to meet growth targets (creating demand) while guaranteeing repayment quality (ensuring borrower loyalty).

Yet although these more personal relations initially put loan officers in touch with the 'demand', they also exacerbated the crisis. Equally, they evolved over time driven by customer-learning phenomena following the crisis and loan officers changing strategy as they adjusted to a new, more stable sector environment, albeit viewed as extremely hostile in that the old drivers (easy credit and relations of trust with borrowers to foster repayment) had disappeared.

Development of creditor–debtor relationships between loan officers and borrowers

In addition to the features of supply (products, price and procedures) and demand, development project stakeholders also have an important role to play. Be they end users, fieldworkers, managers or local leaders, we can assume that they do not apply procedures or consume the financial services passively, but 'co-produce' them. Development projects can be seen as ongoing negotiation processes within which stakeholders engage, interact, cooperate, disagree and often compromise, while attributing values and meaning in keeping with their own frameworks, interests and constraints (Long 2001). Yet few papers address the key role played by field staff and loan officers, in particular in the making of this new market (Dixon et al. 2007; Afonso 2013; Morvant-Roux et al. 2014).

Before the repayment crisis: close, personalized relations with borrowers As already mentioned, the environment of resistance to debt with pockets of feelings of impunity among borrowers hugely complicates the loan officers' daily work on building the market on two levels: i) finding clients willing to borrow money, and ii) finding clients who are also willing and/or able to repay. The incentive to repay may actually be weaker where people do not mind losing access to credit, where competition is strong and where there is no credit bureau to report on information. Before the crisis, and Zakoura's bankruptcy in particular, loan officers drew on personal relations with their clients to promote credit uptake and ensure repayment. Locally based, caring loan officers gained the customer's trust. In addition to leveraging loyalty as a way to get and keep new clients (at least the good ones), loan officers made use of their personal, trusting relationships as social pressure to make borrowers pay their debts. On the client side, these personalized relations shifted the dynamic towards a hybrid form of the creditor–debtor relationship that allowed for a degree of flexibility and distance from formal procedures: 'We borrowed money from Badiha and Jamal [fictitious names of loan officers] ...... She [Badiha] knows the family' (female borrower, branch office in Fez). According to Badiha (the loan officer), who we met later in her new workplace, face-to-face relationships were positive for repayment: 'Some customers pay to keep a good relationship with the loan officer ... Borrowers do not know the institution, they only know the loan officer ... If they had difficulties repaying they would seek a solution anywhere' ... 'Sometimes we find the solution with them, we go to their place' ... 'For some of them, if their business was slow, I would find them some work or I would help women to sell their goods and earn money.' In an illustration of the loan officer's importance to the client, she mentioned that she went on holiday for two weeks at one point before the repayment crisis, but her clients did not want to pay their instalments while she was away because: 'They wanted to repay it to me!' One loan officer was transferred to another branch, but his customers kept asking for him. Branch staff worried about upsetting the relationship with the client and the branch told customers that: 'He was sick or on holiday'. The work set-up was that each loan officer managed his/her portfolio of clients alone. The local, flexible loan officers collected loan instalments from the borrower's home instead of at the branch, making for less formality in the lending process. This approach was designed to close the gap between the supply of microcredit services offered by a provider from outside the social network, neighbourhood or village and the target population. However, the situation became complicated when Zakoura went bankrupt. Although these personalized relations had positive effects ('they were paying me'), they in turn had an adverse effect on the entire sector. Loan officers were the sole executors of the borrowers' relations with the branch (resulting in exclusivity and strong identification with the loan officer at the expense of the institution as a whole). In some extreme cases, borrowers would speak only to 'their' loan officer and rejected any intervention from any other member of the branch's staff.

Close relationships and massive credit delinquency As a result of this situation, part of the repayment defaults that hit Zakoura and other microcredit providers starting in 2008 were rooted in these personalized relations between loan officers and borrowers. Firstly, prior to the credit delinquency crisis, some loan officers took advantage of this face-to-face client portfolio management to steal money from the instalments paid by borrowers, hiding it for some time before the branch manager found out (the mostly illiterate customers trusted the loan officer). Our field observations also show that, during the six-month transition between the announcement of Zakoura's bankruptcy and its takeover by the Fondation Banque Populaire (now named Attawfiq), some of Zakoura's loan officers made the most of the exclusive relationship they had built with borrowers to manipulate them into defaulting. Following the bankruptcy, the new company hired the 'good', trustworthy loan officers and let the others go. Yet the loan officers who knew that the new company would not hire them took advantage of the transition to abuse borrowers by telling them not to repay their loan. This behaviour resulted in higher credit delinquency, but also served as an example and incentive for other borrowers to stop repaying once they found out that defaulters were getting away with it: 'Before [the crisis], they were afraid of prison. Now they know there are no prosecutions' (loan officer, Berrechid). The growing feeling of impunity among clients brought with it a feeling of powerlessness among loan officers. Moreover, the post-crisis situation has prevented them from using the personalized relations strategy that helped them build the market (meet demand while ensuring repayments). The institutions' policies and the customer-learning process have severely challenged this personalization of creditor–debtor relationships.

'Standardization' towards more contractual, albeit distrustful creditor–debtor relationships MFI senior management is now opposed to the personalized relationships that initially allowed for the 'deep' market-building before the repayment crisis hit. Today, senior managers are trying to put some distance between field staff and clients. A number of strategies have been introduced to build more contractual relationships. Human resources managers now arrange to transfer employees from one branch to another (farther away) or change their position: Badiha, for example, changed both workplace and position as she became a cashier and was no longer a loan officer when we met her.[8] Branch managers are also subject to transfer from one branch to another when they have worked at the same branch for a number of years. Branch managers may decide a staff transfer is necessary as soon as they detect a high risk of collusion between a loan officer and borrowers. In this case, the branch manager asks the human resources department to transfer the loan officer to another branch without telling him/her the true reason to prevent any risk of collective defaulting.

Yet this new approach still needs to maintain a good level of repayment (portfolio quality) and customer stability (quantity). In a move to prevent the loss of 'good' clients, the transfer of a loan officer is generally concealed from customers who might be tempted to follow 'their' loan officer. Badiha, for example, explained that her customers followed her when she was transferred to the other MCA (field notes, Morvant-Roux and Roesch, January 2014).

At branch level, collective portfolio management has replaced individual portfolio management. For instance, two loan officers share the responsibility for the same borrowers and may make field visits together and help each other with recovery operations. In some areas, branch managers have set up committees of field employees working for branches in the same area to hold weekly meetings in order to encourage information-sharing on borrowers during the selection process: for example, a husband and wife may ask for a loan from two separate branches in an attempt to outwit the lending procedures. This committee also provides informal support for the most problematic cases. Loan officers with a difficult situation on their hands may seek support from the committee to make a collective visit to the defaulter in order to intimidate him/her. The idea is to put on a united face to make it clear to the client that s/he has a debt with an institution and not just with an individual lender. This new approach is designed to clarify the borrower's perception that his/her contract binds her/him to an institution rather than a single person. This is supposed to impress on the customer the serious implications of non-payment. A branch manager in Rabat explained to us that they make customers feel more accountable by asking for ID and other official papers so they understand that borrowing money 'is something serious'. This new approach is expected to ensure repayment and optimize portfolio quality.

However, loan officers still have to grapple with an adverse situation where credit uptake is concerned. Although they need to ensure repayment, they also need to maintain a good relationship with borrowers so that they keep borrowing from the microcredit institution. Since loan officers can no longer build personal relationships with borrowers, they now gather information on clients' private lives. As mentioned before, loan officers are afraid to grant loans to potential defaulters. Since the legal enforcement mechanisms are weak, they are now looking for new informal enforcement mechanisms. They also try their best to keep previous (good) customers while exercising great caution when it comes to lending to new clients they do not yet know. The social pressure strategy is based on gathering information on the client's private life. For example, it is easier to pressurize a female defaulter into paying if the loan officer knows that her husband is not aware that she has borrowed money. Information sources are informal: from customers' neighbours and the local grocer to informal exchanges of information with loan officers from other branches of the same MCA living in the same neighbourhood as the prospective client. They also make use of the good relations they have with their clients and previous customers to get them to talk about each other. Many loan officers we met said how complicated and stressful it can be to live in the same neighbourhood as the branch and their customers: 'If I know a person, it will make my job easier, but not always since if she knows me, she can come to me to ask for a microcredit when she does not deserve it' (loan officer). So most loan officers live in different neighbourhoods.

Another strategy used is to make careful lending decisions to lower the default risk. Three main strategies are used here. The first is to prioritize previous (good) clients, giving them credit renewal and loans to meet quantitative targets. Given the limited demand for microcredit – reluctance to borrow, economic slowdown, fierce competition in certain areas, etc. (contrary to what senior managers see as being due to low national coverage rates by formal financial services) – finding new clients can be quite a challenge. Branch managers told us that they are generally unable to meet 100 per cent of the monthly growth targets, but that they earn the same wage and are viewed in the same way by their superiors even if they meet just 75–80 per cent of the targets. The priority is the repayment rate. In this environment, loan officers do their best to get 'good' borrowers to renew their loans and go to see previous clients to try to convince them to borrow again: 'We work mainly with former clients – renewals – it is hard to find new clients' (loan officer, branch near Casablanca). 'Many clients stop borrowing. They argue that it is *haram* – forbidden by the Sharia – but we don't let them go, the good ones, we constantly visit them' (branch manager, Fez). Loan officers try to keep their clients even when a new branch of the same MCA opens near the existing one and is closer to some clients. We had the opportunity to visit a client who lives closer to the new branch. We asked her why she did not move to the new one. Her answer was, 'I would like to, but they won't let me!' Then the loan officer added, 'I won't let you go!' (she is a very good client).

One borrower in downtown Fez told us, 'I had stopped borrowing for a while and they came to my place to offer me a loan again' (woman borrower, Fez). Some loan officers say they prefer contracting group loans rather than individual loans, which reduces the face-to-face contact with a single borrower. Although these solidarity groups do not always run smoothly, loan officers can bring social pressure to bear among solidarity group members unbeknown to the borrower in arrears. One strategy used when a group member is late with payment is to arrange a meeting with the other group members without the said borrower's knowledge and have them pay the defaulter's share without informing the delinquent that his or her instalment has already been paid. This strategy has a number of advantages: i) a positive signal is sent back to the (information) 'system' and the group is not penalized; ii) the loan is repaid; and iii) the credit delinquency risk no longer weighs on the loan officer, but on the solidarity group. Another strategy consists of prioritizing loans for women. Two main reasons are put forward for this. Firstly, women are less mobile and easier to find at their homes than men. Secondly, women form the core of the family's solidarity mechanism: 'Female borrowers are more likely to ask for (and receive) family support if they have problems with repayment' (loan officer, Casablanca). Whereas the male code of honour prevents men from showing any signs of having cash-flow management problems, mothers are more likely to get support from a son or brother to make the instalments.[9] This strategy of prioritizing women is at odds with the MCA management's stated policy. Other strategies include debt rescheduling, early renewal of microcredit (after 50–70 per cent of the loan has been repaid), and allowing the potential client to use the loan granted to repay another MCA and as such 'steal' the client (interview with a loan officer in Fez). As highlighted with the Dominican Republic, loan officers are affiliated to different microcredit providers. There is little scope for a competitive edge, other than by offering the borrower special arrangements and flexibility. This is particularly the case here in that microcredit providers do not collect savings. This makes it harder to 'steal' clients from other microcredit providers.

In addition to these strategies, loan officers are careful to strike a balance between a formal stance to ensure repayment and a friendly attitude to encourage borrowers to borrow again. Table 6.1 sums up how the creditor–debtor relationships adopted by loan officers have evolved.

New context and new challenges

The observed shift in the Moroccan microcredit sector towards the 'standardization' of the field staff's work (convergence with the classic banking approach) goes hand in hand with the policy launched to stabilize the sector following the credit delinquency crisis (see Rozas et al. 2014). We have

TABLE 6.1 Creditor–debtor relationships before and after the repayment crisis

	Morocco before the repayment crisis	Morocco after the repayment crisis
Debt-related norms	Reluctance, mutual support and savings in kind first	Reluctance, mutual support and savings in kind first
Perception of informal credit sources	Fear and little use	Fear and little use
Demand for formal credit services	Low in general	Low in general
Perception of microcredit	Ranging from fear to feelings of impunity and little loyalty in urban areas	Customer-learning process and more widespread feelings of impunity
Main constraint	Borrower wariness	Loan officer and borrower wariness
Loan officer's strategy	Quality of personal relationship (proximity) and distance from lending procedures	Intrusion into clients' private lives + respect for lending procedures to avoid problems with the hierarchy
Creditor–debtor relationship	Personalized relationships	Formal/friendly mix
Result	Deep market-building and strong growth	Stagnation (slow growth)

Source: Authors

shown, however, that the customer-learning process has made loan officers more cautious about trusting new borrowers and has encouraged them to favour previous 'good' clients, if not constantly 'harass' them to get them to take out new loans. In an overall environment of low microcredit uptake, the tightening of loan access conditions for borrowers and a downbeat economic climate, especially in tourist areas, could well combine to paralyse demand. Both supply and demand, therefore, are in somewhat of an impasse as it becomes harder and harder for loan officers to find customers who meet the solvency criteria. The case of the female loan officer working for an agency in Casablanca's suburbs shows how officers fear poor clients, but are under pressure from head office. She told us that she was scared of granting credit to a borrower who was not going to pay it back, but that head office put 'the pressure on to contract loans'. She said that only a minority of potential customers met the solvency criteria and gave the example that she had twenty people who wanted a microloan at that point in time, but that she would 'sign no one'. Only one female customer differed in this respect as she had professional premises (proof of business activity). However, the loan officer knew she wanted the money to pay for her daughter's wedding and therefore did not want to give her the loan. In general, though, the credit use criterion purportedly plays second fiddle to meeting growth targets. For example, on the subject of (the many) women who claim to want to invest in the blanket business, but actually use the microloan for consumption, one branch manager said, 'When you see that they are making the repayments, you give anyway. It's hard to find people who are reliable.'

The following charts present the growth in the number of customers for the country's leading microcredit associations. The slight upturn they show in growth falls rather flat in the light of Zakoura's bankruptcy and takeover by the Fondation Banque Populaire pour le Microcrédit (renamed Attawfiq). FBPMC and the other MCAs set out to recoup and indeed netted Zakoura's most reliable customers (Zakoura had nearly 450,000 clients). They should then have posted a sharp rise in client numbers, but only Attawfiq reported a small increase in customers. This could be taken to mean that the number of customers with Attawfiq, and the other MCAs, is tending to stagnate. Note that the loan supply shifted to the urban areas at the same time, as mentioned in the introduction.

This stagnation trend can also be seen across the six urban branches we visited (Figure 6.1). Each branch's business obviously develops and grows based on different factors. Although we observed that loan officers are generally much more wary of trusting clients they do not know, the economic situation of the customers in some areas appeared to be a decisive factor in agency buoyancy. In some agencies, the development of industrial and urban planning activities is giving small traders new opportunities and creating a growth market that is offsetting this stagnation (Rabat 2). Other agencies are

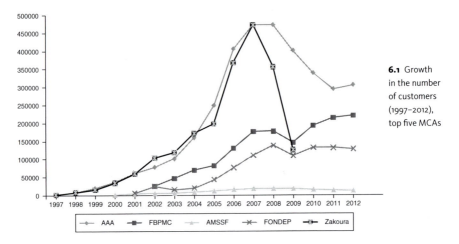

6.1 Growth in the number of customers (1997–2012), top five MCAs

Source: Adapted from Mix Market data

faced with less upbeat environments such as Casablanca 2 (suffering from competition from a new branch of the same MCA in its area), Rabat 1 (district of civil servants not conducive to trade) and Fez 2 in the Medina, where craft trades have been particularly hard hit. Yet with the exception of a few economic growth districts (Rabat 2), the overall situation is one of business stagnation.

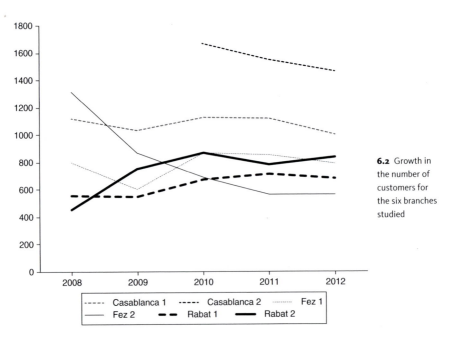

6.2 Growth in the number of customers for the six branches studied

Source: Adapted from MFI's Management Information System data (2008–12)

More recent surveys have found that this trend, already observed by our last credit delinquency study (Morvant-Roux and Roesch 2011), has firmed up. The trade and craft businesses that form the bulk of the MCAs' clientele have been particularly hard hit by the downturn in trans-North African trade following the Arab Spring (trade channels between Egypt, Libya and Tunisia were highly disrupted if not cut off altogether), competition from trade with China and the drop in tourists due to the Arab Spring.

Conclusion

The 'success' of the new microfinance movement in reaching poor households in developing countries was rooted in its ability to promote proximity (see also D'Espallier et al. this volume). This takes in not just geographic proximity (programme and branch location), but also social proximity to overcome social and cultural barriers between potential borrowers and microfinance institution staff. Regular meetings and visits with clients and hiring local staff were strategies designed to build trust and lower social barriers between microcredit providers and potential borrowers (Servet 1996). Yet although proximity has long been viewed as key to the success of the microfinance industry, enabling many stakeholders to combine social mission with strong growth, this chapter argues that it played an instrumental role in the spread of the credit delinquency crisis in Morocco in 2009. The rise in defaults on payments distinctive of Morocco's microcredit crisis was far from simply a consequence of over-indebtedness or some sort of a Ponzi scheme. It was a complex phenomenon, key to which was the perception of the credit, the credit institution and the loan officer. Our findings show that Zakoura's loan officers opted for the social approach to inspire trust in borrowers so that they could meet their growth targets. In an environment where demand proved lower than expected owing to resistance to debt, modest consumer outlays (celebrations, education, weddings, etc.) and, more recently, a less buoyant economic situation, the opposition described by Jean-Yves Moisseron and Hind Malanaïne between society and community (*Gemeinschaft*) initially came down in favour of the community legitimacy of microcredit (Moisseron and Malanaïne 2013). Yet when coupled with internal control failings, the exclusive relationship the loan officers had with borrowers spiralled into widespread abuse of the system (misappropriation, payment default 'attacks', etc.) and ultimately had a hand in bringing down Zakoura. With this collapse, the threat of legal action lost all credibility with the borrowers and the loan officers ran for cover behind a more contractual approach (society or *Gesellschaft*), henceforth shunning any confrontation or exclusive relationship with the borrowers. With the institutions' legitimacy no longer a guarantee of adherence to the contract, what was left was the 'need for credit' or the fear of no longer having access to credit if the borrower did not repay the loan in hand. Given the low propensity to contract debt, the leverage of the non-renewal of credit also failed to guarantee repayment. The loan officers therefore found themselves having to invent new means of pressure. One of them is to pry into their customers' private lives. Yet this strategy also broadens the gap and mutual distrust between loan officer and client. The officer knows the customer, but the customer also knows the loan officer. So to defend themselves, the loan officers hide behind procedures. These procedures also protect them from an ever-watchful hierarchy constantly on its guard. This change of risk management (with the accent placed on contracts and procedures) has brought the situation to an impasse of overcautiousness in seeking new customers and testing new products. This is behind the sector's low growth. The situation clearly shows the delicate balance the microfinance institutions need to strike in an environment of mistrust that is forcing them to juggle 'community' and 'contract'. It also points to the need to take better account of the experiences of the loan officers tasked with building the microcredit market. They form an important link, all too often seen as mere unthinking, unfeeling operatives without any social connection with the customer. Whereas a review of the procedures, products and organization could help prevent further crises, flanking the market stabilization process by redefining the role of loan officers and giving them better training could well be just as decisive.

Notes

1 Note that the Moroccan microcredit sector deals in credit only, given that the country's banking legislation prevents MCAs from handling savings.

2 For a recent detailed and accurate analysis of the microcredit crisis in Morocco, see Rozas et al. (2014).

3 Drawn up by the Centre Mohammed VI de Soutien à la Microfinance Solidaire.

4 The Smart Campaign is an initiative to certify MFIs that comply with transparency and consumer protection rules.

5 Funded by the French Development Agency, the French Deposits and Loans Fund (CDC) and the European Investment Bank.

6 The Atlas foothills south-east of Marrakesh, a rural area of Fez, the major cropping area east of Rabat, and the eastern districts of Casablanca.

7 Unlike in other fieldwork conducted in Mexico and the Dominican Republic, we did not manage to interview any private moneylenders.

8 Formal banks use this kind of strategy as well; see Gloukoviezoff (2010).

9 Fatima Sadiqi (2003) highlights the crucial role of males protecting women from the same family (daughters, sisters, spouses, mothers), or any other close kin in Moroccan society.

References

Afonso, J. (2013) 'Loan officers and preventing overindebtedness – the case of Banco ADOPEM', *Microfinance in Crisis, Research and Policy Brief Series*, 8, Paris: Université Paris 1 Sorbonne, Institut de Recherche pour le Développement (IRD).

Bonzon, M. (2012) 'Le cas du refus de remboursement dans la région de Ouarzazate: symptôme d'une responsabilité sociale mise à mal', Study report, ALDEFI, July.

Bourdieu, P. (1977) *Algérie 60. Structures économiques et structures temporelles*, Paris: Les Editions de Minuit.

Chehade, N. and A. Nègre (2013) 'Lessons learnt from the Moroccan crisis', *CGAP Brief*, 6 August, www.cgap.org/sites/default/files/Brief-Lessons-Learned-from-the-Moroccan-Crisis-July-2013_0.pdf, accessed 14 September 2014.

Crépon, B., F. Devoto, E. Duflo and W. Pariente (2011) 'Impact of microcredit in rural areas of Morocco: evidence from a randomized evaluation', Working paper, JPal, 31 March, www.povertyactionlab.org/publication/impact-microcredit-rural-areasmorocco-evidence-randomized-evaluation, accessed 14 September 2014.

Dixon, R., J. Ritchie and J. Siwale (2007) 'Loan officers and loan "delinquency" in microfinance: a Zambian case', *Accounting Forum*, 31(1): 47–71.

Duflo, E., B. Crépon, W. Parienté and F. Devoto (2008) 'Poverty, access to credit and the determinants of participation in a new microcredit program in rural areas of Morocco', *Série Analyse d'Impact Ex Post*, 2, Paris: Agence Française de Développement, October.

Gloukoviezoff, G. (2010) *L'exclusion bancaire. Le lien social à l'épreuve de la rentabilité*, Paris: PUF.

Guérin, I., M. Roesch, G. Venkatasubramanian and B. D'Espallier (2012) 'Credit from whom and for what? Diversity of borrowing sources and uses in rural South India', *Journal of International Development*, 24: S122–S137.

Guérin, I., S. Morvant-Roux, R. Roesch, J. Y. Moisseron and P. Ould Ahmed (2011) 'Analyse des déterminants de la demande de services financiers dans le Maroc rural', *Série Analyse d'Impact Ex Post*, 6, Paris: Agence Française de Développement/RUME.

Long, N. (2001) *Development Sociology. Actor perspectives*, London: Routledge.

Moisseron J.-Y. and H. Malanaïne (2013) 'The Janus-figure of the microfinance credit-agent between two orders of legitimacy', *Microfinance in Crisis, Research and Policy Brief Series*, 3, Paris: Université Paris 1 Sorbonne, Institut de Recherche pour le Développement (IRD).

Morvant-Roux, S. and M. Roesch (2011) 'Analyser les liens entre impayés, endettement croisé et surendettement en milieu urbain', *Rapport de mission*, Caisse des Dépôts et Consignations, Al Amana.

Morvant-Roux, S., I. Guérin, M. Roesch and J.-Y. Moisseron (2014) 'Adding value to randomization with qualitative analysis: the case of microcredit in rural Morocco', *World Development*, 56: 302–12.

Reille, X. (2009) 'The rise, fall and recovery of the microfinance sector in Morocco', *CGAP Brief*, December, www.cgap.org/gm/document-1.9.48450/Morocco_Brief_FR.pdf.

Rozas, D., K. Pinget, M. Khaled and S. El Yaalaoui (2014) *Ending the Microfinance Crisis in Morocco: Acting early, acting right*, Washington, DC: International Finance Corporation (World Bank group).

Sadiqi, F. (2003) *Women, Gender, and Language in Morocco*, Boston, MA: Brill.

Sami, A. (2009) *Religion et droit dans les pays arabes*, Bordeaux: Presses Universitaires de Bordeaux.

Servet, J.-M. (1996) 'Risque, incertitude et financement de proximité en Afrique. Une approche socio-économique', *Revue Tiers-Monde*, 37(145): 41–58.

— (2011) 'La crise marocaine ', *Rapport de mission*, Caisse des Dépôts et Consignations, January.

Part III
ENVIRONMENT

7 | MALAISE IN THE SENEGALESE MICROFINANCE LANDSCAPE

Eveline Baumann, Abdoulaye Fall and Cécile Godfroid

In contrast to the other countries discussed in this volume, Senegal, which in the 1980s was a pioneer of microfinance in western Africa, has not at first glance been experiencing a microfinance crisis. There have been no signs, such as a dramatic loan portfolio slowdown. On the contrary, MFI portfolios have been growing at a steady, albeit slower pace. Deposits have continued their upward trend, and from 1998 to 2013 MFI client numbers increased more than tenfold, at an annual rate of almost 17 per cent. In 2013, 11 per cent of the value added by the financial sector came from MFIs, with a penetration ratio as high as 15.2 per cent.

But the true nature of the microfinance landscape remains ambiguous. Several ratios, including portfolios at risk, give grounds for potential concern. Levels of concentration are also high. Three of the MFIs account for four out of five members, and two-thirds of the overall loan portfolio. Current legislation, which pushes strongly for commercialization and the key principles of financial profitability, competition and regulation (Christen 2001), may be fostering concentration insofar as it seeks to set up a unique financial landscape, which also includes MFIs. It is also a call for greater professional norms, which only MFIs benefiting from economies of scale are able to achieve. This can mean that small institutions focused on social welfare become crowded out. At the same time, the distinction between 'traditional' banks and MFIs is becoming blurred: the latter are implicitly encouraged to concentrate on supposedly solvent clients, such as medium-sized companies and wage earners, encroaching on the territory of 'traditional' banks and fostering competition. Finally, there has been an overall lack of transparency and recurrent political interference, falling short on the transparency and availability of information required in the market economy.

This situation has fed into a malaise that has been voiced not only by independent experts, but also, although only in private, by MFI staff members, senior officials and MFI clients and non-clients.[1] They are all concerned by what can be called the current mission drift of microfinance.

Before looking at the available data and their limitations, we will discuss the landscape of microfinance in Senegal and its institutional framework. We will then consider the outcome and challenges of the in-depth legal reform that was carried out in the late 2000s. We will finally demonstrate how fierce competition and legislative shortcomings can handicap financial inclusion.

The landscape of microfinance in Senegal

High concentration in the microfinance arena goes back to the very beginnings of financial inclusion in Senegal, when international donors actively backed the movement. While microfinance initially focused on the rural population, who were seen as being in need of 'development' tools, its focus progressively shifted to towns, which helped offset losses from less profitable rural areas. Little by little, the social welfare focus gave way to an explicitly market-centred approach, which legislation has also spurred on.

Rural versus urban MFIs The Senegalese microfinance landscape was affected from the outset by recurrent environmental disasters and high urban–rural migration, as well as by massive lay-offs in the public and semi-public sector in the 1980s and early 1990s in the wake of radical reforms that were labelled as structural adjustment (Doligez et al. 2012; Ouedraogo and Gentil 2008). Unemployment was high, insofar as this can have any meaning in a context where seven out of eight people with an occupation were self-employed, apprentices or family workers (Senegal 2014e: 28), and where jobseekers were neither systematically registered nor in receipt of unemployment benefits. Poverty reduction was on the agenda of international development agencies, and the time seemed ripe for encouraging private initiatives through community-based access to saving and loan products. At a time when development banks had all closed down and usury was widespread, microfinance was thought to be an ideal tool. Cooperative governance was seen as the 'one best way' to manage organizations.

But there was a flaw, insofar as it was taken for granted that there would be (increasing) demand for microloans, and at the same time saving products. Not enough attention was meanwhile paid to existing informal financial tools, where in-kind and cash saving and credit were closely intertwined. These tools were a response not only to concerns for solidarity and reciprocity among family members and friends, but also for protection between people of different social statuses. In Senegal, these are at the heart of strategies for managing risk. They mostly involve women, and considerable flows of money and products such as cloth.[2] There are also more anonymous means of obtaining credit, which are strongly historically embedded. Traders and rich farmers often provide cereals, the same amount of which has to be returned after the harvest, when prices are usually half as high as during the hunger gap. In towns, people in need of cash may turn to cash loan-sharks-cum-middlemen, the so-called *bukkimen*, who sell products on credit, which are immediately sold on, often at a 30–40 per cent lower price than what was initially paid.[3] Given this wide range of tools for coping with risk, it comes as no surprise that people see microloans as just one means among many for helping make ends meet.

Senegalese decision-makers and senior civil servants were active in setting up the institutional framework for microfinancial activities, with the help of bi- and multilateral donors. Three major microfinance institutions came to the fore over a short timescale, each with their own sponsors. ACEP (Alliance de Crédit et d'Epargne pour la Production) was set up in 1986, in the ground-nut regions of Kaolack and Fatick, with the support of USAID. Crédit Mutuel du Sénégal, too, started out in the groundnut region, in 1988, with its first headquarters in Kaolack; it was sponsored by the Frenh cooperation service. In contrast, PAMECAS (Partenariat pour la Mobilisation de l'Epargne et le Crédit), backed by the Canadian International Development Agency, focused from its very outset in 1995 on the suburban population of the capital in Pikine and Rufisque. Its management backed MFIs which seemed to have quick growth prospects and which preferably were in regions not covered by 'formal' financial institutions (Ouedraogo and Gentil 2008: 167).

Sponsors' ambitions were twofold: they were keen to boost their own model of microfinance, and to increase their market share. This contributed to the dominant position of the 'big three', alongside less powerful, small and medium-sized institutions that made a local, but nevertheless significant, contribution to financial inclusion.

But prioritizing rural areas turned out to be economically unsustainable, because the primary sector is extremely risky, with one year out of three experiencing drought, locust invasions or other natural hazards. For this reason, ACEP and Crédit Mutuel du Sénégal increasingly turned to an urban clientele, transferring their headquarters to Dakar. Less affluent service points for rural clientele were thus backed up by urban service points that tended to do better. By contrast, PAMECAS managed to expand its activities into rural areas as the very result of its urban origins (Ouedraogo and Gentil 2008: 253–4). This offsetting formula resulting from 'extensive growth' allowed the three main actors to establish their dominance. High levels of subsidies from various donors facilitated the recruitment of skilled human resources, but also computerization as a means of better control, and boosted competitiveness. As early as 1998, Crédit Mutuel du Sénégal, ACEP and PAMECAS could rely on a strong network of service points, which accounted for 123 out of the 233 credit points across the country (BCEAO and BIT 2000). Two out of three Senegalese microfinance depositors or borrowers are clients of the 'big three'; their powerful position has not flagged over the years.

The institutional framework: from the specific nature of microfinance to a single financial landscape Senegal was the first West African country to adopt a spe-cific law on microfinance (PARMEC) (Lelart 1996). This framework gradu-ally came into force across all the countries of the West African Economic and Monetary Union (WAEMU). From the very outset, the specific features of the region's microfinance sector were cooperative governance and high risk pooling, with members' savings serving as essential resources for loan distribution. The underlying idea was for this business model to foster members' 'sense of ownership' of 'their' MFI and thus to help reduce fraud.

As this legislation was supposed to encourage the development of cooperatives, not only did it regulate fully fledged MFIs, but it also provided for a specific status for pre-cooperatives, the so-called GECs (*groupements d'épargne et de crédit*) which were generally coupled to development projects. In 1996, they had 8 per cent of the microfinance loan portfolio and 10 per cent of the country's microfinance clients, four in five being women, a percentage three times higher than that of women's participation in fully fledged MFIs (BCEAO and BIT 1998). Both types of organization were supervised by the Cellule d'Assistance Technique aux Caisses populaires d'Epargne et de Crédit (AT-CPEC), which was accountable to the minister of economy and finances. Resources were, however, scarce. Under the Abdoulaye Wade regime (2000–12), a specific Ministry for Women's Affairs and Microfinance was set up. The political consequences were twofold. Firstly, the new ministry shadowed the AT-CPEC and limited the dominant position of the Ministry of Economy and Finances. Secondly, it became key in the exploitation of microfinance and gender-related issues for political ends. By contrast, there has been a long tradition of strong links between women's associations and the political sphere in Senegal. As will be discussed in more detail below, this trend was more pronounced during Abdoulaye Wade's presidency, when female development project leaders were instrumentalized in order to mobilize the supposedly malleable electorate of (rural) women (Sall 2012, 2013).

Little by little, demand for microloans outpaced deposit rates, spurring on the search for additional sources. Some MFIs created their own bank, the BIMAO (Banque des institutions mutualistes d'Afrique de l'Ouest), which was particularly funded by the Crédit Mutuel du Sénégal. Other organizations faced growing pressure to move towards commercial banking. MFIs had no choice but to grow quickly to attract cross-border credit lines. But this entailed manifold risks: prudential ratios were neglected, while the supervision and training of beneficiaries became more and more haphazard. And while these factors inevitably lowered loan portfolio quality, the public MFI supervisory board (Direction de la Réglementation et de la Surveillance des Systèmes Financiers Décentralisés, DRS-SFD) experienced a lack of resources that hastened the downward spiral. The national authorities' verdict was pretty alarming, criticizing the MFIs for their 'weak managerial capacity', 'nebulous practices', 'absence of internal control', etc. (Sénégal 2010: 2). Many pre-cooperatives equally stood out for their poor management practices (Fall 2012: 32). There were over four hundred of them in 2003 and they were mostly based in remote areas, addressing the less affluent segments of Senegalese society. Beyond the difficulties the GECs encountered, to which the public at large were oblivious, there were flagrant further shortcomings, with tremendous irregularities festering at Crédit Mutuel du Sénégal, the most powerful MFI. A first warning sign of these irregularities became apparent in 2008, when an internal audit revealed fraudulent investment practices in real estate involving leading staff members.[4] The auditors were dismissed, but the wrongdoers were not prosecuted for several years, until further irregularities were disclosed.

In the second half of the 2000s, there was a clear and urgent need for in-depth reforms, which culminated in a new 2008 law on microfinance (SOS Faim 2015). Its main objectives were as follows:

- ensuring that most of the Senegalese population had access to financial services;
- consolidating and professionalizing the microfinance industry;
- giving high priority to prudential ratios, internal control mechanisms and the audit of the consolidated financial statements;
- protecting consumers' interests.

While the microfinance landscape is now open to for-profit MFIs such as limited liability companies, only licensed cooperatives are authorized. As such, institutionally isolated GECs have had no choice but to join existing MFIs or to disappear. As a consequence, almost 450 organizations closed down (Sénégal 2010, 2013a). The Central Bank has been more actively involved in supervision and licensing than ever before. To meet its requirements, a highly sophisticated information system to cover the most powerful MFIs was set up. These measures sought to bridge the gap between microfinance and the banking sector (Fall 2012; Holmes and Ndambu 2011) and to integrate MFIs into the overall financial landscape.

Undoubtedly, this new legislation has encouraged competition between financial organizations, especially at the high and the low end of the MFI scale. But the professional norms required – procedure manuals, computerization, geographic information systems, etc. – need infrastructure and training investment, as well as adequate salaries, which small organizations cannot afford, resulting in their high turnover.

Basic data on the microfinance industry in Senegal

Remarkable progress has been made in the overall availability of data, but significant gaps remain insofar as not all microfinance institutions have adopted a transparent attitude, be this towards the regulation authorities or international benchmarking companies. Unsurprisingly, this tends to give a mixed picture as to MFIs' viability.

Official data and insider information At the end of the first quarter of 2014, the penetration ratio of microfinance services was 15.5 per cent[5] (Sénégal 2014b: 5). By that time, Senegalese MFIs had approximately two million clients, 92 per cent of whom were physical – as opposed to juridical – persons (ibid.: 6). Forty-three per cent were women, which ratio has barely changed over the past ten years, and which is four points higher than twenty years ago, when data on female membership was gathered for the first time (BCEAO and BIT 1997). MFI clients are first and foremost savers: only one in five is also a credit taker (Sénégal 2014c: 3).

The most striking feature of the microfinance landscape in Senegal is a high concentration, firstly as regards the spatial distribution of MFIs, and secondly in terms of the institutions themselves. In spatial distribution terms, the MFI penetration ratio is by far at its highest in the Dakar region (28.3 per cent in June 2013), which is twice as high as the national penetration ratio (Sénégal 2013b: 7). While one out of five Senegalese people lives in the Dakar region, approximately 50 per cent of all MFI members are concentrated there. It is roughly the same proportion for loan portfolios and savings. In the Dakar region, 85 per cent of the savings and loan portfolios are in the capital. The penetration rate is lowest in regions such as Matam, Kolda and Fatick, which are considered to be the least affluent regions in the country (Sénégal 2013c).

As far as institutional concentration is concerned, there is a wide discrepancy between the institutions, with some powerful ones on the one hand, and a host of small MFIs on the other. Over the years, the 'big three' have successfully consolidated their leading position. Currently, four out of five microfinance members and three out of five active borrowers are clients of Crédit Mutuel du Sénégal, ACEP or PAMECAS. These three actors make up 78 per cent of total MFI assets, 82 per cent of deposits and 66 per cent of loan portfolios (Sénégal 2013b: 4). The Crédit Mutuel du Sénégal has been a particularly remarkable case. Between 2002 and 2011, its loan portfolio registered a mean growth rate of 35 per cent annually, which is twelve points higher than the overall national level (Sénégal 2011: 6, 2013a: 4–5, 2013b: 6). Economies of scale and the aforementioned offsetting of service points have allowed the three main actors to face up to the challenges of professionalization and modernization. Crédit Mutuel du Sénégal has moreover benefited from refunding facilities thanks to BIMAO. In contrast, small and isolated institutions, mostly in rural areas, with less skilled human resources and poor processing tools at their disposal, have often faced tremendous difficulties, as the quantitative data shows. Between the two extremes of the MFI scale there are also a few highly active newcomers such as Microcred and Saint-Louis Finance. In contrast to the three main actors and the small MFIs, their legal status is not that of a cooperative, but of a limited company.

There is evidence that the Senegalese population has been adopting an increasingly loan-driven financial culture. While from 2005 to 2013 client numbers grew at an annual pace of 14 per cent, the growth in active borrowers was three points higher (Sénégal 2014c).[6] Owing to this, and given the strict regulation governing transformation of savings into loans, cross-border funding has become unavoidable. On a national level, the mean loan size has been roughly stable since 2006, at approximately 510,000 CFA francs (XOF) (US$1,040),[7] but the mean loan amount at Crédit Mutuel du Sénégal and ACEP has been at least 50 per cent higher. But as we will see below, these mean figures can hide a great deal of disparity. The primary destination for loans is trade;[8] agriculture is financed by microloans to a far lesser extent.[9] Half of the loan portfolio is used for working capital, breaking away from microfinance's original goal of funding small farmers and providing starting capital to petty commodity producers. Calls for the creation of non-farm (self-)employment have had little tangible impact, because entrepreneurial newcomers have usually lacked collateral for seizure in the event of a loan default.

As in other countries, the trend for commercialization has gone hand in hand with the up-scaling of the best-performing MFIs, bringing them into competition with commercial banks (Seck 2009). This has come about firstly by shifting to a clientele of small and medium-sized companies, the so-called PMEs (*petites et moyennes enterprises*).[10] In 2013, more than 4,400 PMEs received 14 per cent of the loan portfolio of eighteen MFIs, with a mean loan amount of around US$18,300 (Sénégal 2014c). According to our informants, loans as high as 50 million XOF (approximately US$100,000) are commonplace, the highest being 300 million XOF (US$612,000). It may be that MFIs extend credit up to 300 million XOF because there is no clear upper limit on the loans they are allowed to grant, unlike in other countries such as Morocco. MFIs can provide loans as high as those fixed by the WAEMU bank authorities for small and medium-sized businesses, namely 300 million XOF. This practice is all the more worrying given that defaulting appears to be particularly commonplace on substantial loans. It goes without saying that only the largest MFIs have enough resources to distribute loans of this size.

Secondly, up-scaling is also at stake when wages are paid by an MFI, after having been channelled through a traditional bank. There is no official data for the country as a whole, but insiders claim that one single powerful actor can have as many as 60,000 wage earners, which is 16 per cent of the country's 370,000 workers on a permanent salary. This service is quite a profitable business. Firstly, wages are paid on a monthly basis, which helps MFIs to plan ahead in their financial operations. Secondly, for MFIs, the service generates a regular income of 3,000–5,000 XOF (US$7–10) per month. Thirdly, it may be a route to regular saving. Finally, it opens the door to secured consumption loans, which may be as high as 5 million XOF (US$10,000).

As far as operating results and compliance with prudential ratios are concerned, there have undoubtedly been some signs that the microfinance landscape is becoming increasingly insecure. The net operating income was still positive on the national level in 2011, but turned negative in 2012 (Sénégal 2012a, 2013d). In the same year, only three out of fourteen regions recorded positive operating results, as opposed to eleven out of fourteen for the previous year. Dakar was affected by the decline in both years (ibid.). A temporarily high loan rate on one signature can be noted, as well as loans distributed to MFI staff.[11] What is more, the three main actors' financial position may be troubled in that they are experiencing a marked performance decline.[12] At ACEP, for instance, the portfolio at risk greater than thirty days (PAR 30) reached 9.31 per cent in the second quarter of 2012, as opposed to 6.81 per cent in 2011, which is substantially higher than the 5 per cent generally taken as the maximum benchmark. Other than Microcred, one of the aforementioned newcomers, all the main actors have seen a remarkable drop in return on assets and equity as a result of their falling net income. This can partly be explained in terms of the substantial increase in the allocations for provision for risks and charges, as well as for other assets required by the risk-based supervision. It has also harmed the operational self-sufficiency ratio, which, in 2012, fell below the critical point of 100 per cent at PAMECAS and Crédit Mutuel du Sénégal. The latter's debt-to-equity ratio reached 18.96 in 2012, as opposed to 3.96 in 2011, showing that the MFI has only a very small safety net for absorbing losses when all of its liabilities have been repaid. Globally, more recent data has tended to confirm this trend of relatively high portfolios at risk: in June 2013, the PAR 90 of eighteen MFIs was 6.6 per cent (Sénégal 2014c: 3). All this raises doubt as to the long-term stability of the country's microfinance landscape.

Lack of informational transparency The public supervisory board (DRS-SFD) is now in a better position to collect and disseminate information to observers and microfinance professionals, thanks to its sizeable staff of eighty-two in 2013, as opposed to thirty-six in 2009, the creation of regional six offices, and robust investment in technical infrastructure. But it has issued only consolidated data, which is a serious handicap for understanding the underpinnings of the current changes. While nine out of ten microfinance clients are known to be individuals rather than associations, there is no information on who takes out credit, what their income is and whether they are employers, self-employed or wage earners. Such distinctions can be considered to be of the outmost importance, because they are key to understanding the types of loans granted and their potential contribution to 'development'.

As far as loan distribution is concerned, DRS-SFD distinguishes between administrative regions, but gives no breakdown between rural and urban zones. Information on the various economic sectors concerned is also scarce. Firstly, there is little precise data on agriculture and the type of farms funded (such as small-scale family-owned farms, groundnut producers or agricultural enterprises exporting crops). This is in stark contrast to the authorities' commitment to promote agriculture in the *Plan Sénégal émergent*, the country's current vade mecum for economic policy (Sénégal 2014d). Here again, only mean values are given, rather than a more accurate picture of loan distributions. This is the greatest cause for concern because, as stated above, there is no specific definition for microloans, but only an upper limit on loans that can be issued to small and medium-sized companies.

The weaknesses of the data communicated by the DRS-SFD are due to MFIs' general lack of informational transparency. Insiders confirm that practices for withholding compromising information and doctoring figures to improve appearances take place in Senegal. Prudential norms concern, among other factors, the composition of the loan portfolio, as expressed by the percentage of dubious loans (portfolio at risk at thirty or ninety days), of loans on one signature or those distributed to MFI staff. Official targets can be met by subterfuge and dubious loans rescheduled. This means that they are considered as new loans, which helps to keep the portfolio at risk at ninety days under the 3 per cent limit. Loans on one signature or those provided to MFI staff are supposed to be kept under the threshold of 10 per cent of the loan portfolio. If ever the loans to be distributed come close to this limit, frontmen or partner organizations may play a crucial role. While the latter may purchase the loans, the former may be the official beneficiary. These 'informal' techniques are well known among microfinance professionals. They make the figures look better and may explain, at least to a certain extent, the tremendous variations in some ratios from one quarter to another.

Although transparency is supposed to be an intrinsic value in microfinance, some MFIs have been unwilling to share the most basic of data, seemingly viewing their activity reports as confidential documents. Websites – even those of market leaders – give only poor information, and are only sporadically updated.[13] This attitude contrasts to the commercial banks' approach.

A further issue is MFIs' reports to Mix Market, one of the data hubs for microfinance institutions. Although they are not obligated to make a report, MFIs' practices here reflect their attitudes to transparency. A substantial number of Senegalese MFIs publish their reports with significant delays, and the information given is becoming increasingly incomplete. This is all the more worrying because it concerns not only the small institutions, but also the main actors. For instance, the most recent data available on the Crédit Mutuel du Sénégal on borrower and depositor numbers dates back to 2011. PAMECAS has published no data on its portfolio at risk and write-off ratio since 2009. In a break from previous years, none of the three main actors submitted their risk coverage ratios for 2012.

Non-compliance with the 'rules of the game' is thus common. It comes as no surprise that despite the 2008 law intended to restore the soundness of the microfinance landscape, massive irregularities still occur. Their consequences can be particularly dramatic when market leaders are involved. This was recently the case for CMS and PAMECAS. After the initial alarm signals of 2008, further irregularities were revealed at CMS in 2012.[14] These included fraudulent management and investment practices, but also the creation of financial vehicle corporations and leaders' failure to comply with ministry recommendations. Finally, the managing director and leading staff members were replaced. At PAMECAS, irregularities were revealed in late 2014, leading to the dissolution of the executive management bodies.[15] In both cases, given their highly explosive character, official information was scarce. This also concerns potential legal actions against the wrongdoers.[16] To a certain extent, lack of transparency helped to prevent an open crisis in the sector.

Given this situation, one could assume that at least some managers are looking to hide the apparently unfavourable situation, as can also be surmised from the following statement from one of them in February 2013: 'There is a deterioration of the portfolio, which is not linked to a cyclical phenomenon, but to the very structure.' But as long as there is no credit bureau in Senegal, it may be difficult to re-ascertain portfolio soundness. To date, stakeholders including the Central Bank, the organization of MFI professionals (AP-SFD) and the two ministries in charge of microfinance have been unable to reach an agreement over the creation of a credit bureau. Diverging approaches and interests are at work, impeding substantial progress.

Growing competition and challenges

Microfinance's growing commercialization, the highly competitive financial landscape and risky practices developed by MFI managers have harmed Senegalese microfinance and led to malaise.[17] Not only have stakeholders such as microfinance professionals, senior civil servants and clients evoked this, but so have outside observers. Among other factors, this malaise appears to be related to the widening gaps between the high professional norms and everyday practices called for, the manipulation of financial tools for political aims and, finally, to the trend of downscaling commercial banks.

Squaring the circle: financial profitability and social embeddedness Ever since its beginnings in the late 1980s and early 1990s, microfinance in Senegal has been through broad changes, not only as regards membership, resources and distribution of loans, but first and foremost in terms of its formal rules, which are now meant to adhere to those of the market economy. While microfinance was at first roughly assimilated into the development sphere, it can now be viewed as a sub-field of finance, with a habitus adapted to the market economy. One of our interviewees, the director of a leading Senegalese

MFI, put it this way: 'I'm a banker!' Three decades ago, his predecessor would probably have said: 'I'm a development worker!' in order to highlight his commitment to social welfare. The increasingly high educational level of MFI staff members has facilitated this change. Credit officers recruited in 2014 must have a university degree, whereas in the 1990s secondary education was sufficient. The growing supply of relatively well-trained graduates[18] and the profusion of microfinance training have fostered these transformations of the workplace. MFI staff are put under a lot of pressure over targets for membership growth, loans per loan officer, PAR ratios, efficient recovery, etc. They are supposed to prioritize economic efficiency over social welfare. Their commitment to their employer's values is honoured by bonuses. MFI staff members' attitudes towards their clients contribute to eroding the embeddedness of economic relations in the local social matrix, which is one of the characteristics of modernity.

In society as a whole rather than microfinance as a specific field, norms have been changing at a somewhat slower pace over the past decades, from a material point of view, but also with respect to the formal norms and informal rules of social life (Baumann 2003). Although quite an affluent urban upper middle class has emerged, the living and working conditions of the bulk of society have seen only limited change. Those who make a living through self-employment, petty commodity production and small-scale trade face tremendous hardship. Carpenters and tailors are stymied by electricity supply failure, as they were in the 1980s. Organizational shortcomings have forced farmers to cope with irregular input provision and insufficient storage and transportation facilities. Petty trading has change dramatically, with competitive Chinese traders now based in Dakar, where living conditions remain poor. Public distribution mechanisms to compensate for volatile incomes and expenditure are as good as inexistent. It therefore comes as no surprise that small entrepreneurs are spreading their risks by diversifying not only their sources of income, but also their financial tools. As discussed above, microcredit is just one means among many for them to meet their professional and personal obligations. Indeed, in the event of distress over their working capital or consumption needs, people may use their in-kind or in-cash savings, obtain informal loans from friends or acquaintances, make an arrangement with a ROSCA, or turn to a microfinance organization. In other words, they do not necessarily distinguish between the economic andr social nature of motivations and remedies. This means that cross-indebtedness is commonplace, which can either facilitate or handicap MFI loan repayments, depending on how commitments to microfinance organizations and personal connections are prioritized.

To date, the various training workshops organized to 'teach the poor how to spend their money' (Guérin 2012) have not always been very helpful when it comes to bridging the gap between high MFI professional standards and what has been labelled a lax attitude to repayment. Low levels of formal education are undoubtedly a real challenge in Senegal today,[19] but are not necessarily a reason for bad financial resource management.

Blurring the boundary between financial institutions and political tools The embeddedness of financial tools in the social and political context of Senegal today is also at stake when it comes to public development projects to distribute loans. There is often a high degree of interference between the economic goals of job creation through loans, and the political goals of redistribution and gaining voters' support, which can have a spillover effect on microcredit.

Delineating microfinance as a domain is of utmost importance, in terms of the distinctions between microfinance organizations and development projects. The former have precise obligations not only towards their clients, whose deposits are partially converted into loans, but also towards their donors; financial profitability is the key norm. By contrast, development projects generally draw on public funds and grants and are above all tools used by political parties in order to enhance redistribution ... and gain votes. Senegal has a long history of development projects based on funding facilities. *Opération maîtrisards*, which was launched in the early 1980s, was undoubtedly one of the most spectacular of these schemes (Baumann 2015). It was created to fund graduates, mostly economists, to become 'a new race of entrepreneurs'. The creation of a single job cost as much as US$40,000 and not one of the funded neo-entrepreneurs managed to honour their financial commitments. While the government was unable to recover the outstanding loans, the defaults were not penalized. This set a detrimental precedent for the subsequent loan-based development programmes that were launched.

Over time, unemployment increasingly became a serious concern for decision-makers. Pressure, particularly in the capital's working-class suburbs, regularly spilled over into riots, finally leading to Abdoulaye Wade's electoral victory in 2000. The high-water mark of job creation initiatives prioritizing loan distributions was undoubtedly the Wade period, when institutions such as the Agence Nationale pour l'Emploi des Jeunes and the Fonds National pour la Promotion de la Jeunesse frequently had overlapping functions. These are just two of the various organizations which had an ambiguous legal status, paralleling ministries, and fostered subsidy-seeking attitudes among supporters of the regime. As a rule, the funding offered not only lacked serious planning, but also ex-post evaluation. The Senegalese Court of Auditors' reports are clear as to this: none of the organizations was in a position to issue activity reports; none could indicate who had been the beneficiaries of the loans, nor what they had been used for, nor their recovery rates (Sénégal 2007).

What is more, political interference was commonplace throughout the presidency of Abdoulaye Wade. As an example, several of our MFI interviewees mentioned that, when receiving public credit lines, staff members were explicitly asked to show favouritism to particular clients known to be close to the regime. Instrumentalizing both women[20] and young people was a well-known strategy of the Wade regime, especially in the run-up to the 2009 regional elections, when MFIs were set up on a massive scale as a means of political recruitment. There were close links between some MFIs and political elites, opening the door to high levels of permissiveness, and the avoidance of disciplinary sanctions in the event of non-repayment.

Generally speaking, during the Wade period, resources were regularly hoarded by the ruling elites, while non-compliance with legislation went hand in hand with impunity. These practices' spillover effect onto microfinance was undeniable, and contributed to tremendous distortions of detriment to fair competition and the health of the sector. But notably, so far, there has been no widespread collective resistance to this in Senegal.

Traditional banks: bending the bars of the iron cage Ultimately, if we want to understand the challenges MFIs face today, it is worthwhile looking at the financial landscape in terms of a continuum that also includes traditional commercial banks. As highlighted above, there have been no development banks in Senegal since the 1980s. Commercial banks, which are increasingly transnational, face fierce competition. In their traditional field, they have drawn closer to their potential clientele, offering innovative products alongside mobile banking and plastic cards, which have played a crucial role. An example of this is how two leading banks have competed for customers in the relatively enclosed area of the Saint-Louis university campus (Ba 2009).

Commercial banks have tried hard to gain new customers from the traditional clientele of MFIs, which has gone hand in hand with the risk of MFI employees also being poached away. This strategy is the outcome of the Senegalese economy experiencing a serious slowdown, in spite of GDP per capita growth. Indeed, the biggest companies, such as ICS (Industries chimiques du Sénégal; production of phosphate fertilizers), SAR (Société africaine de raffinage; refining of hydrocarbons), Sunéor (groundnut processing) are undergoing great difficulties. Banks have been able to grow only by opening up to new, previously neglected niche markets. In Senegal, this has meant downscaling. Compared to the Côte d'Ivoire and Togo, for instance, Senegal is still poorly banked. To overcome what is an obvious handicap to the spread of the market economy, commercial banks have created service points in secondary towns and opened branches in Dakar's working-class suburbs, Pikine and Guédiawaye, targeting families receiving remittances from abroad.[21] According to preliminary estimates, remittances from abroad amounted to 14 per cent of GDP in 2013, which is three points higher than official development assistance. Ecobank, a transnational bank set up in Senegal in 1999, has exemplified this strategic targeting of remittance beneficiaries. It has thirty-six branches across the country today as opposed to fifteen in 2007 and twenty-two the following year.[22] Not surprisingly, besides money transfer services, mobile banking, plastic cards and ATMs play a crucial role. On its website, Ecobank clearly shows its colours: 'Ecobank is committed to providing the underbanked and the unbanked poor with access to finance. We believe that prospects remain very bright for the microfinance sector, which is arguably larger than the traditional banking sector.'[23] 'Traditional' banks are thus increasingly targeting what can be called lower-middle-class consumers of financial services, who are potential MFI customers and are particularly at ease with mobile phones. High mobile phone coverage is a tremendous leverage in this regard. Indeed, in the first semester of 2014, there were just under 14.4 million registered cell phones in Senegal, which corresponds to a coverage ratio of 112 per cent.[24] The SGBS (Société générale de banques au Sénégal), the most powerful commercial bank in terms of balance sheet total, has fuelled this development by creating Manko,[25] a new concept for providing financial services to the lower middle classes in Pikine, Guédiawaye, Thiaroye and Yeumbeul. Manko allows customers to pay bills, transfer money, acquire loans and save money using their mobile phones. This mobile banking tool was inspired by the Kenyan M-Pesa scheme. Finally, a particularly proactive approach to plastic cards has also been adopted by the UBA (United Bank for Africa), a relative newcomer to the Senegalese financial market. A network of partners gives UBA clients access to 800 points, mostly MFIs, across the country. In a single month, 26,000 plastic cards were distributed as part of the pilot phase.[26]

While commercial banks have been downscaling as discussed above, MFIs have been involved in a process of upscaling. This is in line with the current legislation and its call for a unique financial sector. This can be seen for microfinance as the consequence of consolidation and a sign of maturity (Seck 2009). But it is arguable that some Senegalese MFIs are unequivocally straying from their initial objective of serving poor people in need of small amounts of money, as opposed to the more or less well-established clientele of fully fledged banks. As one of the members of the AP-SFD, the MFI professional association, put it: 'Some MFIs are quasi-banks targeting a vulnerable population.' This is a cause for concern for two reasons. On the one hand, MFI professionals do not necessarily have commercial banking competences, which might explain the high ratio of default over higher loans. On the other hand, until recently, these 'quasi-banks' benefited from the same advantageous fiscal regime as grassroots MFIs, which led to growing ambiguity over the identity of MFIs and to distortion of the (micro)financial scene.

Conclusion

Since its infancy in the late 1980s, the Senegalese microfinance industry has been through remarkable changes, as can firstly be seen in the quantitative data, but also in the institutional environment. Today, one in two of the country's 14.5 million inhabitants has access to microfinance services, one in five of whom are active borrowers. It seems that financial inclusion is within the reach of a growing proportion of the population, even in remote areas. As for the institutional environment, tremendous reforms have been carried out in recent times, with control mechanisms being strengthened, computerization becoming widespread and the central bank having a say in the licensing of new institutions.

On initial consideration, unlike in the other countries discussed in this book, there has been no outright crisis in Senegal, in the sense of a marked discrepancy between legitimate expectations and concrete achievements. But seemingly objective criteria have certainly pointed to a decline in performance and loan portfolio quality. Our field investigations led us to the conclusion that this deterioration has been both global and local, and that it is closely related to what we can call mission drift in the Senegalese microfinance industry. The growing worldwide trend for the commercialization of MFIs and the trivialization of loans and indebtedness has also affected the Senegalese microfinance arena, driving local stakeholders to adopt an increasingly for-profit perspective. This can be seen in the most recent law on microfinance in 2008, which breaks away from the social-welfare-oriented approach that was specifically taken at the outset. It therefore comes as no surprise that local microfinance managers have been actively seeking out profitable market niches such as small and medium-sized duly registered companies on the one hand, and wage earners on the other, as a clientele offering unprecedented opportunities for consumption loans. Interest in funding small-scale agriculture, meanwhile, appears to have waned, although there is a shortage of data for this. We have argued that the high concentration of MFIs and growing competition has not only exacerbated existing imbalances in the microfinance industry, but affected the financial sector as a whole, pushing MFIs to up-scale and 'traditional' banks to down-scale by addressing the better-off clients of microfinance organizations. As a result, wage earners and duly registered companies have been made priority targets by both high-level MFIs and 'traditional' banks. New technological tools such as plastic cards and transfer services have played a key role in this process.

The fierce competition has led to a certain malaise among microfinance professionals and their clientele, undermining the stability of the sector as a whole and especially of those MFIs that are 'small enough to fail'. This malaise is nourished by the impression of a growing discrepancy between grassroots organizations and quasi-banks – those MFIs which are 'too big to fail' – political interference, rumours about the limited soundness of actors, and scandals over fraudulent practices that have been reported in the media. The changes brought about by the current market-oriented approach to microfinance have undeniably engendered self-enforcing dynamics. The increased need for cross-border funding has brought the potential for an exacerbated market-centred approach for poorly performing MFIs to be crowded out.

It is currently difficult to forecast the future of microfinance in Senegal. MFIs might continue targeting wage earners, but there are limited numbers of them and, generally speaking, wage employment remains roughly stagnant. Given that there is no credit bureau, the rise in practices of wooing wage earners could lead to over-indebtedness, as a result forcing families to cut their most basic expenditures on, for instance, food, medical services and housing. So far, there has been no solid data on this phenomenon. Over-indebtedness appears to be taboo, at least in official circles.[27] Meanwhile, mobile banking could conceivably become a new niche, at least for the most competitive MFIs and, surely, for banks, which may increasingly rely on MFI service points. This change would mark a shift from a credit-focused approach to one based more on payment and transfer services (Beck et al. 2011), as, for instance, has been taking place in Kenya. Decision-makers favouring the integration of the financial sector may see it become reality. In this event, there may be renewed calls for what was labelled '*animation rurale*' in the 1960s and 1970s: initiatives targeted at less well-off segments of the population to encourage what was called 'development'. There certainly seems to be something of a shortfall in MFIs promotion of the social inclusion of the poor.

Notes

1 This chapter is based on written sources (comprising academic literature, doctoral theses, internship reports, official papers and data banks) and oral interviews. About eighty in-depth interviews with stakeholders from both the supply and the demand side of financial services, and members of public and private intermediation institutions, were carried out in February and March 2013, and in June and July 2014. Participant observation was focused on baptismal ceremonies and ROSCA meetings. Quantitative data was mostly accessed from official Senegalese sources and MFIs, as well as Mix Market. The preliminary findings were presented in Baumann and Fall (2013a). We are highly indebted to our informants, several of whom requested to remain anonymous.

2 For instance, *tuur* brings together women of the same age group with the aim of mutual assistance; *mbootaay* helps to finance special events; *ndey dikke* is for exchanging gifts. See Bop (1996), Mottin-Sylla (1993), Ndione (1992) and Baumann and Fall (2013b).

3 *Bukkimen* were a common phenomenon during the structural adjustment period. Their numbers have declined since then, although they have not disappeared completely.

4 'Epinglé par un audit interne, le Dg du Crédit Mutuel Sénégal (CMS) licencie cinq inspecteurs', *Nettali.com*, 17 September 2008; 'Micro-Finance – Crédit Mutuel du Sénégal – Audit: Les chiffres des auditeurs, les "armes" du Dg', *nettali.com*, 19 September 2008.

5 Of the population.

6 Over the same period, the population grew at an annual rate of 2.5 per cent, as did GNI per capita (purchasing power parity in current international US dollars). See databank. worldbank.org/.

7 Mix Market.

8 Forty-nine per cent in 2010, 53 per cent in 2011, 42 per cent in 2012 (Sénégal 2013a: 16).

9 Twenty-three per cent in 2010, 13 per cent in 2011, 10 per cent in 2012. (Sénégal 2013a: 16). On the level of the WAEMU, only 3 per cent of the total loan portfolio held by banks and MFIs related to agriculture (BCEAO 2013: 28).

10 Senegalese legislation classifies 'PMEs' as having an annual turnover of below 5 million XOF (US$10,200) and fewer than 250 employees.

11 Various issues of *Situation des SFD* (the quarterly publication of the Direction de la Réglementation et de la Supervision des Systèmes Financiers Décentralisés, www.drs-sfd.gouv.sn/).

12 As one of our informants put it in February 2013, 'The crisis of CMS is far from being overcome.'

13 The most communicative MFI in Senegal is undoubtedly the above-mentioned Microcred. See www.microcred.sn.

14 Very little information about the irregularities was made available to the public, which may explain why at Crédit mutuel du Sénégal – and more recently at PAMECAS – business practically continued 'as usual'. See also 'Un énorme scandale dans la microfinance: camorra mutuelle au Sénégal', *Le quotidien*, 22 March 2012, and 'Bamboula à la FC CMS. Comment le Crédit mutuel du Sénégal a été siphonné par ses dirigeants', *La Gazette*, 5 April 2012.

15 'Détournement au Pamecas: le ministre Amadou Bâ dissout tous les organes de direction', *leral.net*, 20 October 2014; 'Crise à PAMECAS: le PCA et le Directeur se lavent à grande eau et chargent la Directrice de la DRS', *dakaractu.com*, 12 November 2014.

16 Some of our informants claim that the informational quasi-blackout can be explained by the complicity between some microfinance actors and political decision-makers, particularly during the Wade regime.

17 In the sense of 'a general feeling of discomfort … or unease whose exact cause is difficult to identify'. See www.oxforddictionnaires.com.

18 Unemployment is fostered by high enrolment rates in the (partially private)

tertiary education sector, and by extremely limited job creation in the so-called modern sector. For details, see Baumann (2015).

19 In Dakar, two active people out of ten have not been to French-speaking school at all, and those who were enrolled spent less than five years in class; the situation is even worse in rural areas. For details, see Baumann (2015), which draws on official data.

20 Two main actors were the Association des femmes pour la promotion de l'entrepreneuriat (AFEPES) and the Réseau africain pour le soutien à l'entrepreneuriat féminin (RASEF). See Sall (2013).

21 Thus competing with PAMECAS among others.

22 Besides this specific clientele, Ecobank is also targeting agricultural enterprises and development projects, among others in the Senegal river valley.

23 www.ecobank.com/microfinance.aspx, accessed October 2014.

24 Autorité de régulation des télécommunications et des postes, www.artpsenegal.net/, accessed October 2014.

25 See 'Société Générale: lance Manko au Sénégal', *boursier.com*, 2 May 2013; 'Sénégal: Manko ne désemplit plus', *Le Griot*, 19 June 2013.

26 See 'Spotlight on Amie Ndiaye Sow, MD/CEO, UBA Senegal', *The Lion King* (UBA in-house publication), January–March 2014, pp. 13–22.

27 As a director of a powerful MFI put it: 'One can presume that over-indebtedness does exist, but we cannot prove it.' However, there is also one exception worthy of mention: on its website, Microcred calls for 'the prevention of overindebtedness'.

References

Ba, M. (2009) 'Les déterminants du choix du lieu d'implantation des agences bancaires au Sénégal: cas de la SGBS et Ecobank', Master's thesis, Saint-Louis: Université Gaston Berger, UFR des Sciences économiques et de gestion.

Banque Mondiale (2007) *Sénégal. A la recherche de l'emploi. Le chemin vers la prospérité*, Report no. 40344-SN, 2 vols, Washington, DC: Banque Mondiale.

Barthelemy, O. (2013) 'La microfinance et les difficultés de financement du monde rural: l'exemple des impayés au sein de la MEC Feprodes', Master's thesis in Political Sciences, Université de Toulouse.

Baumann, E. (2003) 'Au-delà des performances économiques: microfinance et généralisation du marché en Afrique de l'Ouest', *Dialogue*, 32: 13–31.

— (2015, under review) *Sénégal: le travail dans tous ses états*, Paris.

Baumann, E. and M. A. Fall (2013a) 'Senegal: The rise and foretold fall of microfinance?', Third European Research Conference on Microfinance, University of Agder (Norway), 10–12 June.

— (2013b) 'Représentations de la dette et microfinance au Sénégal', in B. Hours and P. Ould-Ahmed (eds), *Dette de qui? Dette de quoi? Une économie anthropologique de la dette*, Paris: L'Harmattan, pp. 77–90.

BCEAO (Banque centrale des Etats de l'Afrique de l'Ouest) (2011) 'Enquête sur les envois de fonds des travailleurs migrants au Sénégal', Dakar.

— (2013) 'Rapport annuel de la Commission bancaire 2012', Dakar.

BCEAO (Banque centrale des Etats de l'Afrique de l'Ouest) and BIT (Bureau international du travail) (1997) 'Banque de données sur les systèmes financiers décentralisés. 1994–1995', Dakar: PA-SMEC (Programme d'appui aux structures mutualistes ou coopératives d'épargne et de crédit).

— (1998) 'Banque de données sur les systèmes financiers décentralisés. 1996–1997', Dakar: PA-SMEC (Programme d'appui aux structures mutualistes ou coopératives d'épargne et de crédit).

— (2000) 'Banque de données sur les systèmes financiers décentralisés. 1998', Dakar: PA-SMEC (Programme d'appui aux structures mutualistes ou coopératives d'épargne et de crédit).

Beck, T., S. M. Maimbo, I. Faye and T. Triki (2011) *Financing Africa: Through the Crisis and Beyond*, Washington, DC: World Bank.

Bop, C. (1996) 'Les femmes chefs de famille à Dakar', in J. Bisilliat (ed.), *Femmes du Sud, chefs de famille*, Paris: Karthala, pp. 129–49.

Christen, R. P. (2001) 'Commercialisation and mission drift: the transformation of microfinance in Latin America', CGAP Occasional Paper no. 5, Washington, DC: CGAP.

Doligez, F., F. S. Fall and M. Oualy (eds) (2012) *Expériences de microfinance au Sénégal*, Paris: Karthala.

Fall, A. (2012) 'Les mutations juridiques et institutionnelles de la microfinance au Sénégal', in F. Doligez, F. S. Fall and M. Oualy (eds), *Expériences de microfinance au Sénégal*, Paris: Karthala, pp. 27–44.

Guérin, I. (2012) 'L'éducation financière ou comment apprendre aux pauvres à bien consommer', in I. Guérin and M. Selim (eds), *A quoi et comment dépenser son argent? Hommes et femmes face aux mutations globales de la consommation*, Paris: L'Harmattan, pp. 51–72.

Holmes, E. and J. Ndambu (2011) *Diagnostic sur la protection des consommateurs des services de microfinance au Sénégal: enquête auprès des clients*, Frankfurt am Main: Frankfurt School of Finance & Management.

Lelart, M. (1996) 'La nouvelle loi sur les mutuelles d'épargne et de crédit dans les pays de l'UEMOA (Loi PARMEC)', *Mondes en développement*, 24(94): 57–69.

Mottin-Sylla, M. H. (1993) *L'argent, l'intérêt, l'épargne et le temps. Tontines et autres pratiques féminines de mobilisation de moyens observés à Dakar*, Dakar: ENDA-SYNFEV.

Ndione, E. S. (1992) *Le don et le recours: ressorts de l'économie urbaine*, Dakar: ENDA-Tiers-monde.

Ouedraogo, A. and D. Gentil (2008) *La microfinance en Afrique de l'Ouest: Histoires et innovations*, Paris: Karthala.

Sall, A. (2012) 'Les stratégies et initiatives des femmes dans le secteur de la microfinance. Le cas du Sénégal', Sociology thesis, Paris: Université Paris Descartes, Faculté des Sciences humaines et sociales, Ecole doctorale 180.

— (2013) 'Abdoulaye Wade et ses projets pour les femmes. Entre parité et financement des associations', in M. C. Diop (ed.), *Le Sénégal sous Abdoulaye Wade. Le Sopi à l'épreuve du pouvoir*, Dakar/Paris: CRES/Karthala, pp. 283–308.

Seck, F. F (2009) 'Panorama de la relation banque/institutions de microfinance à travers le monde', *Revue Tiers Monde*, 2009/3(199): 485–500.

Sénégal (Rép. du)/Ministère de l'Économie, des Finances et du Plan/Projet d'Assistance technique aux opérations bancaires mutualistes au Sénégal (1991) 'Etude sur les habitudes et besoins des populations-cibles en matière d'épargne et de crédit et sur l'intermédiation financière informelle au Sénégal', Dakar: Cellule ATOBMS, June.

Sénégal (Rép. du)/Ministère des Petites et Moyennes Entreprises, de l'Entreprenariat Féminin et de la Microfinance (2004)

'Microfinance. Lettre de politique sectorielle. Stratégie de plan d'action 2005–2010', Dakar.

Sénégal (Rép. du)/Cour des comptes (2007) 'Le Rapport public 2005', Dakar.

Sénégal (Rép. du)/Ministère de la Famille, de l'Entreprenariat Féminin et de la Microfinance/Ministère des Finances (2008) 'Document actualisé de politique sectorielle de la microfinance et plan d'action', Dakar.

Sénégal (Rép. du)/Ministère de l'Économie et des Finances, Direction de la Réglementation et de la Supervision des Systèmes Financiers Décentralisés (2010) 'Plan d'assainissement du secteur de la microfinance', Dakar.

Sénégal (Rép. du)/Ministère de l'Entreprenariat Féminin et de la Microfinance/Ministère des Finances (2011) 'Etude diagnostique. Protection des consommateurs de services de microfinance au Sénégal', Report by D. Brouwers, D. Mbengue, L. Lhériau, Dakar.

Sénégal (Rép. du)/Ministère de l'Économie et des Finances, Direction de la Réglementation et de la Supervision des Systèmes Financiers Décentralisés (2012a) 'Données consolidées des systèmes financiers décentralisés par régions. 2011', Dakar.

Sénégal (Rép. du)/Ministère de l'Économie et des Finances (2012b) *SNDES 2013–2017. Stratégie nationale de développement économique et social*, Dakar.

Sénégal (Rép. du)/Ministère de l'Économie et des Finances, Direction de la Réglementation et de la Supervision des Systèmes Financiers Décentralisés (2013a) 'Rapport annuel 2012', Dakar.

Sénégal (Rép. du)/Ministère de la Femme, de l'Enfance et de l'Entreprenariat féminin/ Direction de la microfinance (2013b)

'Rapport sur la situation globale du secteur au 31 décembre 2012', Dakar.

Sénégal (Rép. du)/Ministère de l'Économie et des Finances, Agence nationale de la Statistique et de la Démographie (2013c) 'Deuxième enquête de suivi de la pauvreté au Sénégal (ESPS-II 2011)', Dakar.

Sénégal (Rép. du)/Ministère de l'Économie et des Finances, Direction de la Réglementation et de la Supervision des Systèmes Financiers Décentralisés (2013d) 'Données consolidées des systèmes financiers décentralisés par régions. 2012', Dakar.

Sénégal (Rép. du)/Ministère de l'Économie et des Finances, Direction de la Réglementation et de la Supervision des Systèmes Financiers Décentralisés (2014a) 'Rapport annuel 2013', Dakar.

Sénégal (Rép. du)/Ministère de l'Économie et des Finances, Direction de la Réglementation et de la Supervision des Systèmes Financiers Décentralisés (2014b) 'Situation des SFD. 2014 Trimestre 1', Dakar.

Sénégal (Rép. du)/Ministère de l'Entreprenariat Féminin et de la Microfinance/Direction de la Microfinance (2014c) 'Rapport sur la situation du secteur au 31 décembre 2013', Dakar.

Sénégal (Rép. du) (2014d) 'Plan Sénégal émergent', Dakar.

Sénégal (Rép. du)/Ministère de l'Économie, des Finances et du Plan/Agence nationale de la statistique et de la démographie (2014e) *Recensement générale de la population et de l'habitat, de l'agriculture et de l'élevage*, Dakar.

SOS Faim (2015) *Zoom microfinance. Effets de la réglementation en microfinance: le cas de l'Afrique de l'Ouest*, 43, Brussels.

Tellez, A. C. (2012) 'The role of credit officers in over-indebtedness. The case of MEC FEPRODES in Senegal', Master's thesis, Brussels: Université Libre de Bruxelles.

8 | *NO PAGO*, A SOCIAL MOVEMENT AGAINST MICROCREDIT INSTITUTIONS IN NICARAGUA

Jean-Michel Servet

In 2007, Nicaragua entered one of the biggest crises the microcredit sector has seen.[1] Like the Andhra Pradesh crisis in 2010, the Nicaraguan crisis was the subject of media coverage far beyond the country's borders, albeit to a lesser degree. It has been largely misrepresented, with images of borrowers of the *No Pago* (Don't pay)[2] movement demonstrating against microcredit providers[3] for an outright cancellation of their debts. The press, investment fund managers and even some experts point to the government, qualified as 'populist', as having caused or significantly fuelled the crisis.[4] According to this perspective, the indebted were manipulated by the Sandinista government, led by President Ortega. This political explanation exculpates multiple sector stakeholders of any responsibility for the crisis, as does the explanation that points to changes to rural incomes. This chapter argues that deeper causes may be at work, such as fierce competition among microcredit institutions and providers of external capital, who pushed the sector's growth and subsequent over-indebtedness of clients,[5] and primarily examines the political and social dimension of the crisis, analysing elements that are distinctive compared to other crises presented in this book. We question the supposed radical stance of Daniel Ortega's government vis-à-vis microcredit providers, and then analyse the property rights social movement that emerged. The ability of rural elites to rally their clientelist relationships against microcredit providers is examined in detail. Before going farther, however, let us review the signs of the crisis.

Signs of crisis

The development of Nicaraguan microcredit[6] is marked by a post-conflict phase followed by a post-disaster period. From the 1930s to 1979, the population lived under a right-wing dictatorship and armed conflict, followed by a Marxist regime with ties to Cuba and the socialist countries of central and eastern Europe, followed by an anti-Sandinista rebellion supported by the United States between 1982 and 1989. Then, in 1998, Hurricane Mitch hit, devastating much of Central America, causing 3,800 deaths and leaving 500,000–800,000 homeless just in Nicaragua, according to official figures. On top of this, Nicaragua experienced a drought in the first half of 2001.

Microcredit, whether through non-profit organizations or, to a lesser extent, for-profit latecomers, contributed to the construction of a Westernized democratic public space, long thwarted by the Somoza dictatorship (1936–79) and the Sandinista government (1984–90).

'Liberalization' was not just political; it was also economic. The expansion of microcredit occurred as part of an increasingly hegemonic trend towards neoliberalism, both internationally and locally. Microcredit boomed in Nicaragua during the years dominated by economic and financial planning inspired by the structural adjustment concept, starting in 1990 with Violeta Chamorro's government, then in 1996 under Arnoldo Alemán and finally from 2002 to 2006 under Enrique Bolaños. As elsewhere, free market competition in Nicaragua was considered superior to all other interdependent forms of production, trading and financing. The context was marked by the liquidation of government-led financial institutions created under the Sandinista rule,[7] such as BANADES, a state development bank that financed agriculture in the 1980s,[8] and closed in 1997. The bank failures increased the financial exclusion of a large portion of the population and small production units.

Between 2004 and 2008, the three microcredit banks (Banex, ProCredit and FAMA) grew by 42 per cent per year. Membership in the country's microcredit association, ASOMIF, grew by 28 per cent. At its peak in 2008, the sector had a loan portfolio of $560 million (i.e. 16 per cent of all formal loans in the country), with the three microcredit banks covering $314 million, and ASOMIF members accounting for $246 million, of which $219 million was invested in loans for livestock and agriculture.[9] Compared to most microcredit sectors, usually focused on small urban businesses and craft sectors, the Nicaraguan sector was remarkably atypical. We will discuss this further below.

The sector's strong growth from the 1990s until the 2008 crisis was generally unhealthy, in that the sector's defining characteristics made inevitable the difficulties that would come. As can be seen from the other examples in this book, Nicaragua was not the only country subject to excess. This qualification of 'unhealthy' can be justified by:

- The lax regulation and poor supervision (no effective use of the credit bureau pre-crisis, no real financial education of borrowers,[10] weak internal control of microcredit institutions, little cooperation between financial service providers despite ASOMIF's efforts to coordinate the major non-profit organizations and dialogue with public authorities).
- Carelessness about the concentration of risk on 'big clients', insufficient debt and repayment capacity analysis of clients at the branch level, inadequate monitoring of loan usage (larger clients used loans to buy land instead of livestock – the stated purpose). The problem was not so much the large number of 'non-poor' clients,[11] but rather that default risk

was concentrated on a small number of borrowers owing to the high loan amounts granted.
- Widespread opportunism and clientelism.

The result was almost frantic competition to win market share, to attract investor capital and make new loans. Consultant Barbara Magnoni tells the story of a meeting with a senior manager of FINDESA (which later became Banex) in 2007. When asked what FINDESA's main comparative advantage was, he replied 'We are very good at raising money from foreign investors'.[12] Unfortunately, they were less skilled at getting their clients to pay them back.

After this short period of strong growth in client numbers and loan volumes, the microcredit market started contracting in 2009.

In terms of numbers of clients The portfolio of the major microcredit providers, members of ASOMIF, fell from 350,000 clients in 2008 to 297,000 in 2009 to 250,000 in 2010 and 241,000 in 2011 for a total number of loans of 246 million in 2008, 213 million in 2009, 175 million in 2010 and 163 million in 2011. The number of bank and *financiera* (non-bank financial institutions that offer microcredit)[13] clients fell in even higher proportions during the same period, from 166,900 in 2008 to 103,800 in 2009 to 46,000 in 2010 and 45,700 in 2011, for a total number of loans of 216.8 million in 2008, 159.6 million in 2009, 110.4 million in 2010 and 104 million in 2011. The drop in 2010 was sharper than in 2011.[14]

Repayment rates The very high repayment rates – considered in Nicaragua, as elsewhere, an almost unquestioned virtue of microcredit – plummeted within a few months. Between December 2007 and December 2010, the portfolio at risk over thirty days had, on average, climbed from 3.6 to 14.2 per cent. Analysis of regional data, institution-wise and branch-wise, suggests that these averages mask considerable disparities. Regional data allows us to disaggregate and thus better understand the causes for portfolio deterioration. Indeed the PAR 30 reached 40 per cent in some branches. Some institutions were hit harder than others, suggesting either a less resilient business model, or geographical or sector overexposure.

Foreign investments in the microcredit sector also declined sharply Microcredit investment vehicles, by far the largest source of capital for the Nicaraguan sector, were worried about protecting their own interests in the country, and did not immediately apprehend the difficulties, which appeared temporary and could have justified rescheduling and renegotiation of loans. Microcredit providers, in turn, driven by their foreign investors, demanded that their own borrowers repay their loans according to the terms of their contracts. Eight funders quickly deserted the country. It was not until the autumn of 2012 that a few returned, making 'homeopathic' investments. For example, in July 2013 Belgian investors (BIO and Incofin), Swiss investors (ResponsAbility and Symbiotics), Dutch investors (Cordaid and Oikocredit), a German investor (ConCap) and Luxembourgers (LMDF/ADA) jointly contributed $9 million to FUNDESER. Symbiotics also offered a new loan to ProMujer Nicaragua. This return of foreign capital does not cover the sector's needs. The country seems to have gone back to the starting point, when foreign capital was scarce.

The financial sector, especially the microcredit component, was dramatically weakened with the beginning of the crisis in 2008. However, the different causes of this crisis appear so intertwined that the same events are cited as a cause by some and an effect by others, depending on the analyst's perspective.

Daniel Ortega's government's supposedly hard line against microfinance providers

To explain the sector's decline, many outside observers immediately evoked political reasons. They denounced the intervention of President Daniel Ortega and his Sandinista ideology, still considered 'populist' even today.[15] His speech in front of indebted borrowers, in Jalapa (Nueva Segovia) on 12 July 2008, is often quoted as evidence of this: 'to protest in front of the offices of the usurers. ... they were right to protest against the usurers, but instead of being on the roads, they should protest and put themselves in front of the offices. We will support them.'[16]

The title and tone of Elizabeth Rhyne's article 'Microfinance among the populists' reveal a bias against the president, reputed to be a Sandinista.[17] We will explain later the reasons for Ortega's apparent, yet ambiguous, support of the debtors' movement. Six months later, on 26 February 2009, government support had tempered, at the signing of a conflict resolution agreement between the government, ASOMIF, the bank FAMA and the Caruna cooperative (Caja Rural Nacional). 'In Nicaragua, the no payment culture has been buried,' stated the president. This statement largely explains why demonstrators from the movement took to wearing T-shirts and brandishing signs with the words 'Si Pago' (Yes, we pay) to demand debt rescheduling.

What about the conflict itself? Should it be interpreted as nothing more than a pro-Sandinista, anti-credit movement?

During the initial phase, on 22 July 2008, a fire broke out in the offices of FUNDENUSE, a microcredit provider in Ocotal. Demonstrators had blocked access to the branch for the last twenty-four hours, demanding loan restructuring. They were strongly attacked by the riot forces of the Ocotal police, who fired rubber bullets and large amounts of tear gas. In the aftermath of a police charge, one of the protesters lost an eye. Some attribute the fire unequivocally to the protesters[18] By laying the blame for the destruction of a branch office on the indebted borrowers-cum-rioters,[19] this attribution greatly exaggerated the incident, allowing microcredit providers to unilaterally come across as innocent victims, and the demonstrators as dangerous insurgents. On 26 July 2008, the city of Ocotal was still occupied by the anti-riot police and TAPIR forces, while more than five hundred members of the movement had met at the farm of one of its leaders, José Andrés Castillo Urbina. Destruction was limited.

It is possible that the MFI directors, who generally live in the capital rather than in what are sometimes hard-to-reach municipalities, may have been misinformed about the conflict. But it was in the interests of both local and national MFI representatives to publicize – even exaggerate – these disturbances to public order, to provoke police intervention. Presenting the situation this way legitimized the inability of microcredit providers to meet their obligations vis-à-vis foreign lenders. The foreigners who had lent to them in turn did the same thing to those they depended on for their own funding sources. However, the media coverage and exaggeration could have had the effect of quickly amplifying the movement, encouraging more and more people to join. The indebted could have said of those shown in the media, 'if they demand debt forgiveness, why can't we?'

Branches were blocked by protesters, with staff inside.[20] Loan officers were threatened during demonstrations in front of the institutions, as well as during their recovery visits to clients. However, the violence was limited to zones where memories of the civil war between the Sandinistas and Contras[21] were still fresh, and where many people, particularly in rural areas, were armed. The movement took a harder stance when the government distanced itself from the protesters. Bastiaensen and Marchetti (2011: 18) describe scenes of violence in the Matiguas region: 'Bullets were fired at credit promoters, mortar grenades thrown at the local bank manager's house, a car put to fire, and the personnel and clients taken hostage and threatened with gasoline in the local branch.'[22] Nicaragua's microcredit crisis, unlike election crises of the past, resulted in no fatalities among the management or staff of the microcredit institutions, and few were injured. The 22 July 2008 demonstration in Ocotal could have degenerated and had the opposite effect to what external investors expected. Instead of a return to order, it could have led to a defensive attack against the creditors themselves.

We can imagine that the government, in supporting the demonstrators' indignation about the sector's high profitability (hence the accusation that they were 'usurers' by President Ortega), had not considered the possibility that the main microcredit investors would withdraw from the country. Maybe there was a desire to 'make the rich pay'; after all, international aid to the country is sparse and the United States has repeatedly conditioned its aid so that Nicaragua respects the interests of Uncle Sam. The attitude of neo-

Sandinistas may also correspond to a desire to weight actions in favour of so-called 'poor' people. The assertion of collusion between the movement and the presidency of the republic – that the crisis had political origins – appears erroneous. Interviews with movement members revealed former supporters of the extreme right anti-Sandinista Contras along with partisans of right or centre parties.[23] Moreover, Daniel Ortega and his entourage display a dual discourse; on the left is his wife, very much in favour of ties to Venezuela, while on the right is his vice-president from 2007 to 2012, Jaime Morales Carazo of the Liberal Party, who led discussions with the IMF and the United States government. Not one political party criticized the borrowers' calls to demonstrate against microcredit institutions, out of fear of losing the next elections. In Matiguas, where conservatives have long governed, there were fewer signs of calls for support of President Ortega than in traditional Sandinista strongholds. Rio Blanco is anti-Sandinista and emerged as the bastion of the *No Pago* movement. On 10 August 2009, the leaders of the movement reported that two demonstrators were wounded by gunshots during a roadblock.

Some members of the Sandinista party wanted to exploit the movement for votes in the 2008 and 2011 elections, to re-elect President Ortega, Sandinista deputies and other local officials. The government's relationship with the movement was not one of influence, whereby the government triggered, guided and manipulated demonstrators out of hostility to microcredit providers. Indeed, the relationship between the *No Pago* activists and the government was quite the opposite: it was the movement's leaders who strongly encouraged protesters, in municipalities where they could, to openly display support for President Ortega. Their hope was that this would initiate a process that would lead to debt forgiveness, or at the very least renegotiation of repayment over several years. The presence or absence of pro-Ortega banners at the street protests was thus dependent on the municipalities' political leanings. Sometimes the goal was to garner the passive support of non-Sandinista local officials, especially those at the National Assembly, so as to obtain favourable debt relief measures (spread over five or more years of reimbursement with a grace period of at least six months). Similarly, and conversely, MFIs lobbied certain elected officials so that they would pass amendments in their favour. The movement's leaders promised to mobilize votes in favour of the ruling party if it organized the cancellation or repurchasing of debts, the renegotiation of loan maturities, and a drastic reduction in interest rates and fees. However, it is important to emphasize that these demands were not met. President Ortega never officially met with the leaders of the movement,[24] and even declared the end of the no-repayment culture. The movement nonetheless achieved its main objective. Thanks to the strong support of members of the National Assembly, seizures and evictions were stopped.

A social movement in defence of land rights

Many large microcredit providers in Nicaragua made the fundamental error of targeting educated, relatively well-off and socially connected customers. These clients proved capable of organizing themselves to defend their rights, and this in a country where traditions of social and political protest are very much alive. Some of these borrowers went into deep debt, taking large loans from several institutions, and became leaders of the *No Pago* movement. The largest debtors easily incited the smaller ones to join their movement. This explains why the movement started just before the actual decrease in farm and livestock income. It grew dramatically when this decline became widespread.

It is surprising how many microcredit clients are qualified as 'poor' in Nicaragua by institutions or even the clients themselves. Some scarcely meet the usual criteria used to justify this type of financial service. One of the leaders of the *No Pago* movement in Wiwili owns a forty-room hotel and a small truck, and twice a month goes up the Rio Coco in a motorboat to supply shops along the river and collect from the shop owners gold that has been traded by miners against goods. This leader has a reputation for throwing her weight around at the local hospital to avoid queuing. Many of the movement's leaders appeared as mediators; they leveraged their client networks, in the political sense of the term. Some are small traders or artisans with modest incomes, while others are ranchers with large herds of cattle and extensive acreage.

Some segments (rich farmers, for instance) deliberately exclude themselves from commercial bank credit. Willing to open savings accounts, these farmers deem the process for getting a loan from a commercial bank too lengthy, complex and bureaucratic. With their income and land holdings, they could have borrowed from banks, were they willing to provide verifiable information about their land and resources, and accept the time frame required for the loan application process. Given the opacity around land rights and land acquisition, they preferred to go to microcredit institutions, where they could benefit from privileged relationships with the managers – relationships that were absent in their dealings with banks. Microcredit providers were particularly keen to open their doors to this non-poor clientele, given the abundance of foreign investors' funds available for microcredit operations.

It was indeed the microcredit providers themselves – by the nature of the loans they were giving to these clients – who created the conditions for the conflict and ultimately losses for their institutions. A particularity of the Nicaraguan crisis was the supply of 'microcredit' to people not only above the poverty line and in the middle-income strata, but to people whose loan needs exceeded tens of thousands of dollars – in a developing country, this is a level that is more appropriate to banks than microcredit institutions. This new and expanding market brought high margins (given annual effective interest rates of over 40 per cent). The high loan size drove down the administrative cost per dollar lent (compared to a loan of a few tens or hundreds of dollars). For many, the segment appeared both low-risk and highly profitable because it was relatively inexpensive; there were nonetheless notable exceptions, such as Fondo de Desarrollo Local, which already had a strategy to work in agriculture and livestock sectors, as part of their economic and social development objectives.[25]

It is important to note that the first signs of protest against the imprisonment of debtors and guarantors at the request of ProCredit and Banex (ex-FINDESA) were reported in Madriz and Nueva Segovia in March 2008, four months *before* the president's speech and the deterioration of agricultural incomes, often presented as the cause of over-indebtedness and thus the repayment crisis. This deterioration mainly occurred in 2009. The movement started, like many other protest movements in Nicaragua, by blocking roads. The first of these *plantones*, reported on 21 April 2008, blocked the Panamerican to Honduras and united 400 people just outside the city of Ocotal on the Rio Coco bridge. The aim was to elicit government support for the protests against microcredit institutions and banks. Two days later, the roadblocks continued, but negotiations between the government and the movement had broken off.[26] The roadblocks were lifted when a government representative promised that no one would be jailed for defaulting on loans to microcredit providers[27] and that negotiations would be conducted to reschedule repayments and lower interest rates.

The first demonstrations in front of banks and microcredit institutions took place on 12 May 2008 in San Juan del Rio Coco, Ocotal, Murra, Quilali and Jalapa, and fielded roughly a thousand people. Towards the end of June 2008, the movement appeared to have spread to other departments in the north: Jinotega, Matagalpa and Esteli. Protests in front of branch offices united several hundred people, swelling to several thousands in the capital Managua.

In this context, outstanding debt was associated with feelings of revolt rather than hidden shame, as observed among South African miners fighting for wage increases in order to repay their debts during the summer of 2012. In Matiguas, for example, situated in the centre of Nicaragua, a van patrolled the streets to announce the first meeting of the local *No Pago* movement. Farther west, in Wiwili, the movement bought twenty-five minutes of advertising on a local radio station, to call the first meeting of the movement against microcredit; it took place forty-eight hours later and led to periodic protests in front of MFI branches throughout the town. It is remarkable how fast the future leaders of the movement managed to meet each other. The movement's president, Omar Gonzalez Vilchez, and Vice-President Andrés Castillo, lived in Jalapa and Ocotal, respectively, some 130 kilometres apart, in regions where communication is often difficult and roads are not always paved. Vilchez was the former Sandinista mayor of his town. Castillo, a former member of the Sandinista Front, was a candidate for mayor in the 2008 and 2012 elections, the latter under the banner of the Alianza Liberal Nicaragüense, a right-wing party he has led in Nueva Segovia since 2008. The meetings and protests aimed to pressure managers and loan officers and make them renounce collateral seizures. Some local movement members travelled by bus to other municipalities in the region, to support protests.

No Pago can be analysed as a *social movement* in that it promotes shared objectives (Gaillard 2013: 44). It meets three criteria, which together define a social movement, according to Alain Touraine:

- a principle of identity (a group of indebted and over-indebted clients vis-à-vis microcredit providers);
- a principle of opposition (there is a common enemy, embodied by microcredit providers and what are judged to be high interest rates, abusive fees, excessive non-payment penalties, and unfair property and collateral seizures);
- a principle of totality in the sense of the defence of converging interests (farmers, traders, artisans, salaried employees) and a desire to be recognized by the government.

The lack of close and regular contact with clients explains in part why the accumulation of risk factors went unnoticed by MFIs. The movement's influence was initially underestimated by the providers. In some cases, risks were not ignored but concealed from foreign donors, who, deceived by the sector's expansion and immediate investment returns, did not pay enough attention to institutions' operations and the country context. The lack of understanding of local dynamics is illustrated in the *Comunicado de los proveedores of financiamiento internacionales para la pequeña empresa y micro* (Press release by international investors in small and micro-enterprises), published in *La Prensa* (a leading conservative newspaper[28]) on 23 September 2009. The petition was signed by twenty-five foreign investors, including five from Europe, eight from the United States and two from Costa Rica.[29] They asked the government, National Police and judiciary authorities to enforce 'public and constitutional order'. The text reflects either a misunderstanding of the uprising's causes or wilful ignorance;[30] for some observers, the target audience was more external than internal. The title of the petition, which appeared in the *campo pagado* (paid advertising section), is surprising when one considers the profiles of the most indebted defaulters – hardly micro- and small enterprises. Did the signatories expect the government to send the army or police, and risk violence, in order to allow MFIs (themselves indebted to the investors) to seize the assets of defaulting clients? There were accusations of property seizures by people close to MFI leaders and alleged corruption of judges (Bastiaensen and Marchetti 2011).[31] Some institutions had added clauses to their contracts in which borrowers agreed that any judicial recourse would take place in the town of the MFI's headquarters or an otherwise suitable place nominated by the MFI (and not the client's place of residence). This led movement members to organize a defence for those who faced eviction. The stipulation that legal recourse take place far from borrowers' place of residence could have weakened the indebted. Instead, it fuelled the movement, creating interregional solidarity and giving it a national dimension. Corruption notwithstanding, eviction rulings could favour MFIs only when the ruling was made in towns where the *No Pago* movement was weak, and where judges were unswayed by protests or direct intimidation. Were not the foreign institutions that lent to local MFIs without fully assessing the risks also partly responsible, which explained and legitimized their losses? The press release by the foreign investors came at such a crucial point that it is hard to imagine it was a mere coincidence: the adoption of a decree recognizing the unconstitutionality of loan underwriters forcing borrowers to renounce their 'natural judge'. The decree made it impossible to move trials into towns where the debtors' movement had less influence, or where, according to some accusations, judges were biased towards the creditors (corruption charges were filed). One may wonder whether some of the self-identified socially responsible foreign investors that co-signed the appeal of 23 September 2009 did so in full knowledge of the situation at that time; or whether they had been manipulated by some MFI leaders.

There has never been consensus among the people in favour of the movement. Activists from the Sandinista National Liberation Front affirmed their strong opposition to the *No Pago* movement and justified the utility of microcredit and MFIs. In Rio Blanco, there were even clashes between *No Pago* activists and opponents. Based on various testimonies, we estimate that, at its peak, the movement attracted approximately fifteen thousand 15,000 people. The total number of borrowers is thirty times higher.

In fact, the movement referred to as *No Pago* – and recognized under the name El Movimiento de Productores, Comerciantes, Microempresarios y Asalariados del Norte (MPCMAN – Movement of producers, traders, workers and microentrepreneurs North) – had at least three sub-groups in 2012.[32] It was above all a movement against imprisonment of debtors, and therefore a property rights movement (property rights have been a recurring problem in Nicaragua since the land confiscations of 1977–88). The largest loans granted to those involved in the movement had served to purchase land. This explains why they were so hard to repay, a reason entirely independent of the drop in agricultural and livestock prices, which occurred in 2009 (and not 2008). The land purchases were often independent of immediate productive needs, given the extensive nature of livestock farming. When the situation of the agriculture and livestock sectors worsened, with the government defending the interests of agro-businesses more than smallholders, the movement morphed into an organization whose efforts focused on renegotiation of all loans with conditions that were highly favourable to the indebted but much less so to MFIs. They exerted pressure by refusing to repay. In some places, especially in the north and centre of the country, movement participants were convinced that they could achieve debt forgiveness in exchange for votes, and by leveraging existing tensions within the Sandinista movement (this was especially the case just before the municipal elections in November 2008 and the legislative and presidential elections of November 2011).

In October 2008 the movement covered the north-west part of the country. In November 2008, it was in Rio Blanco and Bocana de Paiwa. In December of the same year, it had reached the eastern part of the country and appeared in the Autonomous Region of the North Atlantic in the municipalities of Mulukuku and Siuna, followed by a more muted presence in Rosita, Bonanzas and Puerto Cabezas.[33] On 11 January 2009, a demonstration of more than five thousand people in front of the National Assembly in Managua demanded that lawmakers vote for a moratorium. Clashes between movement protesters and the police took place that week, some forty kilometres north of the capital. The movement gained momentum when microcredit providers began to seize assets and property of defaulting borrowers. Borrowers fought back, faced as they were with declining revenues; or perhaps their reaction was opportunistic, and they were hoping for a moratorium on debt, similar to what they had seen in the past.[34] Together, movement members refused to pay their debts and called for renegotiation of interest rates and fees. To hide interest rates, which were above the legal ceiling, institutions charged very high fees; this undeniable fact gave a sense of legitimacy to the revolt, and to the president's speech in Jalapa. The high level of fees played a crucial role in accusations[35] against microcredit providers.[36] The sum of fees and late payment penalties easily exceeded one third, even half, of the loan. To make matters worse, late payment penalties continued to rise during the conflict.

Microcredit providers accused movement leaders of filling their own pockets by charging indebted clients for a document they would present to MFIs to renegotiate their loans. The document was bought for one cordoba[37] (by MPCMAN) and could be resold by local movement representatives to indebted members. In some regions, movement representatives asked for up to 100 cordobas (US$5) for a signed document, which had no legal value and could actually be accessed for free, as the leaders could simply photocopy it. Local representatives would give a portion of the money collected to the movement's national leader to cover operating costs. The same was done with a monthly membership fee. In addition, funds were raised to cover the costs of participation in events in other cities and meetings in the capital, Managua. Initially meetings were weekly, but were reduced to monthly intervals. A local leader was accused of having fled to Spain after collecting funds on behalf of the movement. Local leaders were also criticized for taking a commission in exchange for serving as an intermediary between an indebted client and his (or her) creditor(s) to renegotiate a debt. As the uprising waned, members appeared to have stopped paying dues; still, a large number of microcredit providers affirm that the system is still in place, enriching local and national movement leaders. The decline in dues suggests that the movement has weakened. We can assume that an increasing number of indebted clients prefer to settle their debts by negotiating a rescheduling solution, rather than continue the conflict, and work with movement leaders to mediate with the financial institution.

The moratorium[38] adopted after lengthy negotiations in the National Assembly (by 87 votes to 24) in February 2010 failed because the eligibility conditions (namely the period during which the debt was contracted) allowed only a small number of clients to benefit. ASOMIF members fielded 380,000 requests; a small number of cases were accepted and only 10 per cent of these beneficiaries ultimately respected their repayment commitments. Once it became clear that many clients still had outstanding debts, those who had signed an agreement to settle their debts probably hoped that the government would cancel their debts, as it had in the past for banks (Jonakin and Enriquez 1999). This was the message intimated by movement leaders, as well. The personal requests to negotiate loans, submitted to MFIs with a letter from the movement, allowed institutions to draw up lists of movement members. These lists are still used today by many to deny loans, even after clients have settled their debts.

The opposition to MFIs was essentially a movement in defence of property rights and against the actions taken by MFIs against clients in default. It did not have the characteristics of a widespread protest movement that demands broad social or economic reform. This is why the movement brought together both Sandinistas and anti-Sandinistas: it was a largely opportunistic attempt to protect individual interests. It also explains why not all the Sandinistas supported the movement.

It is difficult to characterize the movement as a democratic organization, with leadership designated by the base. National and local leaders were key to driving the movement, but they executed services more than they actually represented the members. The membership base appears to validate the choice of local representatives, designated by a national leader. It is therefore a hierarchical relationship designed to provide protection, rather than one based on solidarity, with a delegated representative; the overall rationale is to defend individual interests, collectively.

Conclusion

At its peak, the microcredit crisis in Nicaragua revealed blindness to the sector's functioning and its weaknesses. The survey conducted in July 2012 made it clear that foreign investors' finger-pointing at Sandinista politicians as the cause of the crisis – picked up by the media – in fact obscured a more complex web of causes and systemic failures. This analysis may seem harsh and may appear to underestimate the good-faith efforts of the many stakeholders interviewed in this study – both those who have attempted to foster human and social development through wide access to financial services, and those who have sought to defend indebted borrowers. But it would be wrong to consider the mistakes made as anecdotal or circumstantial, and thereby devoid of lessons for other countries.

We can also question what appears to have been underestimation of risk by industry researchers and experts familiar with Nicaragua. For some, this underestimation was due to a purely macroeconomic analysis that systematically equates a growing credit supply with positive economic growth, without considering the quality of supply, nor the difference between financial development and increased loan volumes (regardless of use). For others, it was largely due to data collection methods. To obtain a large quantity of information from clients, particularly on loan use, these researchers often relied on their privileged relationships with a few organizations or projects (one or two networks become their key informants). Rarely did surveys look at the micro or meso scale to assess all of the cash flows in a given locality. Collecting data from a single institution can turn researchers and experts, voluntarily or not, into vectors of the individual interests or dominant ideologies of the institution, for better or for worse. Insofar as the researcher is confused with the loan provider, without access to credit bureau information, it becomes impossible to identify cases of multiple borrowing or to know when loans are used to pay off other loans – practices that can be hidden from both researchers and loan officers.

Many of the elements considered 'causes' of the crisis were actually consequences, owing to a snowball effect. An analysis of the Nicaraguan crisis must take into account more critical factors than the purely political ones identified by foreign investors. The failure of microcredit institutions to respond quickly to the inability or unwillingness to repay was a crucial factor, as was the lack of governance of many lending organizations, both national and local. All microcredit providers, regardless of their charter type, were taken by surprise. And yet, as some branch managers point out, a simple comparison of the number of MFI branches in a given city compared to the total number of clients reported would have been enough to raise red flags. Just look at the proportion of clients compared to the local population and objective credit needs, i.e. the market absorption capacity (or more precisely cash flows to repay), and it becomes obvious that the same clients were borrowing from different MFIs for reasons far different from those they reported. If repayment capacity had been analysed not just on the basis of cash flow to meet a single loan obligation, MFIs would have realized that clients were borrowing elsewhere and were already or would soon be unable to repay their loans, in the event of a sudden economic downturn or interruption in credit flows ... some of which loans were being used to repay other loans.[39]

Despite, or rather because of, the existence of a credit bureau that sheds light on the financial situation of potential clients and their credit history (provided data is systematically reported), allowing providers to reduce credit risk, and despite strong pressure on delinquent clients to repay, portfolio at risk remains significant. Microcredit institutions may take several years to return to the loan volumes and client numbers from 2007/08 – if they manage to do it at all. Five years after the start of the crisis in 2008, its aftermath is still visible. It is true that ASOMIF[40] data from non-profit members show an increase of 13,030 clients from 2011 to 2012. This could be considered a recovery. However, this increase of roughly 5 per cent is weak when compared to pre-2008 growth rates. And it is worrying that of the twenty member organizations, only two have shown signs of recovery: Pro Mujer Nicaragua and Financiera FINCA Nicaragua. They have seen client numbers rise by 23,273, while others have stagnated or continue to decline. Financia Capital and PRESTANIC have experienced a drop in clients and portfolio; FUNDESER and FDL have see client numbers go down, as well (but not their loan portfolio). The rebirth of microcredit in Nicaragua tends to focus on microcredit as loans for crafts, trade and consumption; the low-income farmers who were so active in the movement, and rural zones in general, appear the main losers in these post-crisis developments.

Notes

1 The field research for this chapter was conducted in June/July 2012. It would not have been possible without the collaboration of ASOMIF (Asociación Nicaragüense de Instituciones de Microfinanzas), which organized a large number of meetings in Managua and throughout the country. I also thank the directors, managers and field staff from the microcredit institutions, banks, the credit bureau and regulatory institutions for their time and availability, as well as the clients and representatives of the *Movimiento de Productores, Comerciantes, Microempresarios y Asalariados del Norte*. Finally, I would like to acknowledge Florent Bédécarrats (Agence Française de Développement), François Doligez (IRAM), Davide Forcella (Université Libre de Bruxelles/CERMi), Jean-Jacques Martin and associates of the International Guarantee Fund in Nicaragua, Solène Morvant-Roux (University of Geneva), Yvan Renaud (Symbiotics SA) and Claudia Rocca. I am also grateful for the first comments received from Johan Bastieaensen, Eveline Baumann, Davide Forcella, Laura Gaillard, Isabelle Guérin, Solène Morvant-Roux and Helena Roux. It was not possible to incorporate all their valuable input owing to limited space.

2 The movement first took its name at its launch on 29 March 2008 following a meeting of more than three hundred producers, traders and microentrepreneurs in Jalapa (Nueva Segovia): *El Movimiento de Productores, Comerciantes, Microempresarios Nueva Segovia* (Movement of Producers, Traders, Microenterprises of Nueva Segovia). The leftist daily *El Nuevo Diario* reported on the movement on 30 March in an article entitled 'Alarmed by efforts to capture bank debtors'. Its second meeting was held on 5 April 2008 and resulted in the election of Omar Vilchez Gonzales, former Sandinista mayor of Jalapa, and Andrés Castillo Urbina as coordinator and vice-coordinator.

3 The term 'microcredit providers' refers to the range of institutions that offer loans in Nicaragua and which were the object of debt forgiveness requests by a large portion of their clients, starting in 2008.

4 See, for example, the posting by Elisabeth Rhyne (managing director of the Center for Financial Inclusion and senior vice-president of ACCION International) entitled 'Microfinance among the populists' from 11 June 2010: www.huffingtonpost.com/elisabeth-rhyne/microfinance-among-the-po_b_609167.html.

5 In this volume, see especially the contributions of Baumann, Fall, Guérin, Morvant-Roux, Picherit and Roesch.

6 Jonakin and Enríquez (1999); Doligez (2002); Greg et al. (2010); Roux (2010); Mendoza (2012); Sinclair (2012: 193–201).

7 Rocha (1998); Jonakin and Enriquez (1999: 164–5).

8 'Between 1978 and 1988, the number of peasant families benefiting from the Rural Credit Programme, begun by Somoza in 1959, rose from 28,000 to 80,511. In 1980, the figure reached as high as 100,700 before dropping to an average of 70,000–80,000 in the succeeding years. Whereas in 1978 the peasant farmers benefiting from the programme had only received approximately 4% of available agricultural credit, this figure grew to 31% by 1985. The newly formed state sector also experienced a dramatic increase in its access to credit after 1979, securing as much as 40% of the total, while the medium and large growers saw their share drop from 90% to 29% during this six-year-period' (Jonakin and Enriquez, 1999: 143).

9 See detailed data and results for the subsequent period in Bastiaensen et al. (2013: 152, 153).

10 For more on the financial education of borrowers, see the case of the Programa de Fomento de Servicios Financieros para Poblaciones Bajos Ingresos in Nicaragua, supported by the Swiss Cooperation (Gaillard 2013). For a more general approach, see Guérin (2012).

11 This is also seen elsewhere, such as Bolivia, where microcredit accounts for a large part of the financial services sector.

12 Financial Access Initiative blog, 25 August 2010, www.financialaccess.org/blog/2010/08/bubble-bubble-banex-trouble,

cited in Roodman (2012: 257–8), accessed 20 October 2014.

13 The 2010 and 2011 data do not include Banex. The figures quoted here are from the FDL 2011 report (p. 10), calculated from statistics published by ASOMIF and SIBOIF.

14 This is explained by Nicaragua's growth rate in 2010/11, higher than that of its Central American neighboors thanks to increased foreign investment flows into the energy, mining and textile sectors, and a rise in the prices of the country's main exports. Added to this is aid provided by the Venezuelan government, and migrant remittances from Costa Rica, the United States and Spain. Between January and May 2012 migrants' remittances to Nicaragua grew more than anywhere else in Central America (+13.6 per cent compared to the same period in 2011) to reach US$415 million. The annual flow of remittances sent by 20 per cent of the 6 million Nicaraguans working abroad (half undocumented) was nearly US$1 billion in 2012.

15 This term does not have the same pejorative connotation in Latin America as it carries in other parts of the world, especially in France. In some countries, populism is a form of social democracy that ties governments to workers' movements in different sectors.

16 'A protestar frente a las oficinas de los usureros. ... Han hecho bien en protestar en contra de los usureros, pero en vez de estar en las carreteras protesten y plántense frente a las oficinas. Nosotros los apoyamos'

17 See the articles by Bédécarrats et al. (2011, 2012), on the attitude of leftist governments in Latin America towards the development of microcredit.

18 For example, Bastiaensen et al. (2013), a well-documented article.

19 As is the case of an otherwise well-documented and balanced article by Bastiaensen and Marchetti (2011: 23, which states: 'One day later [after the speech of President Ortega in Jalapa] the office of the MFI FUNDENUSE was put to fire.' It was stated that offices of this microcredit provider were burned because its leaders were anti-Sandinistas. Our investigation suggests that this needs to be qualified, given the diversity of political opinions of those who work at FUNDENUSE, and even those who oppose it.

20 On 14 July 2008, ASOMIF denounced

the movement for taking hostage FUNDENUSE staff, in Jalapa, for five hours. To protect themselves, institutions closed offices in the city and suspended all new loans. The wave of closings spread to Ocotal and Quilai. ASOMIF members threatened to permanently close branches in some cities. Throughout 2009, fifteen branches ceased operations.

21 However, the regions where the *No Pago* movement was the strongest were not politically homogeneous: Jalapa was strongly controlled by the Sandinistas whereas Quilali was controlled by the Contras.

22 See also the eyewitness account by Bastiaensen and Marchetti (2011: 18, n. 22).

23 Bastiaensen and Marchetti (2011: 18) tell the same story: 'Authoritarian clientelistic practices are however not the monopoly of the Sandinista party as the No Pago movement with its many liberal and even ex-contra (and therefore anti-Sandinista) leaders has proven.'

24 Contact was made with people close to President Ortega and his wife. According to a confidential source, a dinner took place between the president and the main foreign microcredit investors, who had made known their intention to stop funding the sector if their interests were not met.

25 See the work of Bastiansen et al. (2013) for an analysis of the different objectives of MFIs; see the older works of François Doligez (2002) and Helena Roux (2010) on the relationship between financial and agropastoral sectors.

26 The first meeting between representatives of the movement and the government (Minister of Livestock and Forestry Ariel Bucardo, director of Fondo de Crédito Rural Eva Acevedo, and the director of ENABAS, Miguel Diaz) was held on 10 April 2008 in Managua at the ENABAS offices.

27 The law preventing imprisonment for debt was voted on in the National Assembly (by eighty-five deputies) on 12 February 2009. A few days later (26 February), an agreement was signed between the government and ASOMIF; President Ortega declared that Nicaragua had buried '*la cultura del no pago*'. On 12 March, the Matagalpa police held for three hours four leaders of the movement who had come to support the owner of a bus cooperative, indebted to Banex.

28 While the opponents of the *No Pago* movement affirm that it is Sandinista-

influenced, we can question the motives that pushed foreign investors to pay to publish an appeal targeting the country's authorities in a daily that systematically refers to Ortega's presidency as '*ilegal e inconstitucional*' ...

29 From the United States: Kiva, MicroCredit Enterprises, Calvert Foundation, Deutsche Bank US, Micro Vest Capital Management, Working Capital for Community Needs, Global Partnerships and Developing World Markets; Belgium: Incofin, Alterfin and BIO Development through Investment; Switzerland: responsAbility, Symbiotics and BlueOrchard Finance SA; Netherlands: Oikocredit, Triodos Ban, Triple Jump and Cordaid; Italy: CredSud and Etimos; Germany: Bank in Bistum Essen; France: PlaNis (subsidiary of Planet Finance); Luxembourg: ADA; Costa Rica: Omtrix and Locfund. It is not clear whether all the signatories identified with the message in the appeal. Some may have refused to sign the text as written, but found their names added owing to a 'technical glitch' on the part of the promoters.

30 Bastiaensen and Marchetti (2011) and Bastieansen et al. (2013) are among the few works that highlight the real and complex causes of the crisis.

31 Bastiaensen and Marchetti (2011: 17) indicate: 'There was, for example, one particular court where an MFI-friendly judge almost systematically ruled in favor of the MFIs such that many cases against defaulters were concentrated there.'

32 Andrés Castillo Urbina, vice-coordinator of the movement when it was founded in spring 2008, subsequently split off to form a new organization. In 2012, his organization had roughly one tenth of the members of the first. There is a third branch (*Movimiento del Norte Si Pago*), much more radical and mainly active in the central part of the country (especially in Rio Blanco). These splits suggested a weakening of the movement and illustrated the conflict between hardliners and more realistic members who felt a compromise would be necessary or inevitable.

33 According to a survey of MFIs conducted in the Atlantic region by Laura Gaillard at the end of July 2012.

34 Jonakin and Enriquez (1999: 162) point out that prior to its liquidation in 1997, BANADES had seen two debt moratoriums imposed by

public authorities, which benefited the rich farmers that made up much of its portfolio. It is easy to imagine that members of the movement remembered these, and thought the government would once again impose similar debt relief.

35 In July 2008, a few days after President Ortega's speech criticizing microcredit providers for their usurious interest rates, the movement received the support of sociologist and economist Orlando Núñez, as well as the leader of Frente Nacional de los Trabajadores, Gustavo Porras. See the article by economist Manuel Ulloa Arauz entitled 'El limit del interés permitido y el delito of usura', published in El Nuevo Diario, 5 August 2008.

36 It should be noted that in Nicaragua interest rates for loans between individuals

have no cap; they are often 10 per cent per month, especially for pawning.

37 In October 2014, one cordoba = US$0.05.

38 Ley especial para el Establecimiento de Condiciones Básicas y de Garantía para la Renegociación of Adeudos entre las Instituciones Microfinancieras y Deudores en Mora, published by La Gaceta. Diario Oficial, 13 April 2012, pp. 1868–70.

39 From M. Franco, 'Determinantes de la cartera mala en el mercado de las microfinanzas in Nicaragua', Borrador para discussion, ASOMIF, Managua, 2010, an econometric study on multiple borrowing based on credit bureau data, cited by Bastiaensen et al. (2013).

40 www.laprensa.com.ni/infografia/2665, accessed 15 September 2014.

References

Bastiaensen, J. and P. Marchetti (2011) 'Crisis in Nicaraguan microfinance: between the Scylla of business for profit and the Charybdis of clientelism', Working Paper 2011.04, Institute of Development Policy and Management, University of Antwerp.

Bastiaensen, J., P. Marchetti, R. Mendoza and F. Pérez (2013) 'L'issue paradoxale du mouvement social contre la microfinance "néolibérale" au Nicaragua: une analyse politique', Mondes en développement, 163: 151–68.

Bédécarrats, F., J. Bastiaensen and F. Doligez (2011) 'Nouvelles Gauches et inclusion financière: la microfinance contestée en Bolivie, en Équateur et au Nicaragua', Critique internationale, 52: 129–53.

— (2012) 'Co-optation, cooperation or competition? Microfinance and the new left in Bolivia, Ecuador and Nicaragua', Third World Quarterly, 3(1): 143–61.

Brenes, E. (2011) 'Complementary currencies for sustainable local economies in Central America', International Journal of Community Currency Research, 15: 32–8.

Doligez, F. (2002) 'Innovations financières, financement du développement et dynamiques rurales. Etudes comparées au Bénin, en Guinée et au Nicaragua', Doctoral thesis in Economic Sciences, Université de Paris X – Nanterre.

Doligez F., J. Bastiaensen and F. Bédécarrats (2012) 'Crises dans la microfinance au Nicaragua. Éléments d'analyse et mise

en perspectives', Techniques financières et développement, issue on 'Les crises de la microfinance', pp. 135–41.

Forcella, D. (2012) Payment for Environmental Services and Microfinance: Proyecto Cambio in Nicaragua, Master's thesis in Microfinance, CERMi ULB, Belgium, www.proyectocambio.org/, accessed 15 September 2014.

Gaillard, L. (2013) 'Les conséquences de la crise du secteur de la microfinance au Nicaragua: éducation, professionnalisation, réglementation', Microfinance in Crisis Research Project, Research and Policy Briefs Series no. 6, University Paris I/ Institute of Research for Development, www.microfinance-in-crisis.org/wp-content/uploads/Research-and-Policy-Brief_6.pdf, accessed 15 September 2014.

Greg, C., S. Rasmussen and X. Reille (2010) 'Growth and vulnerabilities in microfinance', Focus Note no. 61, Washington, DC: CGAP.

Guérin, I. (2012) 'L'éducation financière ou comment apprendre aux pauvres à bien consommer', in I. Guérin and M. Selim, À quoi et comment dépenser son argent?, Paris: L'Harmattan, pp. 51–71.

Jonakin, J. and L. Enríquez (1999) 'The non-traditional financial sector in Nicaragua: a response to rural credit market exclusion', Development Policy Review, 17(2): 141–69.

Mendoza, R. (2012) 'Gatekeeping and the struggle over development in the

Nicaraguan Segovias', PhD thesis, Instituut voor Ontwikkelingsbeleid en beheer, Antwerp: Universiteit Antwerpen.

Morgan, S. (2011) *Charting the Course. Best Practices and Tools for Voluntary Debt Restructurings in Microfinance*, International Association of Microfinance Investors.

Rhyne, E. (2010) 'Microfinance among the populists', *Huffington Post*, June.

Rocha, J. L. (1998) 'On the death of BANADES', *Envio*, 200, March.

Roodman, D. (2012) *Due Diligence: An Impertinent Inquiry into Microfinance*, Washington, DC: Center for Global Development.

Roux, H. (2010) 'Contre-réforme agraire au Nicaragua, instrument de reconquête du pouvoir 1990–2010', Sociology thesis, Université Paris I (IEDES).

Salgado, W. (2012) 'Apuntes sobre la ley de fomento y regulación de las microfinanzas', *Boletín Jurídico Tributario*, 57, Deloitte Nicargua, March.

Sinclair, H. (2012) *Confessions of a Microfinance Heretic. How Microlending Lost Its Way and Betrayed the Poor*, San Francisco, CA: Berrett-Koehler.

9 | WHEN MICROFINANCE COLLAPSES: DEVELOPMENT AND POLITICS IN ANDHRA PRADESH[1]

David Picherit

Introduction

At the entrance to a village Dalit colony,[2] a rusting billboard partly hidden by weeds and plastic announces that microfinance[3] could save lives. Close by, another billboard has been taken down and used by a family to reinforce the roof of an animal shed. On the boards are the names of famous microfinance institutions (MFIs). In the nearby town, most NGOs have boarded up for good. A similar scene is playing out in other villages and towns across Chittoor district in the southern Indian state of Andhra Pradesh (AP). Like a cemetery for development activities, the successive symbols of development projects are lying under the rubble of the business of poverty.

In October 2010, Andhra Pradesh's government passed an ordinance suspending all microfinance organizations. Four years on from what has been called 'the crisis of microfinance in Andhra Pradesh', MFIs, accused by the state of aggressive tactics in their commercial and for-profit banking activities, have lost millions of rupees and left the state. The crisis has affected the whole development sector and a new deal between actors has come in its wake. NGOs involved in microcredit have had to stop their work in the face of state control, with many NGOs now having ceased operations: staff lost their jobs and NGO leaders had to find new lines of work. Microcredit now operates through the self-help group model, under the regional state's Indira Kranti Patham scheme.

How did Andhra Pradesh, which as a state was long at the forefront of microfinance in India, become the first in the world to ban microfinance?

The impact of the state, politics and civil society has taken Indian anti-poverty schemes in many different directions. These have spanned community-based NGO models, state-sponsored schemes and rights-based organizations. Although microcredit is relatively recent as a tool, it epitomizes the shifting trajectories of sixty years of anti-poverty politics in post-colonial societies.

Microcredit has been credited with every virtue, setting the financial inclusion of the poor at the heart of addressing the issues of poverty, education, health and women's empowerment. From the 1990s, it was at the core of anti-poverty policies, with finance as a driver of change. The idea was that credit and an 'invisible hand' would lead to self-employment, education and empowerment, transforming poor people into responsible, self-starting entrepreneurs. Efficient, transparent non-governmental institutions delivering credit were meant to work completely differently from a bureaucratic, inefficient, corrupt state system.

The neoliberal recasting of poverty into a market-based issue hinging on individual responsibility made 'How to make profit out of poverty?' a major question, to which commercial microfinance was given as the answer. But the rise and fall of microfinance has followed a complex trajectory, in which a variety of actors ranging from global institutions to local politicians and NGOs have led an impressive political staging of those policies. The ban was therefore a major development in the history of anti-poverty policies in India.

Microcredit, beyond its role as a simple banking tool or credit delivery mechanism for tackling poverty, and as a 'small part of the debt that binds poor people' (Guérin et al. 2013), has moral and political dimensions. As a project, microcredit is laden with moral aims for financial education and self-responsibility, along with a culture of enterprise and violence (Guérin forthcoming). But development actors too have moral perceptions of the transformations microcredit has brought about, and of the social relations that have developed between their organizations and targeted recipients. Microcredit, along with debt, violence and dignity, are assessed, legitimized and contested through moral values, which as Shah (2009) and Fassin (2009) argue, are plural, historically constituted, and managed in conjunction with power relations. What is taken to be 'good microcredit' is not fixed over time, and tends to reveal competing perspectives over the financialization of development and the role of politics on local levels.

This chapter therefore explores the relations between politics and development in southern India, drawing on an ethnographic case study of the ban on microfinance in Andhra Pradesh. By investigating the local histories of microcredit and MFIs, it looks at how the conflicting moral and political meanings development actors (the state, NGOs, MFIs) have given to the ban reflect wider transformations in anti-poverty politics over the past twenty years.

A year's worth of ethnographic fieldwork was conducted over a two-year period in the Chittoor district, between July 2012 and May 2014. I spent time with and interviewed staff, bureaucrats, credit agents, clients, NGO and MFI employees and leaders. Extra data could be gathered through everyday interactions with political leaders as part of a project on criminal politics, and with Dalit leaders and organizations as part of a project on caste and development.[4]

This chapter's central argument is that the microfinance ban encapsulates political tensions between politicians, MFIs, NGOs and the state over the control of state resources and poor voters. As I will show, such tensions came about through the dual processes of the financialization of development and of political clientelism, which have strongly influenced the relations between organizations and 'clients', and the moral representations of development actors.

The first part gives an overview of the relations between politics and microcredit in Andhra Pradesh. The golden age of development from 1995 to 2005 is discussed in the second part, with an emphasis on the transformations of the development sector in the district of Chittoor. In the third part, I examine the tensions surrounding the financialization of development. These stem from the impossibility of emancipating the development sector from power relations, as is set out in the final part.

Politics and microcredit in Andhra Pradesh

In 2010, suicides, multiple lending, indebtedness, physical and verbal violence and usurious rates suddenly came to epitomize MFI activities in AP. Such incidents, which had long been considered local and trivial, received a lot of media attention in the state and beyond, ultimately provoking the government's ban. All this gave a window into the everyday workings of microfinance, even if the violence was not unique to MFIs. The debate often dichotomized 'good' NGOs offering 'good' microcredit and social work on a micro level together with good state-linked SHGs, in opposition to 'bad' neoliberalist microfinance organizations (rather than efficient, transparent MFIs in contrast to small organizations).

To examine these distinctions, we must look at how microcredit came about in AP. Taylor (2011) has convincingly linked the growth of microcredit to agrarian changes that stimulated demand for credit, as such refuting the so-called 'natural' demand of the poor for financial inclusion. But microcredit could only grow with the support of the state, in a reminder of how power matters in development issues (Harriss 2009; Mosse 2010). At this point, it is worth looking at how the financialization of development has been linked to politics in a process dating back to the origins of microcredit, involving NGOs, SHGs and MFIs.

Politics' influence on the development of microcredit has mostly been discussed in relation to the global architecture of neoliberal policies. Weber (2001) made a key point by showing how the major global organizations' agendas had transformed anti-poverty policies into banking activities. Yerramilli (2013) relates the microfinance ban to World Bank policies, as well as to state-level politics, showing how caste-based politics and clientelism affected microcredit politics. But few studies have taken into account the concrete impact of local politics and financialization on the everyday practices of NGOs and MFIs.

Microcredit has often been portrayed as a form of alternative economics based on solidarity and inclusion, and part of a wider set of social work (Servet

2006). This viewpoint continues to influence the distinctions made between community-based models of NGOs, state-linked SHGs and commercial microfinance purportedly based on impersonal market relations (Sriram 2010). But these distinctions tend to conceal a more generalized process of financialization in development that is driven by assumptions that poor people strongly wish for financial inclusion, and that providing credit to the rural poor should be at the heart of anti-poverty policies. Broader studies have looked at how politics interferes with microcredit, in a bid to understand the local relations between development, power and politics (Pattenden 2010; Edward and Olsen 2006).

Lending money to the poor to tackle poverty is a political choice which took shape in AP thirty years ago, as Watson (2012) discusses. The Integrated Rural Development Programme (IRDP) set up in 1978 focused on small-scale farmers and rural poor households, offering credit through commercial banks. This failed initiative opened the way to a sub-scheme, Development of Women and Children in Rural Areas (DWCRA). This targeted women, who were put together into groups of fifteen to twenty, as was a later key feature of the self-help groups (SHGs). But DWCRA regularly switched its focus, from cooperatives to small, individual businesses, and to loans as a replacement for grants (Watson 2012: 112–13). And from the mid-1980s, NGOs also developed their own community-based models of microcredit.

A major shift came with Chandrababu Naidu, who was chief minister from 1994 to 2004 and a driver of neoliberal reforms in AP using World Bank sponsorship, making the mid-1990s a key growth period for microcredit. Naidu managed to bring together different initiatives, along with groups of women, village-based models and individual loans. He transformed DWCRA into a credit programme for women (one of his main political targets), giving anti-poverty schemes a gendered face (Rao 2008). Microcredit, at the expense of pro-labour policies and universal rights for the poor, soon became the flagship theme of the liberalization process, in a way designed to transform the state from a provider into a facilitator.

Microcredit was given local names and a 'myth of origin' fitting the idea of it emerging from grassroot movements. For example, in 1991, a women-led anti-arrack (local rum) campaign in a small village grew throughout the state. The story goes that this campaign against arrack vendors chose the slogan 'Save one rupee a day'. They advocated saving (*podupu Lakshmi*) what men would have spent on alcohol each day, in order to build collective infrastructures in villages (Pande 2000). As has been discussed elsewhere (Reddy and Patnaik 1993; Suri 2002), alcohol continued to be tolerated (as a major source of funding for political parties) and most of the women's political demands were dropped (Jakimow and Kilby 2006). But the campaign met with a lot of political support, which Naidu linked to the promotion of microcredit. It was a huge popular success: according to the AP government, the number of

SHGs rose from 10,000 in 1994 to 365,000 in 2001. Eight million women were mobilized over fifteen years, giving AP the biggest programme in India (Taylor 2011).

Microcredit grew hand in hand with the state-sponsored welfare schemes that were launched in Andhra Pradesh in the wider context of political clientelism. Politics in AP revolves around two major caste-based political parties, the Telugu Desam Party – TDP – supported by the Kammas and the Congress Party for the Reddys. The onset of electoral competition with the creation of the TDP in 1983 fostered the rise of welfare schemes targeting electoral categories in the 1990s, which have continued to grow ever since (Yerramilli 2013). Naidu used SHGs as a way to win women's loyalty and to promote programmes (through health and education meetings) (Srinivasulu 2004). Political clientelism's role in controlling state anti-poverty resources and their distribution by politicians (Piliavsky 2014; Picherit 2014) has been detailed with a focus on the blurred boundaries between state and society (Fuller and Harriss 2000). Mosse (2000) shows how the state is multilayered, decentralized and reincorporated into different forms of overlordship. This is very much the case in Chittoor district, where criminal and factional politics are what shape everyday political life (as discussed below) and welfare policies, and where SHGs are partly tied up in politics.

Microcredit activities are incorporated to various extents into local forms of power. The development of commercial microfinance in the 2000s was a major threat to the political role SHGs had been given. MFIs, as pure business players, betted on the vulnerability of rural labourers in the wake of the agrarian crisis in AP (Taylor 2011; Reddy and Mishra 2010), entering into what was considered a 'market of the poor'. The proliferation of actors lending money and the ideological stand for 100 per cent repayment transformed local practices, pushing people into over-indebtedness (Guérin et al. 2013). Smaller NGOs faced huge competition from MFIs and state-sponsored welfare schemes in what they had seen as 'their territories'. But the major threat to clientelist politics was the growing influence of MFI leaders supposedly in a position to link up to hundreds of thousands of clients-cum-voters.

But making strict distinctions between NGOs, SHGs and MFIs is of little help in understanding their complex articulations, and the relations between the financialization of development and politics. Microfinance has in fact firmed up a financialization process that began with SHGs and NGOs. The poor's demand for financial inclusion has been the driving force behind most of the politics of NGOs (and later MFIs). Many NGO leaders have accepted the rhetoric and aims of neoliberal principles for transforming practices (Jaoul 2012; Pattenden 2010). Microcredit, which could once be a way for NGOs to sustain their social work, became an end in itself, which was reinforced in AP by the decline of funding from foreign donors. NGOs are not homogeneous, moreover. Dalit NGOs are not like upper-caste Gandhian NGOs, which, for example, promote a romantic image of villages with harmonious social relations. Such a perspective is thoroughly refuted by empirical data on rural India showing that the violence of caste, class and gender relations pervades NGOs' community-based models. My research in the district of Mahabubnagar in AP from 2002 to 2006 (Picherit 2013) brought to light an example of this: physical, sexual and verbal forms of violence were regularly used to deal with credit issues. The SHG cluster's manager was the village head's henchman (a local powerful politician) and was regularly verbally and sexually abusive to women.

The golden age of development: the road to microfinance

The district of Chittoor has a particular place in AP's development politics. In the 1990s, a large number of Dalit social movements, networks, labour unions, NGOs and caste movements emerged to challenge the power of the dominant castes in AP, Reddys and Naidus. Fierce debates between caste- or class-based movements, and between development- and rights-based organizations, shaped the local history of political activism. Most of the Dalit organizations were funded by international donors supporting pro-Dalit and pro-poor political activities. Huge flows of money sustained NGOs and networks, boosting finances and the prestige of leaders capable of attracting funding from Christian organizations and global organizations like OXFAM.

The 1990s and 2000s saw huge growth in the development sector. By the end of the 1990s, many of those NGOs started to set up microcredit programmes in rural areas as a way for people to become self-sufficient and to sustain other social activities (using a percentage of funds from microcredit), or to attract external funds.

In the early 2000s, conflicts between castes (Malas and Madigas) and between the leaders of local development organizations brought about the demise of Dalit networks. Those conflicts were also fostered by the end of foreign support: it almost completely dried up when southern India was pronounced 'developed' after a wave of government discourses against foreign subsidies. This reinforced microcredit as a major NGO activity, which soon faced competition from MFIs. Major MFIs managed by businessmen ('all from upper castes', as Dalit NGO leaders often stress) came onto the market with aggressive commercial terms, while the NGOs faced state forms of harassment against their political activism.

Banning microfinance was a late sign of the end of the golden age of development. The district's rare remaining active NGOs became subcontractors with cheap staff to implement non-political state programmes (orphanages, etc.). This contrasted greatly with the preceding period.

Commercial microfinance does not fall outside these processes, however, but is the concrete expression of a move towards the neoliberal financialization of poverty. Microcredit was often the first step in the process. The case of the Financial Services Society (FSS) exemplifies the social, economic and judicial trajectories of some NGOs over the past two decades.

FSS is based in Chittoor and typifies how some NGOs have transformed into business organizations. In 1982, Gopal Reddy, who was then in his twenties, joined the Indian Rural Reconstruction (IRR) programme. This is a training school for encouraging young people to found rural NGOs. After a few years of training, he started his own NGO (Rural Development Organization – RDO) in 1986 in the constituency of the leader of the regionalist Telugu Desam Party (TDP), Chandrababu Naidu. His NGO implemented various land and water conservation programmes, as well as vocational skills development in a few hamlets, receiving national and international subsidies.

The IRR was a key player in developing rural NGOs, and a lot of the district's NGOs leaders took the same route. Other, Christian, organizations also encouraged young educated Dalits to go into this sector. It offered a platform for influencing political debate to Dalits who had absolutely no chance of finding a place in the powerful political parties.

In the 1990s, a major UK development organization offered training courses on financial independence for NGOs in India, which Gopal Reddy, the head of RDO, took closely to heart. He became independent in three years by shifting his activities to credit and savings. In line with this new focus, he used the juridical provisions available for him to turn his NGO into a Mutually Aided Cooperative Society – MACS. To achieve sustainability for his organization, he expanded his financial activity from a few to 100 hamlets in five sub-districts (*Mandals*), on the advice of his influential IRR mentors.

Financial services thus became the operational focus of his organization, just as with other NGOs in the district and beyond.

Krishnamurthi, who is now the only freelance 'development project'[5] proposal writer for all the NGOs in one sub-district, recalls well how a single page with key development words would suffice to attract money: 'It's always the same story, isn't it? A poor woman who is married to a violent, alcoholic man in an Indian village and who needs a loan to start her own economic activity. Thanks to SHGs, she can take part in microcredit meetings and invest in a productive activity to create her own employment. Easy! I just had to change the names to get the funding!'

This discourse stresses how instrumental a perspective has been taken on development, notwithstanding the decline of NGOs. Chittoor development actors are aware of the political necessity to keep up the appearance of autonomy and resistance to foreign-donor-imposed themes. They must find a balance between taking advantage of the easy funds available and fending off moral criticism for the transformations of the field. Gorrappa, a former NGO leader, discussed the risks of enjoying those facilities, while justifying his choice in terms of the benefits for his children: 'With a single email, they [foreign donors] funded a car and three bikes. I once mentioned the cost of my son's education and they offered me three lakhs. How could I turn an offer like that down?'

Moral ambivalence such as this is the outcome of the funding which has dramatically changed NGOs' organizational structure and development activities, as well as their relations with other organizations. One had to face moral and political criticism from Marxist and Dalit activists who were calling for radical transformation as opposed to financial and technical debate.

The consequences for daily life were huge: report-writing, working using computers and recruiting English-speaking staff from educated backgrounds. NGOs' working culture was transformed, as were client relations: new offices, new cars and new boards constituted the visible signs of the success of NGOs. In 2003, Gopal Reddy's mentors (FSS) again encouraged him to develop commercial credit with higher interest rates in urban areas in Chittoor district. The resulting expansion was impressive. Gopal Reddy also used various legislative provisions to set up an NGO for his credit activities in the neighbouring states of Tamil Nadu and Karnataka: 'There was huge competition with Spandhana, SHARE, SKS and other MFIs. But in a few years we reached fifty crores,[6] sixty crores, like that up to on hundred, two hundred crores.'

In 2007, to cope with the growth, he turned his enterprise into an NBFI, a non-banking financial institution. FSS was born. Comfortable open-plan offices were symbolic of the growth of those financial companies: guards, computers and badges were the ultimate signs of corporate culture (such as in the offices of Basix in wealthy parts of Hyderabad), setting the tone for (not-so-micro) financial companies in smaller towns. The professionalization of the development sector, which was called upon to be modern, efficient and transparent, contrasted with the supposed amateurism of smaller NGOs.

Growth was, however, steady, with profits of 5 to 10 crores annually up to 2010. But capitalization was low and fresh investors were needed. Finally Gopal Reddy opted for a group of private investors, who took the majority stake and full management decisions in the companies they invested in (across all sectors). He sold his share in October 2010, a week before the AP ordinance was passed: 'In a month, microfinance collapsed and we lost sixty crores.'

As Reddy had always been the manager, he had no choice but to go through corporate restructuring.

FSS exemplifies the transitional path from rural NGO to for-profit organization. It was the very same people who started out in rural NGOs who ended their careers as MFI managers. A strict distinction between community-based models, state SHGs and commercial microfinance obscures those transitions, which became a sign of upward leadership mobility in tandem with with one's organization.

There is, however, segmentation along caste and class lines: most MFI leaders are upper-caste. But while such caste status facilitated the mobility of NGO leaders-turned-businessmen, their social backgrounds also brought limits: 'The activity was expanding so drastically that it required a professional approach for the future, from human resources to planning. More than six hundred staff. As you know, I have an NGO background and to some extent only I can control my people'.

Gopal could only partly rely on banking and state institutions to cover his financial activities. The growth rate of activities made controlling people more difficult, and the impressive repayment rates were kept up by encouraging loan juggling and the use of personal violence.

Kondaïah, a credit agent, explains: 'We know that people get loans from every MFI, NGO, moneylender and shopkeeper in their area! This is circulation; we help them to circulate the loan from one source to the next. That let me keep my job as I was repaid, and so could the other agents.'

A former FSS employee commented: 'There were no specific orders to use our muscle, but everybody knew the way to get the money back. We are in Rayalaseema,[7] this is a land of political factions and *goonda* -ism [musclemen]. And my job was to get repayments right away, before the other MFIs came to collect the money.'

The violence the credit agents discuss resorting to is a direct relation to the financial logic and political violence so prevalent in this area of Andhra Pradesh. The credit agents state that competition and the 100 per cent short-term repayment credo reinforced the violence, at the expense of longer-term ties that could have had some leeway for negotiation and compromise. FSS's offices are covered with pictures of its leader, who its employees, always ready to trot out his success story, call *guruji*. But as far as I know there were no official or direct instructions on the collection methods to be used, power relations being such that employees responded to the company's implicit demands.

Gopal Reddy conceded that 'there might be some excess here and there', but that 'our clients expect better credit delivery mechanisms'. MFIs pride themselves on achieving high repayment rates regardless of the local context, as a sign of efficiency. Gopal Reddy made a point of recruiting agents who were not 'local' – in contrast to NGOs' pride in their local roots and cultures of compromise.

FSS typifies the transformations of the development sector in the district over the past thirty years. It shows how financial activities have taken the lead in tackling poverty or making profit out of it, which has been furthered by the relative abandonment of political debate on development, owing to most actors participating in financial activities.

Changing social relations in development

The microfinance crisis pushed many actors to reassess the relations they had established between their organizations and the population they claimed to represent. In a bid to rewrite their history, microcredit actors pointed out moral arguments concerning trust and patronage, highlighting changing social relations in rural development. These tended to stress how moral issues went hand in hand with the financialization of development. 'None of us started an NGO to issue loans. In the beginning, we were talking about developing rural areas, bringing education and for many to radically transform rural societies. No one could imagine us talking only about money!' Ramaïah commented.

NGO leaders based their initial activities around alternative economies and/or social activities, but tacitly accepted, more or less voluntarily, the financialization of their activities: 'This is like a circle. You start, it works then you go on. When you wake up, it is too late. Twenty years ago, people used to show me appreciation for the work done; now they reject us, they behave like clients. Everyone here has forgotten how and why we have done all this.'

This somewhat pessimistic perspective is widespread: the neoliberalization of development issues has been extremely fast and swept along both organizations and clients (Pattenden 2010). This contrasts with the expected paternalistic relations between the population and the personalization of NGOs around leaders proud of their social mobility: 'I am a son of a debt-bonded labourer; I have been educated and built such a big NGO from nothing. I used to go to villages on foot to convince them at that time. Things have changed,' Kondaïah explained.

Staged social relations (garlands, touching feet, organized crowds), the myth of trust relations and local engagement (leaders working in their native villages are very rare, with most preferring to avoid family and caste pressures) and repayment schedule flexibility serve to play down recurrent forms of violence incorporating patronage, sexual harassment of women and honour threats, treating them as market-based relations.

The changing vocabulary permeating most NGOs working in microcredit was one of the many compromises NGOs had to accept. They talk about the livelihoods of 'clients' and 'beneficiaries', projecting an image of the poor as responsible, consumerist and entrepreneurial, and of their organizations striving to innovate. The money flowing into microcredit led to the neglect of alternative sustainable activities, as well as of social relations. NGOs built new offices far away from the village, invested in four-wheel-drive vehicles, and their leaders stopped going to villages. The gap between the NGOs and the working poor's expectations grew to the point that NGOs lost control, stressing the rise of pragmatic and miniaturized social relations. The debts people had to learn to juggle (Guérin et al. 2013) encouraged pragmatic relationships with NGOs at a time when rural villages were being demobilized for collective work. The changes did not mean there was no resistance, or that the neoliberal credo was fully adhered to, but they did lead to huge pragmatism as a way to adjust: 'We just gave donors what they expected to get and they knew it: could anyone meet their expectations? Every NGO had double or triple book accounts, every report was a fake: how could we spend time making reports about issues no one cares about?' the head of a leading NGO in the district asked.

The microfinance crisis heightened leaders' growing bitterness at the surprise of having people behaving like clients: 'We helped them for years and then they stopped repaying and treated us without respect. Since we have no projects, they left us. NGOs are all finished now; we have no pensions, nothing.'

Instrumental relations between 'clients' and NGOs were in evidence from the start of the crisis: the public discarded NGOs which could no longer offer sustainable social support. Criticism of NGOs supplying microcredit was nothing new and was directed at the changes credit supply had brought about: new staff, 'responsibility' for the staff and their families, as well as new relations with the population, as Ramappa, a Dalit NGO leader, thought: 'With our NGO we have always refused to do microcredit. I know every single person, their wages and living conditions. Even people who want to repay loans are sometimes in trouble. How could I force them? If I do so, I lose the support I have built over twenty years.'

In small places, NGOs could not get their money back, because politicians and *goondas* told villagers they didn't need to repay. This caused a lot of problems, even for NGOs not supplying microfinance: 'There is no trust relationship any more. We are bonded to them. If we don't deliver services, they move on. We are not responsible for the suicides, but we are paying the price. Before, they used to respect us, but now there is nothing left.'

Leaders like to reimagine a past where there were trust relations between a leader and 'his' people. This is the sign of a deep change of perspective on social relations among those who always claimed to represent groups. But it pertains to an ideological point which has never held true; most villagers have always had to adjust to the NGOs that settle in their villages and which they never asked for.

While NGOs have contributed to the monetarization of social relations in villages, many morally denounce the practices of MFIs: 'MFIs had no limits, they were all competing: how many people do you cover? What is your quote rate? Those were the only issues. The MFI leaders did not want to know about anything other than one hundred per cent repayment. So credit agents even stopped some funerals to force the family to repay the debts.'

Those public anecdotes well illustrate the moral limitations of financial activities. Unlike many forms of business legitimized in terms of services, proximity and/or redistribution, development actors attack MFI-led microfinance for being foreign, having profit as its sole aim, and of lacking ethics in social relations. Moral questions get in the way of assessing financial activities and compromise is legitimized. One major moral issue is a shift from the collective aims of development organizations (be these about villages, the poor or Dalits) to individualized financial negotiations between a person and a MFI.

The rare people who attempt to promote another perspective are usually those who have left the state for better employment opportunities: 'People don't need us any more and that might be the mark of our success. We started NGOs to help people and now the NGOs are complaining and asking people to support them. But people know where to get credit; they know how to manage bureaucrats and the upper castes,' Rajakrishna, who nowadays works in Hyderabad, commented.

This perspective helps to highlight the transformations of a sector and public expectations from what is a somewhat overoptimistic perspective. Changed expectations are not (necessarily) a sign of empowerment: political middlemen and musclemen protecting/helping people, as well as caste associations politicizing such support, have had a strong impact.

Markets and politics

The uneven implementation of anti-poverty programmes in India stresses the role of local forms of power in giving specific forms to schemes, including microfinance. Rayalaseema has long been a land of political factions between dominant castes (Reddy and Naidus). Political leaders are well known for their criminal activities and violence, and for the power they exercise over the state and its resources. The logic of democracy seems to foster political clientelism; the development sector represents a very instrumental way to reach populations and their votes. In the district, NGOs have to maintain close relations with different levels of politicians who often inspire fear in exchange for protection. Beyond NGOs set up by politicians' relatives, others have their lives and activities helped along by political leaders (paperwork, authorizations, relations with different state offices): racketeering is commonplace and a percentage of funds received from donors is expected to finance politicians and/or political parties.

All these factors point out the limits of NGOs' activities and their capacity to hold out. By the end of 1990s, during the boom period of development organizations, state and political parties reinforced their control over NGOs which were too critical of programmes and their implementation. The TDP started to harass NGOs from the 2000s, and Congress Party members from 2004, as Venkatamma, the head of a Dalit NGO, recalls: 'They used to come to my office to threaten me, telling me that we should not do this or that, otherwise we would not have their support any more'.

Tactics for controlling the sector have included silencing NGOs by hampering sit-ins or public demonstrations, and threatening to withdraw organizations from the Foreign Control Regulation Act (FCRA).[8]

But the sector had been sufficiently well organized to resist in various ways. Major NGOs had to fund smaller ones to extend their control over a territory, while other NGOs linked up or set up labour unions to diversify potential sources of funding and opportunities to lead protests.[9] This was helped by the success of microcredit, which boosted NGOs' financial positions.

This general state of affairs was transformed, to much protest, when the MFIs started developing. According to the NGOs, MFIs went to villages with huge amounts of money which they supplied to the population, who saw them as linked to the NGOs. An NGO leader remembers the struggles: 'They were cheating Dalits; we didn't want the MFIs there in our villages. They came from Hyderabad with money and we had to fight. Their agents had a very tough time around here. In fact we told the villagers not to pay back the MFIs and that we would protect them. And we did.'

This highlights how the MFIs and NGOs competed territorially for control of the poor. The MFIs radically changed the local positions of NGOs and their leaders, who saw some poor people as 'belonging to them'. This was an everyday source of tension, with resistance to MFIs on the basis of caste, class and locality, and MFIs being associated with capitalism, upper castes and/or non-local origins (including Hyderabad).

Such tensions were amplified by MFIs' view that impersonal relations were key to their 100 per cent repayment rate. MFIs differentiated themselves by stressing the weak repayment rates to NGOs, which depended on personal ties with the population. Those relations were seen as a brake to efficient economic models, while SHGs were seen as the puppets of politicians: local leaders kept a stronghold over groups locked into village power relations in order to mobilize them for any political purposes. MFI leaders saw this dependence as a weakness, as Gopal Reddy explained: 'During the elections, repayment rates go down because political leaders ask to postpone to get votes. Everything depends on who is collecting the money and we were successful. We had money and people enjoyed our services, so politicians were afraid that we might play a role in politics.'

During the most recent general elections in May 2014, SHG women went to meetings, distributed candidates' flyers and undertook other political activities (in exchange for wages and food). On the eve of the May 2014 election in Chittoor, it was common to see groups of women walking towards the villas of candidates. They were all collecting money for the votes, stressing the relations between SHGs and politics. In a neighbouring district, money was transferred through SHG bank accounts that had been set up as technological tool against corruption.

SHGs are more than microcredit groups. They have been supported for conveying and promoting the programmes of the state. The microfinance crisis is part of a broader movement to control the activities of development organizations as a whole, and to limit their spheres of intervention to implementing state programmes. In the 2000s, the government set up growing numbers of anti-poverty schemes to address issues that had been seen as the domains of NGOs. At election times, these schemes for the poor (the 'beneficiaries') were key tools and the flagships of political parties. Public schemes, foreign subsidy shortages and political pressure have radically changed the development landscape and entrenched divisions between organizations, which have failed to stay united.

But MFIs have also been a great threat to state-sponsored SHG programmes sustained by the Word Bank (Yerramilli 2013). Gopal Reddy (FSS) argues that the World Bank's influence was decisive for the government: 'The state cannot renew its grants from the World Bank with its low records of SHGs, and their main argument is that as long as MFIs are successful, they cannot move forward.'

Some MFI and NGO leaders claim that the huge flows of money and the lifestyles and salaries of some microfinance leaders, as well as MFIs' growing independence, have begun to irritate many political leaders. The rumour of the links between the head of a major MFI and a political leader of the Congress Party in Delhi visiting his organization rather than state SHGs has made an impression on development actors: it proved to be a symbol of the political ambitions of MFI leaders, a threat other powerful political leaders took seriously with the ban. In a region where politics matters and where most chief ministers come from, every decision constitutes a political tactic.

Indeed, the ban of microfinance has had a considerable impact: most microcredit is now controlled by the state, and politicians played an active role in banning microfinance. In the days following the ordinance, Chandrababu Naidu, former chief minister, appeared on television to urge people to throw their sandals at credit agents and to stop making repayments. Four years later, Chandrababu Naidu promised during the general election campaign to waive all loans granted by SHGs. He was elected chief minister in May 2014.

Conclusion

This chapter has shown how the financialization of poverty issues and political clientelism have shaped forms of rural credit to the poor, from microcredit to microfinance. Those political choices have had a huge impact on the social relations constructed between different organizations and their target populations.

I have set out to argue that a strict distinction between SHGs, MFIs and NGO-run microcredit can hamper our understanding of structural changes that have been marked by a shift towards finance-based development programmes. This process has involved most development organizations, despite their lack of homogeneity. Staff professionalization, workplace culture and the sudden economic boom behind microcredit drastically changed the development sector. Caste, state and politics have played important roles in fragmenting different paths, yet the violence and monetarization of social relations have characterized relations of debt built by organizations and 'clients'.

This is an important point when stressing that the microfinance ban cannot be understood as the outcome of MFI excess or any contrast with virtuous state-run SHGs. Such opposition is first and foremost the continuation of a political struggle for the control of the poor that goes back to the beginning of microcredit, continuing through to its development and the ban on microfinance.

Microfinance as an ongoing key political issue, and its subsequent ban is part of political competition to control the state and development resources that are central to AP's caste- and clientelism-based political system. Banning microfinance is the ultimate step in various attempts to silence the remaining politicized social organizations, and to assume political control over the poor (who are also voters). Yerramilli (2013: 219) has even suggested that the embeddedness of AP's microfinance market in the political system is what distinguishes it from other parts of the world.

But the relations between politics and microcredit are complex and take different forms according to local forms of power, leading to very different configurations of social relations in the development sector. As discussed, Chittoor district has historically seen the politicization of Dalit and anti-poverty issues. As with similar contexts in India such as Uttar Pradesh, as Jaoul (2012) has discussed, politics' resilience has affected the moral assessment of microcredit and social relations between development actors.

But the current weakness of civil society at large in Andhra Pradesh may nevertheless signal a repoliticization process. NGOs have been the only way for low-caste leaders to influence political debates: the decline of NGOs might have been an unintended consequence of empowerment. Many NGO leaders have become involved in politics. To quote Ramappa: 'this is where power is; as NGOs, we were always begging'.

Notes

1 This chapter relies on data collected thanks to two research projects: Caste out of Development – ESRC RES-062-23-2227 – led by David Mosse (SOAS, UK) and Microfinance in Crisis, led by Isabelle Guérin.

2 Dalit (oppressed) refers to a political aim to unite the castes of ex-untouchables, notably the Malas and Madigas in Andhra Pradesh. While people mainly refer to the name of their caste, Dalit is a category mainly used in the political and development arena. Malas and Madigas are strongly divided and organized through their own caste movements (Mala Mahanadu and Madiga Reservation

Porata Samiti). The government stipulates a quota of employment reserved for Scheduled Castes (ex-untouchables) and both Malas and Madigas fight to get a better quota for their own castes. The Dalit colony is the neighbourhood where Dalits live separately (and Malas and Madigas hardly mix in the same neighbourhood).

3 Throughout the chapter, the categories of 'microcredit' and 'microfinance' refer to their local understandings and practices in Chittoor district. As explained, both categories are clearly distinct: microcredit refers to credit activities run by small, local organizations,

while microfinance relates to a wide range of financial services (savings, insurance ...) run by major, for-profit MFIs. SHGs are widely associated with state-run programmes.

4 The names of people and organizations quoted in the chapter have been modified to protect their anonymity.

5 He got a good reputation through his English and development skills for responding to calls for funds. NGOs pay him to write most of their project proposals and funding applications.

6 One crore amounts to 10 million.

7 Rayalassema is the name of a region of Andhra Pradesh covering four districts, including Chittoor.

8 Six hundred and sixty-seven NGOs lost their FCRA accreditation in July 2012.

9 Unions and NGOs are not subject to the same regulations. Unions have greater freedom of speech and actions, while NGOs are not supposed to interfere in politics.

References

Edward, P. and W. Olsen (2006) 'Paradigms and reality in micro-finance: the Indian case', *Perspectives on Global Development and Technology*, 5(1/2): 31–54.

Fassin, D. (2009) 'Les économies morales revisitées', *Annales. Histoire, Sciences Sociales*, 6: 1237–66.

— (2012) 'Vers une théorie des économies morales', in D. Fassin and J. S. Eideliman (eds), *Economies morales contemporaines*, Paris: La Découverte, pp. 19–47.

Fuller, C. J. and J. Harriss (2000) 'For an anthropology of the modern Indian state', in C. J. Fuller and V. Bénéï (eds), *The Everyday State and Society in Modern India*, New Delhi: Social Sciences Press, pp. 1–30.

Guérin, I. (forthcoming) *La microfinance et ses dérives. Emanciper, discipliner ou exploiter?*, Paris: Demopolis.

Guérin, I., S. Morvant-Roux and M. Villarreal (eds) (2013) *Microfinance, Debt and Over-indebtedness: Juggling with Money*, London: Routledge.

Harriss, J. (2009) 'Bringing politics back into poverty analysis: why understanding of social relations matters more for policy on chronic poverty than measurement', in T. Addison, D. Hulme and R. Kanbur (eds), *Poverty Dynamics: Interdisciplinary Perspectives*, Oxford and New York: Oxford University Press.

Jakimow, T. and P. Kilby (2006) 'Empowering women: a critique of the blueprint for self-help groups in India', *Indian Journal of Gender Studies*, 13(3): 375–400.

Jaoul, N. (2012) 'La société civile transnationale adopte les Dalits (Inde). Le politique aux prises avec "l'ONGisation"', *Regards Sociologiques*, 43/44: 81–96.

Mosse, D. (2000) 'Irrigation and statecraft in Zamindari South India', in C. J. Fuller and V. Bénéï (eds), *The Everyday State and Society in Modern India*, New Delhi: Social Sciences Press, pp. 163–93.

— (2010) 'A relational approach to durable poverty, inequality and power', *Journal of Development Studies*, 46(7): 1156–78.

Pande, R. (2000) 'From anti-arrack to total prohibition: the women's movement in Andhra Pradesh, India', *Gender Technology and Development*, 4(1): 131–44.

Pattenden, J. (2010) 'A neoliberalisation of civil society? Self-help groups and the labouring class poor in rural South India', *Journal of Peasant Studies*, 37: 485–512.

Picherit, D. (2013) 'Protection and over-indebtedness in rural South India: the case of labour migrants of Andhra Pradesh', in I. Guérin, S. Morvant-Roux and M. Villareal (eds), *Microfinance, Debt and Over-indebtedness: Juggling with Money*, London: Routledge, pp.151–69.

— (2014) 'Neither a dog, nor a beggar. Seasonal labour migration, development and poverty in Andhra Pradesh', in N. Gooptu and J. Parry (eds), *Persistence of Poverty in India*, Delhi: Social Sciences Press.

Piliavsky, A. (ed.) (2014) *Patronage as Politics in South Asia*, Delhi: Cambridge University Press.

Rao, S. (2008) 'Reforms with a female face: gender, liberalization, and economic policy in Andhra Pradesh, India', *World Development*, 36(7): 1213–32.

Reddy, D. N. and S. Mishra (2010) 'Economic reforms, small farmer economy and agrarian crisis', in R. S. Deshpande and S. Arora (eds), *Agrarian Crisis and Farmer Suicides*, New Delhi: Sage, pp. 43–69.

Reddy, N. and A. Patnaik (1993) 'Anti-arrack

agitation of women in Andhra Pradesh', *Economic & Political Weekly*, 28(21): 1059–1066.

Servet, J.-M. (2006) *Banquiers aux pieds nus. La microfinance*, Paris: Odile Jacob.

Shah, A. (2009) 'Morality, corruption and the state: insights from Jharkhand, eastern India', *Journal of Development Studies*, 45(3): 295–313.

Srinivasulu, K. (2002) 'Caste, class and social articulation in Andhra Pradesh: mapping different regional trajectories', Working Paper 179, London: Overseas Development Institute.

— (2004) 'Special articles: Political articulation and policy discourse in elections Andhra Pradesh, *Economic and Political Weekly*, 39(34): 3845–53.

Sriram, M. S. (2010) 'Microfinance: a fairy tale turns into a nightmare', *Economic & Political Weekly*, 45(43): 10–14.

Suri, K. C. (2002) 'Democratic process and electoral politics in Andhra Pradesh, India', Working Paper 180, London: Overseas Development Institute.

Taylor, M. (2011) '"Freedom from poverty is not for free": rural development and the microfinance crisis in Andhra Pradesh, India', *Journal of Agrarian Change*, 11(4): 484–504.

Watson, S. K. (2012) 'The limits of self help: policy and political economy in rural Andhra Pradesh', Thesis, University of Manchester.

Weber, H. (2001) 'The imposition of a global development architecture: the example of microcredit', CSGR Working Paper no. 77/01.

Yerramilli, P. (2013) 'The politics of the microfinance crisis in Andhra Pradesh, India', *Journal of Politics & Society*, 24(1): 190–225.

CONCLUSION

Media coverage of microcredit, as of other industries, has long focused mainly on acclaimed initiatives and successful organizations. International recognition of and interest in microcredit has grown with the boom in the industry. A vast number of organizations now serve over two hundred million customers (Maes and Reed 2012; Reed 2014), some of them with millions of clients themselves (Roodman 2012). The United Nations even declared 2005 the 'Year of Microcredit' to further 'raise awareness about the importance of micro-entrepreneurship and to further enhance existing programs that support sustainable, inclusive financial sectors around the world' (Year of Microcredit 2012). Since 2008 and the crisis in Andhra Pradesh, however, we have seen something of a turnaround with some severe criticism of microcredit (Bateman 2010, 2011; Sinclair 2012; Mader 2015) and a spotlight on the part played by consumer credit and the fact that it sometimes raises the risks of over-indebtedness (Guérin et al. 2013). Not only is microcredit considered as having little or no positive effects on increasing incomes and on local economic dynamics[1] but it has also been accused of creating a process fostering underdevelopment owing to a reinforcement of informal practices. As a result, these informal practices, initially transitional, have now expanded (Bateman 2014). The aim of this book was not to enter the discussions on the definition of impact and its measurement in different dimensions, but to address the economic effects of microcredit only in the cases where they are likely to cause, reinforce or absorb crises. Yet sound, respectable financial services (far beyond microcredit) remain in high demand in many countries. A huge number of people still do not have access to financial services to meet their needs. Granted, microcredit institutions have no doubt made inroads into addressing these needs, even though it is far from certain that all these new clients can really bear the cost of these credits and the pressure that goes with them (Dichter and Harper 2007). Then there is the fact that MFIs have often concentrated too much on short-term credit, without properly factoring in other key considerations such as adequate savings and insurance services and the negative externalities sometimes generated by microcredit practices.

Thriving microfinance institutions have been studied in detail and their best practices quickly disseminated. Yet scholars have tended to overlook the less successful ventures. Admittedly, some criticism has been expressed, sometimes with due reason, but also at times without taking in the full picture. The majority of microcredit research into problem or crisis situations has hitherto tended to target specific institutions and specific sets of circumstances. Yet we really need a more rigorous analysis of certain crises and also of the situations in which the crises are not apparent (yet), but where some negative effects of microcredit are already observed and can be considered as seeds of crises to come if we are to gain a broader understanding of the issues at stake. This book sets out to contribute to this aim. Given the high profit margins made (outside crisis periods) by some microcredit institutions (especially compared to the margins made by the banking sector in general) and the market rates of bonds, it is clear that those who invest in microcredit can balance their losses with the subprime rates realized outside crisis periods, provided that several major crises do not happen simultaneously. That is the reason why the actors of the financial sector (and particularly private asset managers in Switzerland) present microfinance investments as 'alternative' investments and offer them as such to their clients.

The book contains a collection of chapters that build on a number of cases to help drive forward a more systemic approach. Crises can be examined from many different angles. The demand, supply and environment angles are taken as a way of gaining deeper insights into the key issues to be borne in mind by all those looking to promote more inclusive financial systems.

We believe that four factors are crucial to understanding how microcredit institutions become vulnerable to crises: governance and related factors (including mission drift), regulation and political intervention, saturation of the local economy, and collective resistance practices driven partly, but not solely, by a lack of credibility and trust and the social and cultural mismatch of the financial services available. These four factors can obviously be viewed through the lens of our three proposed dimensions (demand, supply and environment). This book combines these angles in a move to paint a fuller picture of microcredit crises.

Demand is covered mainly by the chapters on India (Tamil Nadu), the Dominican Republic and Senegal. The case of rural Tamil Nadu, studied by five French Institute of Pondicherry researchers (Isabelle Guérin, Cyril Fouillet, Santosh Kumar, Marc Roesch and G. Venkatasubramanian) drawing on surveys conducted since 2003, reveals that borrowing is needed mainly for consumption and multiple needs. Loans are used to meet rising urban lifestyle needs for household appliances on fertile cultural ground for both borrowing and lending (India). In the case of the Dominican Republic, Solène Morvant-Roux, Joana Afonso, Davide Forcella and Isabelle Guérin show that similar borrowing pressure and using loans to buy consumer goods do not produce the same level of over-indebtedness. This is mainly due to the fairly widespread use, including by private lenders, of one of two credit bureaux and also to cultural standards conducive to moral pressure to repay (as observed by other researchers in South Africa, for example, unlike the findings here for Nicaragua). Households may well be found to be over-indebted and financially vulnerable, but this vulnerability is contained, albeit at the mercy of an economic downturn that would reduce incomes. Morocco, held up as a microcredit growth model until it hit crisis in 2008, is addressed by Solène Morvant-Roux and Marc Roesch. The Moroccan case shows that demand for microcredit is by no means uniform, even in the same country. Some local environments are highly conducive to microcredit, while others are much less so, and the pressure that microcredit providers can put on lenders to repay also varies. Researchers can find very different evaluations of potential demand for microcredit in one and the same country depending on where the surveys they use have been conducted and whether they have chosen to take a micro or macro approach.

The book addresses the environment mainly from a socio-economic angle, directly in the last part of the book, with reference to it in other chapters. In the case of Senegal, Eveline Baumann, Abdoulaye Fall and Cécile Godfroid find a country that is extremely opaque when it comes to the dissemination of information. Despite the fact that there has been no microcredit supply growth slowdown or credit delinquency crisis in Senegal, the sector still displays worrying tensions (doubtless behind the exposure of governance problems in two of the leading MFIs – Crédit Mutuel du Sénégal and PAMECAS – in 2014). The final two chapters focus on the areas hit by the sector's worst crises: north-west Nicaragua (chapter by Jean-Michel Servet) and Andhra Pradesh in India (by David Picherit). Both cases flag up that an all-out rush for customers with a great propensity to borrow, attracted by the massive ease of taking out a loan, is key to explaining the collapse of these markets. The two chapters also highlight the intricate economic and political phenomena involved in triggering and escalating these crises.

A key element here is to look beyond the workings of a single institution to focus on the state of an entire industry in its own particular economic and financial environment. Some crisis factors are not related to institutions' practices, but to factors such as a decrease in customers' disposable income following a drought, a downturn in remittances sent by migrants, a cut in income supplements for low-income populations, and a reduction in the price of an income-generating commodity. Organizations suffer from these factors even though they are not responsible for them. Naturally, they could be criticized for failing to anticipate such events and the subsequent crisis and for failing to take suitable measures in response to that crisis. In other circumstances, however, these factors may also explain why some microcredit 'markets', often described as teetering on the edge, for example Peru[2] and

Cambodia, have not (yet) hit crisis despite the worrying level of many customers' over-indebtedness and market saturation. An economic recession or slowdown in the growth rate would probably be all it would take to tip these countries over the edge into a microcredit crisis. This also shows the importance of demand: an increase in unpaid debts or a decrease in demand for credit also depend on the organizations' capacity to anticipate and respond to such potentially threatening developments by, for example, rescheduling repayments or changing their model, as Grameen Bank did when it switched massively from collateral-backed group lending to individual lending in 2001 (Hulme 2012).

Supply is the central theme of the first three chapters. Together, these chapters show that MFIs often play a major role in sowing the seeds of their own crises. In many cases, strategies may not be suited to market potential, since too much growth all too often gives rise to challenging situations at best and crises at worst. Emmanuelle Javoy and Daniel Rozas focus on market understanding to show how MFIs (and other stakeholders) could improve their understanding of market saturation and hence prevent too much growth where the market cannot handle it. However, there are obviously many more MFI-driven pitfalls ready to trip up institutions (or groups of institutions) than just choosing the right growth for the right market. This is why Bert D'Espallier, Marc Labie and Philippe Louis suggest a holistic management approach that sets out to identify the major management and governance issues to consider when developing a growth strategy in order to avoid unexpected losses of control.

The mismatch between supply and demand, which is a constant theme of the book, is directly addressed by Guérin and Servet. The examples presented in the chapter by them on economic loan absorption capacity limitations show the role played by insufficient income in driving consumer demand, competition from informal financing and the way households operate, which can be far removed from an accumulation logic (hence restricting the level of loan renewal). When loans are used for consumer spending, the borrowers' growing over-indebtedness also gradually undercuts future capacities to lend. Analysis of the Indian, Moroccan, Senegalese and Nicaraguan situations shows that it is just as vital to take on board the political environment.

These chapters form a body of studies that make for a deeper understanding of the causes identified at the start of the book. Crises may originate in the market itself or in MFIs' practices. When markets are saturated or cultural practices are not adequately addressed, people will eventually fail to comply with the requirements of any financial system put in place. Yet crises may also erupt in safe, sound markets with a valid demand where the microcredit institutions are managed and governed in such a way that poor practices ultimately beget poor behaviour among their customers and/or employees. Last but not least, safe, sound microfinance institutions can also get into trouble not so much because of their customers' behaviour, but because of the political and regulatory environment in which they operate. All in all, then, many potential catalysts can give microfinance institutions a headache, and any number of these can easily combine to generate a full-blown crisis. Prudence and systemic thinking encompassing demand, supply and environment concerns should therefore be top of the agenda.

To conclude, questions naturally need to be asked about the future of microcredit. In order to elaborate the possible or likely scenarios for the evolution of the microcredit sector, we should remember the major successive phases of microfinance since the 1970s (Servet 2015). Organizations appeared at different stages of these phases, starting from small-scale NGO projects benefiting from strong support from private and public development aids. The affirmed necessity of covering their costs resulted in commercialization models of financial services in which the development aspect progressively diminished until it became more of a stated pretext, for many large structures, or it totally disappeared. This led to an increasing predominance of neoliberal financialization, marked from 2007 on by dominant competitive relationships and several major crises inherent in competitive markets. We should point out that the sector set itself new objectives, such as aiming for financial inclusion instead of fighting poverty, or shifting interest from the sector's historic cases to impact financing and social business, even though the reasons for past failures had not yet been analysed. These evolutions may lead to the favouring of consumer credit over productive credit, or to the privatization of public services such as water and electricity supplies, sewerage or education, mainly by seeming to make these needs solvable thanks to microfinance. The same evolution can be observed in access to medical care thanks to micro-insurance. Even if these projects may nowadays seem to have very limited scales compared to the boom of microcredit, the question of the sector's future must still be analysed. There is a common factor to all these initiatives designed, in the eyes of some people, to revive microfinance: the limits of the anti-statist logics that went with their development are only rarely called into question. However, putting forward the competitive logics as responsible for the crises in the sector does not mean that non-profit or state structures can automatically and systemically be solutions to prevent crises. The case of Morocco, where microcredit structures were given the status of non-profit associations and foundations, is a clear example of the consequences that hypercompetitive and opportunist strategies can have.

As raised in the introduction to this book, these crises sound the alarm regarding what is going fundamentally wrong with the tool. Yet this does not mean that there is a need to purely and simply drop the supply of loan services to individuals excluded from the commercial banks, especially if we consider the needs for other financial services such as transfers, local and remote payments, insurance and savings.

In today's financialized world, everyone needs these types of service for at least two fundamental reasons. First, because, when properly set up, financial services help people to manage their liquidity, giving them a safe place to put their savings when they have an excess of liquidity and allowing them access to additional liquidity through credit when they need it. Secondly, because informal sources of financing, however largely present (as shown in the three chapters focused on the demand side in this volume), almost never meet all the financial needs of a given population. Besides, when people look at the history of how excluded segments of populations have succeeded in organizing by themselves the improvement of their economic situation, very often the setting up of some sort of financial organization was involved. The European history of the poor farmers' cooperative movement as well as the workers' mutuals are good examples of that. So, as in those cases, the main thing is to make the system user-centric, not provider-centric. Obviously, there is no silver-bullet solution, and there are many avenues and organizational options, even for the microfinance institutions that really want to get back to basics with more of a focus on social and even market-oriented issues. We have found in the past that different institutions respond to different needs and situations. This will probably be the case in the future. Yet, as capitalist and commercial microcredit continues to expand, initiatives might be sought to promote what could be called 'solidarity finance' as part of the broader movement of the commons-driven 'inclusive' or 'human' economy. Building on the lessons of these alternatives, past and present, could help reshape the future of the financial inclusion process.[3] Rather than reproducing the state–market nexus, these initiatives could seek to free the poor and marginalized members of society from the oppression and unfairness of the market, the state and the 'community' by building new relationships of solidarity based on equality, mutuality, cooperation and reciprocity. Solidarity finance, rather than being imposed by top-down policies, often emerges from forms of collective and cooperative self-organization driven by different populations and/or organized groups in their respective localities or communities to enhance their capacity to manage their own economic resources.[4] Within these new frameworks, economic and financial practices are subordinated to social and human relations, reversing the classic logic of competition. It is indeed necessary, at least, to ensure that the financial expenditures necessary to remunerate the capital do not lead to the impoverishment of the populations. This is why, rather than using external, often foreign, funds, they promote the mobilization of local resources. Rather than inserting local communities into global value chains, their main commitment is to create local networks by linking up producers, service providers and local consumers. Rather than encouraging the neglect of local resources, their main goal is to act as a stimulus for local development by relying on the multiplier effects of local trade and consumption. Some of these initiatives are associated with alternative instruments to stimulate domestic spending (i.e. local credit cards and local complementary currencies), which are recognized by local producers, traders and consumers and thus have the potential to boost the local economy. Rather than strengthening pre-existing links of dependency between the 'North' and the 'South' with loans made in strong currencies that are expected to produce high returns, some of these initiatives also seek to create and sustain new forms of international solidarity, for instance by creating guarantee funds that make accountable use of local resources. These solidarity finance initiatives often operate in the shadow of capitalist and commercial microcredit. They are much more realistic about their potential effects. They know that social and economic change can occur only in the medium to long term. They therefore find it much harder to attract media coverage and donors often obsessed with quick, clear 'impacts'.[5] Their practical implementation is probably easier said than done. It is also likely that market forces or pressure from the state or donors through the promotion of 'best practices' may force their promoters to make many compromises. Nevertheless, solidarity finance has the great merit of seeking to promote new forms of trade and finance, within different calculation frameworks, and eliciting new social relations upon which to base economic and financial practices.

In their workings, microfinance organizations are subject to internal and external tensions between different rationales. Those organizations have generally been set up based on the administered credit approach that led to the bankruptcy of many of the programmes supported by development banks. Yet if, rather than looking at the current leading organizations, we look at their past and the myriad of small organizations, it would be wrong for redistribution incentives to disappear (either from public administrations or private foundations). In response to the failings of this government-funded approach, the associative and cooperative sector has historically established most of the current microfinance organizations (including those that became for-profit, stock companies) at grassroots level (mainly by means of redistribution by private foundations and public programmes). This approach explains the origin and pervasiveness of the claim of poverty reduction in its economic and social dimensions. This opportunity for socially responsible institutions and alternative investment funds (with financial returns not related to those of the leading financial sectors' cycles) to invest in the sector explains why these stakeholders are increasingly present and why we are seeing the phenomenon that has been called 'mission drift' in the microcredit sector. The profitability goal is now prevailing over social objectives in many cases.[6] In addition, the microcredit sector is subject, at all levels, to three – more or less binding – rationales that coexist and can be combined: a financial build-up rationale, an administered logic of domination over benefit recipients, and an approach that sees financial resources as common goods at the service of communities. The first rationale plays an important, but not exclusive, role in triggering the microcredit crises presented in this book. This logic is closely linked to the belief that, in principle, markets are able to regulate themselves as long as there is no public intervention deemed harmful. This explains why the microcredit sector, left to its own devices, is unable to comprehend the dangers of an unharnessed boom in highly competitive institutions and to regulate its imbalances by itself. We have also seen, though, that the administered approach, far from solving or easing these crises (as in Morocco), can actually exacerbate them, as illustrated by one of the most publicized cases: the Andhra Pradesh crisis. As for the logic of solidarity considering finance as a common good, it can only respond to the diversified needs for financial services if it is combined with the other two rationales. Seeing financial resources as a common good is at odds with the search for maximum (hence excessive) profitability for the sole benefit of the fund providers.

But how to institute a common resource? Finance and its different branches have specificities that also meet the imperatives of general criteria. The recognition and management of a common resource are subject to several conditions that must be recapped here. It is only logical to present them in a hierarchical order, as they follow on from one another.

- The first condition is to define a group of co-producers or users (multiple and independent) and, subsequently, to determine the boundaries (more or less open to the outside) and roles, duties and responsibilities of each one in this group. This group can be defined at a more or less local level, in a global process of bottom-up subsidiarity (as opposed to a top-down 'deconcentrated' decision-making process), in order to address the problems at the different levels where they need to be solved.
- The second condition is to establish the conditions for the access, appropriation, exclusion, distribution, withdrawal and reproduction of this resource, and to make those conditions public.
- The third condition is to control the use of the resource and its revenue-generating capacities.

Once these three conditions are satisfied, the organizations managing the resource must:

- arbitrate potential conflicts in the joint activity or use, for instance of the funds;
- introduce a scale of sanctions and define the best way to repress, or even exclude, those who do not conform to informal norms and collectively agreed rules. These norms are values promoted by prescribing actions or results that, in a way, allow or force them. These rules, which can be

constraining or prohibiting, are modes of organization with sanctions applied when prohibited actions are committed or when the prescriptions are not respected. These rules and norms are therefore constitutive and regulating. We observe here that the access to financial resources has predominance over the right to individual property. The resource can then be shared, as this rule extends the access to the resource beyond the population that is directly profitable (according to the processes of cost and market return integration). The 'sharing' dimension can be observed in the obligation to save in an organization before being allowed to take on a loan, and with the potential provision of this financial resource to all members.

However, this logic can have adverse effects, for example when most of the savings are collected from rural populations (such as farmers trying to protect their assets and considering their savings – obtained thanks to credit – as a potential insurance they can resort to in extreme situations) and those accumulated funds mainly benefit urban populations (often employees with higher revenues looking for cheap credits). We can often observe, in mutual organizations and in savings and credit cooperatives, a ratio of number of borrowers to number of savers ranging from 1:8 to 1:12. In this case, the balance cannot be respected, and the notion of common resource may continue to exist only if the interest rates for the savers are significantly positive; otherwise, it's only a matter of financial transfers from savers to borrowers, and, from a certain angle, a kind of exploitation if the investments made by the borrowers do not benefit the whole community involved in this savings and credit scheme.[7] Setting an interest rate can be considered here as a rule governing the use of this common resource and enabling wealth equalization, or at least preventing the deepening of economic inequalities of revenues and assets between social groups and geographical areas, as those who 'lend' (through savings) and those who borrow are generally from different social groups and represent categories of population with different needs for financial services.

Another essential element in the organization and functioning is the decision-making process. The definition and recognition of a common resource cannot be achieved in a top-down relationship, otherwise it is a kind of 'pseudo-common' resource. This allows the clear distinction between a public collective good and a common good. The question is whether the decision-making is shared equally between the stakeholders, rather than based on rights granted proportionally to property.

With this requirement of democratic functioning, the promotion of common resources cannot be assimilated with:

- either the issue of social or societal[8] responsibility of organizations, in which the clients of financial service providers may be considered as beneficiaries not involved as actual stakeholders co-producing the service tighter;

- or, a fortiori, the issue of consumer protection, another form of top-down relationship, or the issue of the financial education of clients with the aim of instilling the functional norms profitable for lenders (Guérin 2012).

A commons-driven approach, however, fosters an approach balanced between the contributions and gains of each of the stakeholders at different levels in the financial relationship. This includes the extra-financial and even extra-economic effects of the credit (especially social effects such as child labour and environmental effects such as the consumption of charcoal). It also means having to ask questions about the effects of injecting financial flows at micro, meso and macro level: credit in the form of external contributions of funds can prove to be one man's meat, but another man's poison. In this case, other financial services, if not other forms of intervention, are often needed more than credit. Such is the main challenge that providers of financial services will need to take up in the coming years, especially in response to the growing manifestations of market saturation and over-indebtedness. At the very least, we need to turn the page from sweeping sector standardization based increasingly on bank standards, with the main aim of attracting external capital to the sector. In this way, we could promote other forms of financial inclusion beyond the public–private, state–market and solidarity–competition nexuses. In this way, too, microfinance (over and above microcredit) could become a model that serves to remake the entire financial sector.

Notes

1 See note 5.

2 See the Peruvian microcredit market in late 2013, Hugh Sinclair's blog (6 February 2014), blog.microfinancetransparency.com/trouble-brewing-in-peru-mibanco-in-dire-trouble/.

3 This paragraph is inspired by Servet (2010, 2015) and Guérin (2015).

4 See also Paranque (2014).

5 Despite the results of the field surveys, which show little impact and even negative effects, some large organizations focused on reaffirming their beliefs in a positive impact of microcredit, but always at a level that can be considered as anecdotal. See, for example: ACCION International, FINCA, Grameen Foundation, Opportunity International, UNITUS and Women's World Banking – 'Measuring the impact of microfinance: our perspective',

www.grameenfoundation.org/sites/grameenfoundation.org/files/archive-devo9/Measuring-the-Impact-of-Microfinance-Our-Perspective.pdf, 1 April 2010. However, new impact studies commissioned by the British Cooperation (DfID) and J-PAL show that the positive effects are extremely limited. See, for instance, Duvendack et al. (2011), Stewart et al. (2012), Banerjee et al. (2015).

6 Environmental responsibility goals have always been marginal in the sector, even though they appear to be gaining currency owing to media coverage of this kind of intervention. See Allet (2014), Servet (2011a), Forcella (2012).

7 We should point out here that in bidding tontines, such as those existing in Cameroon, we can observe cases of indirect

redistribution when the first beneficiaries of the tontine, who pay high interest, are merchants and the other members are public or private employees who take over the bids in the last turns, when the

accumulated interest at the end of the tontine cycle is shared equally between the members.

8 On the distinction between social and societal responsibility, see Servet (2011b).

References

Allet, M. (2014) 'Why do microfinance institutions go green? An exploratory study', *Journal of Business Ethics*, 122(3): 405–24.

Banerjee, A., D. Karlan and J. Zinman (2015) 'Six randomized evaluations of microcredit: introduction and further steps', *American Economic Journal: Applied Economics*, 7(1): 1–21.

Bateman, M. (2010) *Why Doesn't Microfinance Work? The Destructive Rise of Local Neoliberalism*, London and New York: Zed Books.

— (2011) *Confronting Microfinance. Undermining Sustainable Development*, Sterling, VA: Kumarian Press.

— (2014) 'The rise and fall of Muhammad Yunus and the microcredit model', Working Paper Series 0001, International Development Studies, Saint Mary's University, January.

Dichter, T. and M. Harper (eds) (2001) *What's Wrong with Microfinance?*, London: Practical Action.

— (2007) *What's Wrong with Microfinance?*, London: Practical Action.

Duvendack, M., R. Palmer-Jones, J. G. Copestake, L. Hooper, Y. Loke and N. Rao (2011) 'What is the evidence of the impact of microfinance on the well-being of poor people?', London: EPPI-Centre, Social Science Research Unit, Institute of Education, University of London.

Forcella, D. (2012) 'Payments for environmental services and microfinance: proyecto Cambio in Nicaragua', Master's thesis, Université Libre de Bruxelles/CERMi.

Guérin, I. (2012) 'L'éducation financière ou comment apprendre aux pauvres à bien consommer', in I. Guérin and M. Selim, *À quoi et comment dépenser son argent?*, Paris: L'Harmattan, pp. 51–71.

— (2015) *La microfinance et ses dérives: émanciper, discipliner ou exploiter?*, Paris: Demopolis/IRD.

Guérin, I., S. Morvant-Roux and M. Villarreal

(eds) (2013) *Microfinance, Debt and Over-indebtedness: Juggling with Money*, London: Routledge.

Hulme, D. (2012) 'A short history of the Grameen Bank. From subsidized microcredit to market-based microfinance', in F. Hossain, C. Rees and T. K. Millar, *Microcredit and International Development*, London and New York: Routledge, pp. 12–20.

Mader, P. (2015) *The Political Economy of Microfinance: Financialising Poverty*, London: Palgrave.

Maes, J. P. and L. R. Reed (2012) *State of the Microcredit Summit Campaign Report 2012*, Washington, DC: Microcredit Summit Campaign.

Paranque, B. (2014) 'Microfinance as cooperation between private property and collective action to reconnect consumption and societal development', in P. Phan (ed.), *Conversations and Empirical Evidence in Microfinance*, Imperial College Press, pp. 23–62.

Reed, L. R. (2014) *Resilience: The State of the Microcredit Summit Campaign Report 2014*, Washington, DC: Microcredit Summit Campaign.

Roodman, D. (2012) *Due Diligence: An Impertinent Inquiry into Microfinance*, Washington, DC/Baltimore, MD: Centre for Global Development/Brookings Institution Press.

Servet, J.-M. (2010) *Le Grand Renversement. De la crise au renouveau solidaire*, Paris: Desclée de Brouwer.

— (2011a) 'La microfinance: une finance au service du développement durable?', *Cahiers français*, 361: 23–6.

— (2011b) 'Corporate responsibility versus social performances and financial inclusion', in B. Armendariz and M. Labie (eds), *The Handbook of Microfinance*, Singapore: World Scientific Publishing, pp. 301–22.

— (2015) *La vraie révolution du microcredit*, Paris: Odile Jacob.

Sinclair, H. (2012) *Confessions of a Microfinance Heretic. How microfinance lost its way and betrayed the poor*, San Francisco, CA: Berett-Koehler.

Stewart, R., C. van Rooyen, M. Korth, A. Chereni, N. Rebelo da Silva and T. de Wet (2012) 'Do micro-credit, micro-savings serve as effective financial inclusion interventions enabling poor people, and especially women, to engage in meaningful economic opportunities in low and middle income countries. A systematic review of the evidence', London: UKAid/Centre for Anthropological Research, University of Johannesburg/EPPI Centre, Institute of Education, University of London, September.

Year of Microcredit (2012) 'International Year of Microcredit', www.yearofmicrocredit. org.

ABOUT THE CONTRIBUTORS

Joana Afonso is a PhD researcher at the Economics and Finance Department of the University of Portsmouth, UK, within its Development Studies Group. She works on microfinance field practices both from the supply (loan officers) and demand (clients) perspective, with a particular interest in client protection issues and over-indebtedness prevention.

Eveline Baumann is a socio-economist and Research Fellow at the Institute of Research for Development/Centre d'études en sciences sociales sur les mondes américains africains et asiatiques (CESSMA). She holds a PhD in African studies, and has field experience in Senegal, Mali, Cameroon and post-Soviet Georgia. Her main areas of research are microfinance, employment, social protection, artisanal fishery and small-scale agriculture.

Bert D'Espallier is assistant professor at the Faculty of Economics and Business (KU Leuven, Belgium) and guest lecturer at the Antwerp Management School (AMS, Belgium), where he teaches courses in the area of corporate finance, business analysis and valuation. His research interests involve microfinance, corporate finance and governance, and he is affiliate researcher at the Centre for European Research in Microfinance (CERMi, Belgium) and the Norwegian Centre for Microfinance Research (NOCMIR, University of Agder, Norway). Ongoing research efforts include MFI transformation, the impact of subsidies on MFIs, the relation between cooperative banks and the formal financial sector, and gender issues in microfinance.

Mouhamedoune Abdoulaye Fall is lecturer at the Gaston Berger University in Saint-Louis (Senegal). He holds a PhD in socio-anthropology and is a member of a research team on transformations in rural Sahel (ERMURS). His research interests include development issues and modernity in Africa in the current context of globalization, as well as the appropriation of social sciences in Africa.

Davide Forcella holds a PhD in physics and a master's degree in microfinance. He is a researcher in theoretical physics at the Université

Libre de Bruxelles, and an associate researcher in microfinance at the Centre for European Research in Microfinance (CERMi, Belgium). He has extensive research experience in microfinance and the environment: energy, climate change, ecosystems, rural development, and the design and implementation of environmental indicators for MFIs, both in developing and developed countries. Moreover, he has expertise in credit risk, crisis, over-indebtedness and microfinance in post-disaster/conflict areas.

Cyril Fouillet is an assistant professor and head of economics at the ESSCA Business School in Angers, France. As a research fellow at the French Institute of Pondicherry, he spent three years in India conducting fieldwork on the economic, geographical and political dimensions of microfinance. His latest contribution is an edited special issue on Microfinance Studies with J. Copestake, B. Harriss-White and M. Hudon (*Oxford Development Studies*, 2013).

Cécile Godfroid is currently undertaking a PhD in microfinance, focusing on credit officers' management, at the Centre for European Research in Microfinance (CERMi, Belgium). She is based at the University of Mons (UMONS, Belgium), where she also works as a teaching assistant.

Emmanuelle Javoy is an independent consultant specializing in the analysis of the performance of microfinance institutions and microfinance investment vehicles. She has worked for eleven years for Planet Rating, a rating agency specializing in microfinance, as an analyst, quality manager and then as its managing director for six years. Emmanuelle has supervised the production of more than two hundred rating reports, which gives her a very deep knowledge of microfinance institutions' operations and risk profile.

K. S. Santosh Kumar is a research associate in the field of sociology. He has worked with many different researchers over the past eighteen years, with a specific focus on women's empowerment in the field of health and economic development. Presently, his special areas of interest are the role of credit and debt in women's daily life and decision-making.

Philippe Louis received his PhD in Business Economics from the KU Leuven, Belgium, in 2013. His areas of specialization are microfinance, credit risk, survival analysis, and panel data. He has published several papers in peer-reviewed journals and, in 2011, he was a co-recipient of a special fund from the National Bank of Belgium. In 2014, he was employed as a postdoctoral researcher at the University of Mons (UMONS), and currently he is working as a researcher at the KU Leuven.

Solène Morvant-Roux is a senior researcher and teaching fellow in socio-economics at the Institute of Demography and Socioeconomy, University of Geneva, and an associate researcher at the Centre for European Research in Microfinance (CERMi, Belgium). She has conducted several research projects on microfinance in rural and urban settings in various countries (Mexico, Morocco, the Dominican Republic) with an interdisciplinary approach based on first-hand data and an original mix of quantitative and qualitative methods.

David Picherit is an anthropologist and a research fellow at the CNRS – Laboratoire Ethnologie et Sociologie Comparative, Paris. He is interested in labour, migration and development in Andhra Pradesh. His current research focuses on criminal politics and business in south India. He participates in ERC- and ESRC-funded research programmes on political cultures in South Asia, based at University College London.

Marc Roesch is an independent consultant based in Montpellier. He holds a PhD in agroeconomics and is a retired researcher from the CIRAD (Centre International de Recherche Agronomique pour le Développement). He has worked on microfinance in West Africa, Madagascar and India for the past fifteen years.

Daniel Rozas is a consultant and researcher on a broad range of microfinance topics, including credit bubbles. Besides MIMOSA, Daniel's work includes studies of Andhra Pradesh (he first wrote of a large and growing bubble in the Indian state of Andhra Pradesh a year prior to the subsequent crisis), and an IFC-funded study of the Moroccan microfinance sector during its post-crisis period. Daniel learned his first lessons in market saturation and credit crisis working at the US mortgage investment company Fannie Mae, 2001–08.

G. Venkatasubramanian is a sociologist in the Department of Social Sciences at the French Institute of Pondicherry (India). His research areas include rural geography, migration, labour, finance and rural–urban linkages.

INDEX

30 95